STATIC

Also by Amy Goodman and David Goodman

The Exception to the Rulers:
Exposing Oily Politicians, War Profiteers,
and the Media That Love Them

Amy Goodman

and

David Goodman

STATIC

Government Liars,

Media

Cheerleaders,

and the People

Who Fight Back

HYPERION *New York*

Excerpt from *Gedichte*, Vol. 4, by Bertolt Brecht, copyright 1961 Suhrkamp Verlag, reprinted by permission of Suhrkamp Verlag.

Excerpt from Martin Luther King, Jr.'s "Letter from Birmingham Jail" reprinted by arrangement with the Estate of Martin Luther King, Jr, c/o Writers House as agent for the proprietor, New York, NY.

Copyright 1963 Martin Luther King, Jr., copyright renewed 1991 Coretta Scott King.

"Be Nobody's Darling," by Alice Walker, reprinted by permission of the author.

Excerpt of "Instant-Mix Imperial Democracy," by Arundhati Roy, reprinted by permission of the author.

Parts of Chapter 14, "Anti-Warriors," originally appeared in the article "Breaking Ranks," by David Goodman, *Mother Jones*, November/December 2004.

The Library of Congress has catalogued the hardcover edition of this book as follows:

Goodman, Amy
    Static: government liars, media cheerleaders, and the people who fight back / Amy Goodman and David Goodman. — 1st ed.
       p.   cm.
    Includes bibliographical references and index.
    ISBN: 1-4013-0293-9
    1. United States—Politics and government—2001– . 2. United States—Foreign relations—2001– . 3. Mass media—Political aspects—United States. 4. Political activists—United States. I. Goodman, David. II. Title.
JK275.G66 2006
973.931—dc22   2006043625

Paperback ISBN-10: 1-4013-0914-3
Paperback ISBN-13: 978-1-4013-0914-5

Hyperion books are available for special promotions, premiums, or corporate training. For details contact Michael Rentas, Proprietary Markets, Hyperion, 77 West 66th Street, 12th floor, New York, New York 10023, or call 212-456-0133.

Design by Fritz Metsch

FIRST PAPERBACK EDITION

10 9 8 7 6 5 4 3 2 1

To our late grandparents,

Benjamin and Sonia Bock
Solomon and Gertrude Goodman

Immigrants all
Who fled persecution
seeking a kinder, more just world

Contents

Acknowledgments

We are grateful for all the inspired interference we have had to help us create *Static*.

Mike Burke, a producer at *Democracy Now!*, has provided us with invaluable support as an editor and researcher on this project. Barely flinching when the hours grew late, Mike has helped us to ferret out the stories and people that form the heart of this book.

Denis Moynihan is the master of keeping everything—and us—on track. We are grateful for the countless talents, good humor, and intelligence that he brings to all he does.

We are grateful to Peternelle van Arsdale, our editor at Hyperion, whose insightful feedback has made this a better book. Thanks also to Christine Ragasa for her talent at letting the world (and bookstores) know about our book. And thanks to the folks who have been cheerleaders (the good kind) for our writing: Bob Miller, president of Hyperion, and editor in chief Will Schwalbe. Thanks also to Katie Wainwright, Jane Comins, Claire McKean, and Miriam Wenger.

Thanks to our agent, Luke Janklow, an enthusiastic matchmaker for our efforts. And to Anthony Arnove, our talented and wise foreign agent and friend.

From Amy: The staff of *Democracy Now!* works tirelessly every day (and night and weekend) to find the creative resisters, whistleblowers, and activists who are on the air every day. A huge and humble thanks to Karen Ranucci, co-host Juan Gonzalez, and to producers Sharif Abdel Kouddous, John Hamilton, Mattie Harper, Frank Lopez, Aaron Mate, Ana Nogueira, Elizabeth Press, Yoruba Richen, and Jeremy Scahill. Thanks also to Angela Alston, Taishon Black, Jerome Bourgeois, Russell Branca, Mike Castleman, Samantha Chamblee, Ting Ting Cheng, Jim Carlson, Andres Conteris, Julie Crosby, Mike Di Filippo, Jenny Filippazzo, Uri Gal-Ed, Nell Geiser, Robby Karran, Angie Karran, Mike Kimber, Kieran Krug-Meadows, Jory Leanza-Cary, Errol Maitland, Nick Marcilio, Peter Yoon, Jillian O'Connor, Edith Penty, Isis Phillips, Jon Randolph, Dave Rice, Orlando Richards, Chuck Scurich, Neil Shibata, Nikki Smirl, Danielle Strandburg-Peshkin, Keiko Takayama, Jen Utz, Bernard White, Megan Whitney, Suha Yaziji, and Chris Zucker.

Thanks to my colleagues at Link TV, Free Speech TV, public access and public TV stations, and public and low-power FM stations around the country. My gratitude especially to colleagues at the Pacifica stations—WBAI, KPFK, WPFW, KPFT, and KPFA. All of these people carry the torch high for independent media.

Thanks to Jon Alpert and Keiko Tsuno of Downtown Community TV, who provide a home for *Democracy Now!* in countless ways.

Thanks also to Israel Taub, Michael Ratner, Patrick Lannan, Jaune Evans, Laurie Betlach, and Andy Tuch for their essential support.

We honor the memory of the late great Damu Smith, founder of Black Voices for Peace. We will miss him, but his contributions will live on.

For their friendship, Caren Spruch, Elisabeth Benjamin, Dan Coughlin, Maria Carrion, Diana Cohn and Brenda Murad, and to the little and not-so-little ones, Ariel and Jasper, Anna, Sarah and Eli, Sara and Aliza, Rory and Cecilia, Leila and Maria, Andrew and Valentina, Maren, Fergus, Maeve, Sesa, Gabriela, and Dakota. And to David, whose patience, skill, humanity, and determination made this book happen . . . once again.

From David: My gratitude to the late David Weber, my musical mentor, who taught me the meaning of bel canto. And thanks to my sister Amy, for putting her heart and soul into the remarkable work that she does every day, from which so many of us draw strength. Thanks to my family, Ariel and Jasper, whose love, soccer tournaments, and music lessons lure me back home from my writing sojourns. And to my wife and love, Sue, who has always been, and will always be, my muse and inspiration.

Finally, we are grateful to our family: brothers Dan and Steve Goodman have always lent an ear and good advice when we need it most. Our mother, Dorrie Goodman, amazes us with her energy, travels, insights, food, and love. She and our late father, George, have taught and inspired us to make the world a better place. We hope this book (of which she has read every word several times) helps create the static to do just that.

Introduction: Unembedded

Either you are with us, or with the terrorists.

—President George W. Bush, addressing Congress, September 20, 2001

As Hurricane Katrina ripped into America's Gulf Coast in late August 2005, the Bush administration had a crisis on its hands. Not the tens of thousands of people who had been abandoned in downtown New Orleans. Not the levees that had been breached, drowning the city.

No, the big disaster that the Bush administration acted decisively to solve was its loss of control over the news media. Images were coming out of New Orleans of a disaster of biblical proportions—and a federal response that ranged from inept to nonexistent to blatantly racist.

So the administration acted on instinct: The Federal Emergency Management Agency (FEMA) requested that the media not photograph the dead bodies that were floating down the main boulevards of New Orleans. The military followed by announcing a "zero access" policy for journalists.[1] A FEMA spokesman said it was "out of respect for the deceased" and their families.[2] This was the same rationale President Bush used to justify the administration's ban on photographing the caskets of soldiers returning from Iraq. FEMA was forced to back down in the face of a lawsuit by CNN.

For one horrifying week at the end of August 2005, the world was treated to something it had rarely seen: an unembedded American press showing raw footage of human suffering. The Bush administration's insistence that it had the crisis under control fell flat, as on-the-ground reporters, literally floating free of government handlers, presented the devastation and the failed response in real time. The world was shown photos of abandoned African-American residents of New Orleans struggling to survive the floods, alongside images of Bush in California on August 30— the day after he was informed that the New Orleans levees had broken—chuckling and riffing on a guitar given to him by country singer Mark Wills, whose signature hit, "Wish You Were Here," could have been the Katrina victims' theme song. With one unscripted, uncensored image, the entire Bush presidency was captured: Bush strummed while New Orleans drowned.

This was the response of an American leader to a long-forecast calamity. As even the Republican investigation into the Katrina response noted, "It remains difficult to understand how government could respond so ineffectively to a disaster that was anticipated for years, and for which specific dire warnings had been issued for days. This crisis was not only predictable, it was predicted."[3]

But top Bush administration officials simply didn't care. For years, these antigovernment zealots had preached that the federal government could do no good. When Katrina hit, we saw a self-fulfilling prophecy play out, as the Bush administration suddenly had to rely on the inept political hacks and gutted federal agencies that it had substituted for the functioning bureaucracies that once existed.

There was also the cold political calculus: The victims on the Gulf Coast were just too black and too poor for their suffering to register high on the priority list for this administration. What else can explain the behavior of America's leaders during the days when a major American city was being destroyed? President Bush was vacationing at his Texas ranch. Vice President Cheney was fly-fishing in Wyoming. Condoleezza Rice was in New York City, where she took in the Monty Python play *Spamalot*, went shopping at Ferragamo for shoes, and played tennis with Monica Seles. Donald Rumsfeld attended a San Diego Padres game. And Michael

Chertoff, who, as head of the Department of Homeland Security, was supposed to oversee the country's responses to this catastrophic hurricane, didn't seem to know he was in charge and stayed home the day before the storm hit.

A Media Off Its Leash

At long last, the powerful images of devastation swamped the vaunted Bush spin machine. Even the viewers of Fox News, the house organ of the Bush administration, were treated to the spectacle of Fox reporter Shepard Smith in New Orleans lashing out at right-wing pundit and anchorman Sean Hannity, who insisted that a distraught Smith put the images of abandoned New Orleans citizens in perspective. "This *is* perspective!" shouted Smith, pointing toward the people trapped in the darkened, flooded city behind him.

Then there was an incredulous Paula Zahn of CNN, responding to FEMA boss Michael Brown's admission that he was unaware until Thursday, September 1, that thousands of people were stranded and some were dying at the New Orleans Convention Center. "Sir, you aren't just telling me you just learned that the folks at the Convention Center didn't have food and water until today, are you? You had no idea they were completely cut off?" asked Zahn.

"Paula," replied Brown, "the federal government did not even know about the Convention Center people until today."

The next morning, CNN's Soledad O'Brien sputtered at Brown in exasperation, "How is it possible that we're getting better intel than you're getting? . . . In Banda Aceh, in Indonesia, they got food dropped two days after the tsunami struck."

It was as if the corporate media, long since domesticated as a White House–trained poodle, was surprised by its own bark. After years of passing off White House and Pentagon spin as news, of cowering before administration operatives, Hurricane Katrina reminded the media of what a free press is actually supposed to do. With no troops to embed with, reporters at long last reported what they saw, not what they were told.

"It's refreshing in a way to *not* have the official line, where your only choice is just to see it in front of you," an awed *New York Times* correspondent, Kate Zernike, told the *New York Observer*. She seemed astonished by the power of journalism when it simply reports the realities on the ground, through the eyes of the victims.

The media also missed and distorted plenty of stories during Katrina—such as when white people taking supplies from a store were described as "just trying to survive," while African-American residents doing the same thing were characterized as looters. That was inexcusable, because the media missed the biggest looters in New Orleans: the Halliburtons and Bechtels getting huge no-bid disaster relief contracts—the same Bush-connected profiteers that are making a killing in Iraq.

On *Democracy Now!*, Loyola University law professor Bill Quigley described the situation in New Orleans from inside Memorial Hospital, where his wife worked. Hospital personnel were instructed not to speak to the press—and it quickly became clear why the image managers were so fearful. He reached us at midnight on Tuesday, August 30. With backup generators barely working, and people's cell phones dying, he knew the situation was too desperate to remain silent: "Tens of thousands of people are left behind, and those are the sickest, the oldest, poorest, the youngest, the people with disabilities and the like. . . . There was no plan for that. . . . There's a huge humanitarian crisis going on here right now."

Quigley compared the situation in New Orleans to Haiti, one of the poorest countries in the world, where he has worked for years as an attorney: "I had always hoped that Haiti would become more like New Orleans. But what's happened is New Orleans has become more like Haiti."[4]

Two days later, as cell phones died, Bill sent a text message to a friend's phone: "No water, sick, no heat, call somebody for help."

The American public reacted swiftly and viscerally to the images of the drowned and abandoned Gulf Coast. In response to the unembedded reporting, millions of dollars poured in to relief agencies. And a week after the hurricane hit, President Bush's approval ratings tanked to a then-record low 38 percent.

Meanwhile, another American war zone burns out of control—and out of sight. Thousands of American soldiers and tens of thousands of Iraqis are dead as a war based on lies drags on with no foreseeable end. Mindful of the power of images, the Bush administration has been careful to ensure that the war casualties do not appear on the evening news. Reporters who are embedded with the U.S. military are perpetually spun by their military handlers, and the grateful journalists ensure that their dispatches are carefully "balanced" by official caveats. Images of war are sanitized as a result of outright government censorship—such as the Pentagon ban on photographing flag-draped coffins—and helpful American networks that purge pictures of carnage and death that they deem to be "in poor taste."

The result: When it comes to Iraq, Bush—with the help of the media—can fake his way past the electorate. When it comes to Katrina, the images shock the nation, giving the lie to official explanations, forcing the resignation of the incompetent FEMA chief (though he continued to receive a paycheck), and foisting unprecedented fury on the ever-vacationing commander-in-chief. Even Republicans have raised their voices in outrage at the administration. With Bush's popularity in free fall, his entire second-term political agenda was suddenly in danger of being derailed.

If only the media acted in Iraq as they did in New Orleans, a consistent theme would become apparent: When it comes to death and destruction, George W. Bush is an expert. But when it comes to saving lives and rebuilding societies, as goes New Orleans, so goes Iraq—and the world.

The War on Truth

President George W. Bush has long preferred illusion to reality. "See, in my line of work you got to keep repeating things over and over and over again for the truth to sink in, to kind of catapult the propaganda," Bush explained of his approach at a public forum in 2005.[5] For Bush, the only crises are when his poll numbers fall.

Bush administration officials are obsessed with controlling the flow of information. Their strategy for maintaining their grip on power is simple: Perpetuate fear. We must remain in a state of total war. The implications for democracy are chilling. President Bush has asserted a right to unlimited wartime powers. Thus the Constitution, Bill of Rights, Geneva Conventions, and the very notion of a balance of power have been shredded. The official rhetoric is that we are now in a Long War, led by the president, *über alles*.

The media, so cowed for so long, has failed to present a coherent picture of this frontal assault on our democracy. Alarming stories emerge, piecemeal, of warrantless wiretaps, of U.S.-sanctioned torture, of offshore prisons where thousands are being held at the whim of a president who invokes sweeping life-and-death powers and dispatches propagandists to cover his trail.

Information is a crucial weapon in Bush's war. In a February 2006 speech Defense Secretary Donald Rumsfeld declared that "information warfare" will be vital to fighting terrorism. He lashed out at the media for "an explosion of critical press stories" that exposed secret U.S. anti-terror programs, including propaganda efforts in Iraq. He declared: "We are fighting a battle where the survival of our free way of life is at stake and the center of gravity of that struggle is not simply on the battlefield overseas; it's a test of wills, and it will be won or lost with our publics, and with the publics of other nations. We'll need to do all we can to attract supporters to our efforts and to correct the lies that are being told, which so damage our country, and which are repeated and repeated and repeated."[6]

He responded to the images of and charges about American torture of detainees in Guantánamo Bay and Iraq by dismissing them as fabrications. "The terrorists are trained . . . to lie. They're trained to allege that they've been tortured. They're trained to put out misinformation, and they're very good at it," he declared.

In a speech a month later, Rumsfeld made clear that he believes the real problem in Iraq is simply the coverage: "Much of the reporting in the U.S. and abroad has exaggerated the situation. . . . Interestingly, all of the exaggerations seem to be on one side. . . . The steady stream of errors all seem to be of a nature to inflame the situation and to give heart to the terrorists."[7]

The "truth" that Rumsfeld prefers can be found in the articles that the Bush administration is planting in the "free" Iraqi media, written by American psychological warfare operatives.

IRAQI ARMY DEFEATS TERRORISM blared an October 2005 story in Iraqi newspapers that said, "The brave warriors of the Iraqi Security Forces (ISF) are hard at work stopping al-Qaeda's attacks before they occur." Another planted article crowed, "The ISF has quickly developed into a viable fighting force capable of defending the people of Iraq against the cowards who launch their attacks on innocent people."[8] The latter story was published in the Iraqi press around the time that the United States conceded that no Iraqi battalions were capable of fighting on their own.

The audience for this cartoonish propaganda is not just Iraqis: The Bush administration has turned psychological warfare, which by U.S. law can only be targeted at foreign audiences, on Americans. Rumsfeld dismissed the legal prohibitions against using foreign propaganda at home, declaring in February 2006: "The argument was, of course, that it was taking taxpayers' dollars . . . and propagandizing the American people. Of course, when you speak today, there's no one audience. . . . Whatever it is we communicate inevitably is going to be heard by multiple audiences."[9]

Rumsfeld is leaving nothing to chance. A Pentagon briefing for Army Gen. George W. Casey Jr., the top U.S. commander in Iraq, identifies the "home audience" as one of the major targets of American propaganda. The *Washington Post* reported in April 2006 that U.S. psychological operations soldiers produced a video about atrocities committed by Saddam Hussein that was "seen on Fox News."[10] The Bush administration also attempted to hype the role of Abu Musab al-Zarqawi, the Jordanian who was killed in Iraq in June 2006. Bush officials used Zarqawi to falsely connect Saddam Hussein with the 9/11 attacks, and to bolster their dubious claim that the Iraqi insurgency was led by al Qaeda-backed foreign fighters. "Villainize Zarqawi/leverage xenophobia response," stated one U.S. military briefing. As part of this effort, U.S. psy-ops soldiers in 2004 leaked a supposed letter from Zarqawi to the *New York Times* that boasted of foreigners' role in suicide attacks in Iraq. Other reporters questioned the authenticity of the document that wound up in a widely cited front-page *Times* story. Brig. Gen. Mark Kimmitt, the U.S. military's chief spokesman in Iraq in 2004, boasted later, "The Zarqawi PSYOP program is the most successful information campaign to date."[11]

The "information war" Rumsfeld describes is deadly serious. ABC News reported in May 2006 that the government was tracking the phone numbers dialed from major news organizations in an attempt to root out whistle-blowers. Attorney General Alberto Gonzales added that it "is a possibility" that journalists will be prosecuted for publishing classified information. The message is clear: The media can either participate in Bush's war, or become a target of it. As Bush administration officials have warned, journalists who do not follow the party line are promoting terrorism.

Declaring war on the media is a desperate and risky move. But the corporate media, so compromised and atrophied by its own complicity in promoting the lies of the Bush administration, is woefully unprepared to do battle. If the past is any guide, as the government aims a sword at the heart of our civil liberties and freedoms, the media will provide sporadic resistance at best, and at worst, will help drive the sword home.

Covering for Power

When the Bush administration launched its PR blitz to sell the Iraq War in September 2002, the American public never stood a chance of learning the truth behind the massive fraud emanating from the White House. Bush and his propaganda czars knew something the American public had not quite grasped: The American media was little more than a megaphone for those in power. This was especially true for celebrity journalists like Judith Miller, the now-disgraced national security correspondent for the *New York Times;* and Bob Woodward, once a crusading muckraker at the *Washington Post,* now father confessor to the political elite.

For three years, the Bush administration called the tune, and the *New York Times* danced. In the run-up to the Iraq War, the newspaper, led by Miller's dispatches, acted as a conveyor belt for the lies of Iraqi exiles, channeling their self-serving distortions right onto the front pages. Miller's sources were the key players in the Iraqi National Congress, an outfit first created by the CIA and later funded by the Pentagon. Its leaders, such as Ahmad Chalabi, conjured fantastic tales about the menace posed by Saddam Hussein's weapons of mass destruction. They hinted darkly about bioweapons labs buried beneath hospitals, aluminum tubes that the Iraqi dictator was intent on using to develop nuclear weapons, and secret meetings held between Saddam Hussein and Osama bin Laden.

This was propaganda in the purest sense: disinformation that was bought and paid for by the U.S. government. The only thing needed was for respected news outlets to legitimize these fairy tales by running them as fact. The American media rose to the task, and carried out the Bush administration's dirty work with gusto. The consequences of the media's abdication of its role as watchdog of democracy are now written in new front page dispatches—about the bloody quagmire in Iraq.

Yet the media can't seem to shake its instinct to defer to power. In December 2005, the *New York Times* published a shocking exposé by reporters James Risen and Eric Lichtblau. Their story revealed that following the 9/11 attacks, the Bush administration ordered the National Security Agency (NSA) to begin wiretapping people inside the United States, including U.S. citizens, in direct violation of the Foreign Intelligence Surveillance Act of 1978, which expressly forbids warrantless wiretaps inside the country. To read the article, you might have felt alarmed by the picture of creeping fascism that it describes. But you would have felt vaguely reassured that the press was on the job as a watchdog . . . until you came to the ninth paragraph:

> The White House asked the *New York Times* not to publish this article, arguing that it could jeopardize continuing investigations and alert would-be terrorists that they might be under scrutiny. After meeting with senior administration officials to hear their concerns, the newspaper delayed publication for a year to conduct additional reporting. Some information that administration officials argued could be useful to terrorists has been omitted.[12]

Let's do the math: Thirteen months before this story was published there was . . . a national election. Won by George W. Bush. The guy who ordered laws to be broken, because he felt he didn't have to answer to anyone. The last president to behave in this way was Richard Nixon. He faced a public outcry and was forced to resign in disgrace in the face of almost certain impeachment. Indeed, when the wiretapping story was finally published in the *Times,* it sparked congressional investigations and even calls for impeachment of the president for violating the law.

It turns out the *Times* did, in fact, have this story ready to go before the 2004 election but decided to wait—at the request of the people running for reelection, who rightly feared how the public might respond to the revelations.

Imagine, just for a moment, how different things might have been if this explosive exposé had been published when it was written.

The *Times* delayed publication because it might "jeopardize continuing investigations"—ignoring, as the media watch group Fairness and Accuracy in Reporting (FAIR) has pointed out, that "placing illegal and unconstitutional programs in jeopardy is the whole point of the First Amendment."

More astonishing was *Times* executive editor Bill Keller's explanation of why the story was delayed for so long. He said that the Bush administration had "assured senior editors of the *Times* that a variety of legal checks had been imposed that satisfied everyone involved that the program raised no legal questions." Mind you, this is the regime of George W. Bush we're talking about—the folks who assured us that torture was legal, that preemptive war was legal, and that holding prisoners incommunicado in an offshore gulag was legal. But for the editor of the *Times,* it is enough just to take the government's word when it says something is legal. The *Times* finally published the story—which won reporters Risen and Lichtblau a 2006 Pulitzer Prize—only when it became apparent that Risen was planning to publish the revelation in a book a month later.

In spite of all that we now know about how the media failed to challenge government liars and instead became cheerleaders for a fraudulent war, the corporate media still covers for power. That may explain why an explosive report in the London *Times* on May 1, 2005, which caused a sensation around the world, was ignored or played down in the American media. The British paper revealed the contents of the so-called Downing Street memo, minutes of a July 2002 meeting between British prime minister Tony Blair and his top advisors, at which British intelligence chief Richard Dearlove reported to

Blair on his meetings with CIA Director George Tenet. Dearlove explained that Bush "wanted to remove Saddam Hussein through military action, justified by the conjunction of terrorism and WMD. But the intelligence and facts were being fixed around the policy."[13]

This bombshell from a top British official—that Bush had decided to attack Iraq and would simply cook the intelligence to suit his aims—was greeted with a yawn by the American media. It was only after bloggers promoted the story that the corporate media acknowledged it—and only then, to dismiss it. The *Los Angeles Times* insisted the memo was not a "smoking gun." The *Washington Post* dismissed it as old news. The *New York Times* barely mentioned it at all. And the network nightly news shows virtually ignored the story.

It's a sad day when the government no longer has to cover up its dishonesty because the American media does it for them.

The Access of Evil

This is the state of the corporate media today. It's a symptom of what we call the access of evil: journalists trading truth for access. The public unwittingly mistakes the illusion of news for reality. This also applies to the one-sided debates that are the rage on the networks and cable news. Viewers don't even know what they don't know. The media watch group Media Matters did a study of the Sunday morning talk shows. During Bush's first term as president, 69 percent of the journalists appearing on the Sunday shows were conservatives, and 58 percent of all guests were Republicans/conservatives.[14] This echoes a study done by FAIR in the run-up to the Iraq War. In the two weeks surrounding Colin Powell's infamous 2003 speech to the UN in which he made the case for the invasion that was to occur six weeks later, 393 "experts" appeared on the major nightly network news shows. Of these, *three*—less than 1 percent—were leaders of antiwar organizations.

We can't even call this a "mainstream" media. It's an extreme media—a media that cheerleads for war.

Instead of learning from the media what is actually going on in the world, we get *static*—a veil of distortion, lies, omissions, and half-truths that obscure reality. As bodies pile up in Iraq and New Orleans, many people are mystified, wondering where it went so wrong.

We need a media that creates static of another kind: what the dictionary defines as "criticism, opposition, or unwanted interference." Instead of a media that covers for power, we need a media that covers the movements that create static—and make history.

We are not waiting for this alternative media; people are building it right now. Blogs, Indymedia centers, independent filmmakers, and other grassroots media have opened a new way to understand what is happening in the world today.

Democracy Now! is part of this independent media tradition. Every day, this grassroots, investigative news hour brings forth the dissidents, activists, whistle-blowers, artists, poets, and those most affected by the decisions of the powerful. These are the courageous people who speak truth to power. Since its first broadcast in 1996, interest in *Democracy Now!* has exploded, as people seek out the rich diversity of voices that is missing from the corporate media. Around 500 radio and TV stations now carry the show—including Pacifica and NPR radio stations, public access TV and PBS stations, and both TV satellite networks—and it is aired on stations around the globe, and on the Internet at democracynow.org. The daily video and audio podcasts of *Democracy Now!* are among the most popular online.*

Now, with lives and freedoms on the line, we need a media that

---

*Democracy Now! airs on the five Pacifica radio stations, many NPR stations, low-power FM stations, and college and community stations throughout North America, Europe, and Australia. It can also be seen on the TV satellite networks Free Speech TV and Link TV (Dish Network channels 9415 and 9410, respectively; Link TV is also broadcast on DirecTV channel 375).

cuts through the lies and fakery that obscure the truth. A media that is fiercely independent. Unembedded. Journalism that works to inform, not to deceive. The soldiers and civilians in harm's way in Iraq deserve no less. The citizens of the devastated and abandoned Gulf Coast are counting on it. And the people shackled in America's secret gulags cry out for it.

Free speech is democracy's last line of defense. We must demand it. Defend it. And most of all, use it—now.

Liars and Cheerleaders

1. Outlaw Nation

I always knew the Americans would bring electricity back to Baghdad. I just never thought they'd be shooting it up my ass. —**Young Iraqi translator, Baghdad, November 2003**[1]

Maher Arar was on his way to Canada from a family vacation, changing planes at JFK Airport in New York. His wife and his kids would soon follow.

He would not make it home to Ottawa for over a year.

At JFK, he was pulled over and detained by the FBI and New York City police. After two weeks in a New York immigration facility, he was shackled and put aboard a Gulfstream jet in New Jersey despite his pleas and protests that he would be tortured in Syria. He wept during the entire flight. His family didn't even know where he was being taken. In Syria he was put in a cell the size of a grave. And he was tortured, repeatedly and brutally.

Three hundred seventy-four days after he landed at JFK, Maher Arar was released from the Syrian prison. Charges were never filed against him.

Days after Arar's release, President Bush gave a speech in Washington criticizing Syria. "Dictators in Iraq and Syria [have left] a legacy of torture, oppression, misery, and ruin," he declared.[2]

Thanks to the United States, Arar knew this misery firsthand. He had been kidnapped and tortured at the behest of the most powerful nation in the world.

And he was not alone.

The United States is an outlaw nation.

The laws that used to govern the behavior of American leaders evolved from basic codes of conduct for civilized nations. In 1215, the Magna Carta asserted that no one, not even a king, was above the rule of law, and it established the concept of habeas corpus—a prisoner's right to challenge his or her detention in a public court of law. Kidnapping, murder, and rape, all nations agree, are crimes. The four Geneva Conventions, the first of which was adopted in 1864, established that even in wars, civilians and combatants have rights. The conventions prohibit murder, torture, hostage-taking, and extrajudicial sentencing and executions.

These have long been the publicly proclaimed ideals of Western nations. In private, they have been routinely violated. From the Native American conquest, to slavery, to Vietnam, where torture and extrajudicial killing were staples of the CIA's Phoenix program, to Latin America, where U.S.-backed death squads rained terror on civilians throughout the 1970s and '80s, to the U.S. Army School of the Americas, which counts among its graduates a who's who of Latin American dictators and human rights abusers, the United States has been secretly involved in the torture business for years.

Yet even by these sordid standards, the United States is now probing new lows.

For this, we must credit President George W. Bush. A failed oilman, he lost the 2000 election but was selected as president of the United States by the Supreme Court. Having lost the popular vote nationally that year—including, as recounts proved, losing in Florida—Bush proceeded to declare after the attacks of 9/11 that he had a God-given mandate not just to rule America, but to wage war across the globe. He reportedly told Palestinian Prime Minister Mahmoud Abbas, "God told me to strike at al Qaeda and I struck them, and then he instructed me to strike at Saddam."[3] Bush decreed that neither international law nor U.S. law applied to him or his administration.

Bush was not able to achieve all this on his own. A compliant Congress, lubricated by contributions from self-dealing lobbyists and multinational corporations, together with a deferential American media have been essential parts of his arsenal.

In the Outlaw Nation that has risen up where the United States once stood, holding humans in offshore cages and denying them fair trials is fine. Kidnapping has become an essential tool of foreign policy. The vice president personally lobbies the Senate to legalize torture, while the secretary of defense decides which medieval torments are acceptable (drowning and freezing are in; disemboweling is out). The secretary of state trots around the globe to forcefully and unequivocally reassure squeamish allies—on whose soil the kidnappings and torture occur—that what they know is happening (and secretly assisted) is not really happening. The U.S. media speaks politely about possible "abuse" and refers delicately to things like "stress positions."

Torturing its enemies in secret is not new for the United States. But the open—even proud—embrace of it is unprecedented.

Let us take a look into the dark alleys, behind the iron bars, and into the dungeons to shed some light on the secret actions of the Outlaw Nation.

Tortured

It was around noon on September 26, 2002, and Maher Arar was wearily waiting his turn in the immigration line at John F. Kennedy International Airport in New York. He was en route from Tunisia, where his family was vacationing, to his home in Ottawa, Canada. The 33-year-old computer engineer was familiar with the routines of world travel, working as he did for a high-tech company called MathWorks in Massachusetts. Arar was born in Syria, but left the country with his family when he was 17 years old. He went on to graduate from prestigious McGill University in Montreal.

The immigration officer typed Arar's name into a computer, then paused. He suddenly looked up and motioned for Arar to step aside and wait for further instructions. Two hours later, uniformed officers took him to be fingerprinted and photographed. He was told this was regular procedure, and his bag and wallet were searched. Officials from the New York Police Department and the FBI arrived to question him, and they assured him he would be able to catch his flight to Montreal. When Arar asked for a lawyer, he was told he had no right to an attorney because he was not an American citizen.

As he was about to learn, in this Outlaw Nation he had no rights at all.

At 4 P.M., an FBI agent came to interrogate Arar. According to Arar's affidavit, the agent wanted to know about his connection to Abdullah Almalki, another Syrian-born Canadian, whom Arar said he knew only casually. The agent constantly yelled at Arar, calling him a "fucking smart guy" with a "fucking selective memory." When Arar took more than a few seconds to respond to a question, the agent became angry.

After this five-hour interrogation, Arar was questioned for another three hours, this time by an immigration officer. The new interviewer asked Arar about his membership in various terrorist groups. The Canadian computer engineer strenuously denied any such affiliation. Arar was then chained, shackled, put in a vehicle, and driven to another building at JFK Airport, where he was placed in solitary confinement with no bed. He did not sleep.

The next morning, two FBI agents interrogated Arar for another five hours, asking him about Osama bin Laden, Iraq, and Palestine, among other things. Arar again denied any connection to terrorists or terrorist activity. He repeatedly asked to see a lawyer and to make a telephone call; the officials ignored him. It had been nearly two days, and he had still not eaten.

Early that evening, an immigration officer came to Arar's holding cell. He asked Arar to "volunteer" to be sent to Syria. Arar refused, insisting that he be sent to Canada or Switzerland. At around 8 P.M., Arar was shackled and driven to the Metropolitan

Detention Center in Brooklyn. For thirteen days, Arar remained imprisoned. After days of insisting, he was finally allowed to call his mother-in-law in Ottawa, who promptly got him a lawyer. The Canadian consul visited, and Arar told her that he was afraid the U.S. authorities were going to deport him to Syria against his will. She reassured him that would not happen.

But she was thinking of another America, a civilized nation of laws. Maher Arar was discovering that that America no longer exists.

At 3 A.M. on October 8, 2002, Arar was awoken in his cell and informed that he was leaving. A woman read to him from a document that said that based on classified information that she could not reveal to him, and because he knew a number of men, including Abdullah Almalki, the director of the Immigration and Naturalization Service had decided to deport him to Syria.

Arar recounted on *Democracy Now!* in November 2003: "I explained to them very clearly that if they send me back to Syria, I will be tortured. They accused me of being a member of a terrorist organization. I told them repeatedly that I am not a member of this group. They were just not believing me. I said if you send me back to Syria, the Syrians will try to extract information, and the only way to do that is just to torture me."

The officials ignored his pleas. Instead, they chained him, took him to a waiting car, and drove him to an airport in New Jersey where an unmarked white Gulfstream V corporate jet was waiting. As investigators later learned, this was one of the CIA's fleet of torture taxis that take suspects to foreign countries—typically Egypt, Morocco, Jordan, or Syria—for brutal interrogations. Arar's flight stopped in Washington, then continued to Portland, Maine, and on to Rome and Amman, Jordan.

Flying at thirty thousand feet while CIA agents watched action movies, Arar sat in the luxury jet, terrified. "I just couldn't believe it. I felt at first it was a dream. I was crying all the time. I was disoriented. I wished I had something in my hand to kill myself because I knew I was going to be tortured and this was my preoccupation. That's all I was thinking about when I was on the plane."

Arar was taken off the plane in Amman at 3 A.M. He was chained, blindfolded, and put in a van, where he was beaten by guards. They then drove him to the Syrian border, where he was handed over to Syrian authorities, who drove him to Damascus. He was taken to a building known as the Palestine Branch of Syrian military intelligence. Once inside, his worst fears came true. A group of men sat in a bare room. Arar recounted:

"One of them started questioning me and the others were taking notes. The first day it was mainly routine questions between eight and twelve of us. The second day is when the beatings started. The first day they did not find anything strange about what I told them. Later, they started to beat me with a cable."

The cable beatings were especially harrowing, as Arar has recounted to journalists: "The interrogator said: 'Do you know what this is?' I said, 'Yes, it's a cable.' And he told me, 'Open your right hand.' I opened my right hand and he hit me like crazy. And the pain was so painful, and of course I started crying. And then he told me to open my left hand, and I opened it and he missed, then hit my wrist. And then he asked me questions. If he does not think you are telling the truth, then he hits again. An hour or two later he put me in this room where sometimes I could hear people being tortured."[4]

"In my view, they just wanted to please the Americans," Arar told Democracy Now! just after his release. "They had to find something on me because I was accused of being an al Qaeda member, which is nowadays synonymous with Afghanistan. They told me, 'You've been to a training camp in Afghanistan.' I said no. And they started beating me. I had no choice. I just wanted the beating to stop. I said, 'Of course, I've been to Afghanistan.' I was ready to confess to anything just to stop the torture."[5]

Arar's false confession helped decrease the severity of his daily beatings. But his torture took on a new dimension when he was put in what amounted to an underground grave.

"The worst of all of this is the cell that they put me in. It was an underground cell. It was dark—there was no light in there. It was three feet wide, six feet deep, and seven feet high, with an opening in the ceiling. That's where a little bit of light came in. There was no heating in the winter. There was only two blankets on the hard floor." He paused, sighing as he recounted the horror. "It's a disgusting place to be. There were rats. Cats above the cell peed from time to time in that opening. There was no hot water, especially no toilets. . . . It was a torture chamber. And I stayed in that place for ten months and ten days."

Arar was allowed periodic brief visits with the Canadian consul, but only in the presence of his Syrian torturers, so he did not dare discuss what was happening to him. Meanwhile, back in Canada, his wife, Monia, mounted a tireless human rights campaign on his behalf. Finally, the Canadian government took up his case at the highest levels, demanding that Arar be released. On October 5, 2003, Maher Arar was taken from his cell, told to wash his face, and driven to a courtroom in Damascus, where he was turned over to officials from the Canadian Embassy. There were no charges against him.

Now reunited with his family in Canada, Arar's ordeal continues. He told us in early 2006, "The main thing that is driving me crazy is that when they accuse someone of being a terrorist, directly or indirectly, this brand is gonna stay for life. You are not gonna be able to find a job. Even though people have sympathy for you, always in their head they have, 'What if? What if?' "

Years after his ordeal, Arar is still haunted. His work as an engineer used to involve travel, and these days he is invited to speak all over Canada. But he can't accept. "I don't dare to take a plane. I am so scared to fly," he says. He says that he still has nightmares and flashbacks. "People don't realize what goes through the head of someone who's been tortured," he explains. "The other day I was picking up my daughter from school. So I went to the gym and I said, 'Bring your things with you and come with me.' And suddenly

I had some fear in my heart. Minutes later, I realized that I just used the same expression that the guards in Syria used when they asked people to leave the cell." Two days earlier, he had "a terrible nightmare. Sometimes I see myself being beaten; I fall on the ground and they make me stand up again and they beat me." His distress is obvious. "It's like it's not going away. I just wanna forget about it. But I'm not able to. I've lost confidence in myself.

"I never thought that human beings could treat other human beings like that. For me it was a huge cultural shock. I go from a world where human dignity is respected, where there are values such as people being treated justly and fairly and in a humane way, and I go to another world, in a matter of hours, where human beings are treated worse than animals—there is no respect, there is torture.

"I think the healing process is going to be long and, frankly, my life and future have been destroyed even though I'm working right now to clear my name. But it is just the accusation to label someone as a terrorist—it's not going to be easy to make people believe that I was not a terrorist. I'm just very worried if I'm going to be able to get back to my normal life. One thing is for sure, I don't think I'll go back to the same career. . . . There's so much injustice out there in the world. I don't know, I'll probably become a human rights activist."

He reflects, "I just still can't believe what happened to me. A country like the United States, which is supposed to be a country that praises democracy and respects human rights, to do this kind of thing to me."

Global Roundup

Maher Arar was the victim of what the U.S. government calls "extraordinary rendition"—sending suspects to foreign countries to be harshly interrogated. The program began in 1995, under the Clinton administration, when the CIA undertook a series of kidnappings of suspected terrorists in Europe. Suspects were shipped to Egypt, where some were tortured and others were killed. One of the more spectacular operations took place in the spring of 1998 in Albania. According to the *Wall Street Journal*, Albanian secret police, with their CIA advisors observing from a waiting car, kidnapped an Islamic militant named Shawki Salama Attiya. Over the next few months, four other suspected Islamic militants were abducted in Albania, and another suspect was killed in a gun battle. The men were bound, blindfolded, and taken to an abandoned air base, from where they were flown to Cairo on a CIA plane and handed over to Egyptian security officials for interrogation. Attiya charged later that he was hung from his limbs, was given electrical shocks to his genitals, was dragged on his face, and was imprisoned in a cell with knee-deep fetid water. Two other suspects captured that day were executed by hanging.[6]

A CIA official involved in the rendition program boasted of the closeness between Egyptian security and the United States. The Americans could send Egyptian interrogators the questions they wanted detainees to answer in the morning, and they would have answers by the evening.[7]

The rendition program has been "extraordinary" not only for the brazenness with which it flouts international law, but for how many lives—primarily American—have been lost as a result of it. On August 5, 1998, an Arab-language newspaper in London published a letter from the International Islamic Front for Jihad. The letter promised revenge for the Albanian operation, vowing to retaliate against the United States in a "language they will understand." Two days later, the U.S. embassies in Kenya and Tanzania were blown up, killing 224 people.[8]

Since September 11, 2001, the extraordinary rendition program has morphed into a global roundup. Suspects are being abducted around the world and dumped in places like Guantánamo Bay and Bagram, Afghanistan. By mid-2006, these two offshore American prisons held about one thousand people. Almost all of these prisoners have never been charged, and they languish out of view and outside protection of the law.

In the case of Maher Arar, the Bush administration insisted that it had information linking him to al Qaeda. The administration claimed that Syria promised he would be treated humanely. Syria has denied Arar was tortured. U.S. officials have said that sending Arar to Syria was "in the best interest of the security of the United States."[9]

Human rights groups estimate that over one hundred people have been rendered to countries well known for torturing prisoners. In the case of Syria, the Bush administration could be confident that Arar and the other prisoners it sent there would be savaged. According to the U.S. State Department *2001 Human Rights Report*, published seven months before Arar was sent to Syria:

> Former prisoners and detainees [in Syria] report that torture methods include administering electrical shocks; pulling out fingernails; forcing objects into the rectum; beating, sometimes while the victim is suspended from the ceiling; hyperextending the spine; and using a chair that bends backwards to asphyxiate the victim or fracture the victim's spine. In September Amnesty International published a report claiming that authorities at Tadmur Prison regularly torture prisoners, or force prisoners to torture one another. Although torture occurs in prisons, torture is most likely to occur while detainees are being held at one of the many detention centers run by the various security services throughout the country, and particularly while the authorities are attempting to extract a confession or information regarding an alleged crime or alleged accomplices.[10]

In fact, President Bush has cited Syria's abysmal human rights record as a reason to isolate and possibly attack the country. But as Maher Arar learned, when it comes to torture, Syria and the Bush administration think alike.

Rather than suffer in silence, Maher Arar is pursuing justice. In January 2004, the Center for Constitutional Rights filed suit on Arar's behalf against former attorney general John Ashcroft, former Homeland Security secretary Tom Ridge, FBI director Robert Mueller, former Canadian prime minister Jean Chrétien, and others, charging them with knowingly sending Arar to Syria to be tortured in violation of U.S. and international law. Arar's demand for justice has also resulted in a Canadian government inquiry into the role of Canadian officials in his arrest and detention. In hearings held in Canada in 2005, it was revealed that the Royal Canadian Mounted Police provided unverified (and inaccurate) information about Arar and several other Canadians—who were also tortured in Syria—at the request of U.S. attorney general John Ashcroft. In August 2005, the U.S. Justice Department tried to block Arar's lawsuit, claiming that all information about him was covered by a rarely used "states secrets privilege."

In February 2006, U.S. district judge David Trager dismissed Arar's lawsuit. Judge Trager wrote in his opinion that "Arar's claim that he faced a likelihood of torture in Syria is supported by U.S. State Department reports on Syria's human rights practices." But, the judge added, when "national security" is involved, decisions, even if they lead to torture, "are most appropriately reserved to the Executive and Legislative branches of government." Judge Trager explained that in dismissing the lawsuit on grounds of national security, "The need for much secrecy can hardly be doubted. . . . Governments that do not wish to acknowledge publicly that they are assisting us would certainly hesitate to do so if our judicial discovery process could compromise them."

Michael Ratner, president of the Center for Constitutional Rights, responded on *Democracy Now!*, "You know, this was one of the most remarkable and infamous and worst decisions I've ever read by a federal judge. What it really is saying is it gives a green light to the U.S. to take people like Maher Arar and send them overseas for torture.

"What's happened here is the idea that torture is somehow a

legitimate means in the so-called war on terror is now seeping into not just the administration and the executive, [but] into the judiciary, into the pundits, and everything else," Ratner added. "This is [former Chilean dictator Augusto] Pinochet saying 'I can torture in the name of national security.'"[11]

Maher Arar was astonished by the court's acceptance that "torture happens." "If the courts will not stop this evil act, who is going to stop this administration?" he told the *Toronto Star*. "Where do we go? The United Nations? We—me and others who have been subjected to this—are normal citizens who have done no wrong. They have destroyed my life. They have destroyed other lives. But the court system does not listen to us.

"When a court will not act because of 'national security,' there is no longer any difference between the West and the Third World," he said.[12]

Arar's case hits at the heart of all that is wrong with the rendition program. That's why both the Canadian and American governments are trying desperately to hide everything associated with it. On January 21, 2004, *Ottawa Citizen* reporter Juliet O'Neill had her apartment raided by some twenty agents of the Royal Canadian Mounted Police. She had written about Arar's case several months earlier. Her articles quoted from leaked documents and revealed the contents of Arar's tortured confessions; the implication was that the RCMP had received these confessions either from the Syrians or the United States. The RCMP claims it raided O'Neill's apartment while investigating a national security leak. O'Neill and the *Citizen* have sued the RCMP, and it has become a major press freedom case in Canada.

In January 2006, the Center for Constitutional Rights filed suit against President Bush and the head of the National Security Agency (NSA). The suit claimed that the NSA warrantless electronic eavesdropping program violated attorney-client privilege, since it presumably spies on phone calls between its lawyers, including those representing Maher Arar, and other foreign clients.

In the United States—the cause of his pain—Arar is hardly known, but his relentless quest for justice earned him "Newsmaker of the Year" in 2004 from the Canadian edition of *Time* magazine. For him, to fight is to survive. "The main thing that gives me relief is that people are now listening," he told us. "People have woken up. The media, too."

He reflects, "This campaign started to stop people from terrorizing other people. But what is happening now, this so-called campaign is ending up destroying people's lives in a different way, under the disguise of protecting other people's lives. You can't protect people's lives by destroying other people's lives."

Kidnapped

As people strolled down Via Guerzoni in Milan just after noon on February 17, 2003, a man with a long beard and a flowing djellaba stood out among the fashionably dressed Italians. He was on his way to daily prayers at a nearby mosque. Suddenly, two Westerners clutching cell phones approached and stopped the man. They asked him, in Italian, for his documents, as if they were police.

A witness described what happened next: "At the junction with Via Croce Viola there was a pale-colored van on the pavement. Then, all I heard was a loud noise like a thud. The van suddenly shot backwards and then set off again, away from the mosque, passing me at high speed. And the three people I'd seen, they weren't there any longer."[13]

The man was an Islamic cleric named Hassan Mustafa Osama Nasr, an Egyptian refugee also known as Abu Omar. When the Italian police investigated his disappearance, the trail led to a surprising source: the CIA.

By tracing cell phone records and piecing together eyewitness accounts, the Italian authorities learned that the CIA had sent a "special removal unit" to Italy consisting of about nineteen agents. For months before the abduction, the American agents lived like royalty.

Staying for up to six weeks in $450-a-night hotels, drinking $10 Cokes, running up $500-a-day dining tabs, and jetting off to seaside resorts, these government agents, some of whom appear to have been romantically involved with one another, were living out a James Bond fantasy. Operating under the cover of President George W. Bush's "war on terror," the agents worked in a world beyond laws.[14]

After capturing their prey, the CIA agents whisked the cleric to Aviano Air Base, a joint U.S.-Italian military facility. A few hours later, he was secreted onto a Learjet and taken to Ramstein Air Base, a U.S. military base in Germany. Then he was transferred to another plane and taken to Cairo. A Milan-based CIA agent turned up in Cairo five days later, around the same time as Abu Omar.[15] As for the other CIA agents, they were not yet done partying. Four of them stayed on in luxury hotels in Venice, while two others relaxed for a few days in the Italian Alps.

While the Americans partied, Italian authorities were busy chasing shadows in the war on terror. That's because in March 2003, the CIA sent an urgent message to the Italians that Abu Omar had fled to the Balkans. The Italian police frantically chased down the lead into dead ends. It turns out "the CIA's tip was a deliberate lie, part of a ruse designed to stymie efforts by the Italian anti-terrorism police to track down the cleric," according to Italian investigators interviewed by the *Washington Post*.[16] The Americans didn't want word leaking to squeamish European governments that Abu Omar's real destination was Egypt, where he was brutally interrogated and allegedly tortured. His treatment included electric shocks and being subjected to freezing temperatures.[17]

Which is just the treatment the Bush administration would have expected—and presumably wanted. The U.S. State Department *2002 Human Rights Report*, published a month after Abu Omar was kidnapped by American agents, said this about Egypt:

There were numerous, credible reports that security forces tortured and mistreated citizens. . . . Principal methods of torture reportedly employed by the police included: Being stripped and blindfolded; suspended from a ceiling or door-frame with feet just touching the floor; beaten with fists, whips, metal rods, or other objects; subjected to electrical shocks; and doused with cold water. Victims frequently reported being subjected to threats and forced to sign blank papers to be used against the victim or the victim's family in the future should the victim complain of abuse. Some victims, including male and female detainees, reported that they were sexually assaulted or threatened with the rape of themselves or family members.[18]

Notwithstanding President Bush's absurd claim in 2005 that "we do not render to countries that torture,"[19] he and his administration have found Egypt's abysmal human rights record to be irresistible. Egyptian Prime Minister Ahmed Nazif told the *Chicago Tribune* that the CIA had handed over to Egypt between sixty and seventy terrorism suspects captured from around the world. Indeed, Egypt has become a destination of choice for governments wishing to outsource torture: Human Rights Watch estimated that between 2001 and 2005, Egypt worked with other countries to arrest more than sixty Islamic militants living abroad and return them to Egypt.[20]

Former CIA agent Robert Baer explained the cold logic behind where the United States chooses to outsource torture: "If you want a serious interrogation, you send a prisoner to Jordan. If you want them to be tortured, you send them to Syria. If you want someone to disappear—never to see them again—you send them to Egypt."[21]

As for Italy, it has learned that being a U.S. ally offers no protection from being burned. "The kidnapping of Abu Omar was not only a serious crime against Italian sovereignty and human rights, but it also seriously damaged counterterrorism efforts in Italy and Europe," said Armando Spataro, the lead prosecutor in Milan. "In fact, if Abu Omar had not been kidnapped, he would now be in prison, subject to a regular trial, and we would have probably identified his other accomplices."[22]

But that would have been so . . . legal. In the war on terror, laws and human rights are nuisances to be ignored.

Unfortunately for the CIA, laws still apply in the real world, and kidnappers are considered common criminals. In July 2005, Italian authorities issued arrest warrants for twenty-two alleged CIA operatives, including the head of the CIA Milan substation. The agents, who were named, were charged with kidnapping and other crimes. The Italians say that the kidnapping was overseen by the CIA's Rome station chief at the time, Robert Seldon Lady, and directed by U.S. Embassy officials there. Lady's Italian homes have been raided, and he, like the other defendants, has been unable to return to Italy for fear of being arrested. The CIA and the U.S. Embassy in Rome have refused comment about the charges.

This case is the first in which a foreign government has attempted to bring U.S. intelligence operatives to justice.[23] Whether or not the prosecution succeeds, it signals that even if the United States has decided that international law is irrelevant, other countries still cling to the old-fashioned notion that no one is above the law. It is a sign that rogue Bush administration officials may yet be held accountable for their actions.

The torture-happy Bush administration is now itself feeling some pain. First it must contend with the problem of what to do with all the people it has tortured around the world. If these detainees go to trial, their accounts of abuse will spill forth, and their cases may well be thrown out.

"It's a big problem," explained Jamie Gorelick, a former deputy attorney general and a member of the 9/11 Commission, in *The New Yorker*. "In criminal justice, you either prosecute the suspects or let them go. But if you've treated them in ways that won't *allow* you to prosecute them, you're in this no man's land. What do you do with these people?"[24]

Then there's the problem of how false confessions "blow back" to the United States. It turns out that Ibn al-Shaykh al-Libi, the detainee whose bogus claims on links between al Qaeda and Saddam Hussein were championed by President Bush to justify the invasion of Iraq, fabricated his claims after being tortured while in the custody of—guess who?—Egypt. Al-Libi was handed over to Egypt by U.S. agents in January 2002. The disclosure of his fabrications in 2005 was the first public evidence that bad intelligence on Iraq may have resulted from the administration's reliance on third countries to interrogate and torture detainees.[25]

The problem—that tortured detainees will say or make up anything to stop their abuse—was recognized early by key intelligence officials. In a February 2002 report that was widely circulated within the Pentagon and White House, the Defense Intelligence Agency said it was probable that al-Libi, who was the highest ranking al Qaeda member in U.S. custody when he was captured in December 2001, "was intentionally misleading the debriefers" when he claimed there was Iraqi support for al Qaeda's work with illicit weapons.[26]

Unfortunately, this intelligence assessment conflicted with President Bush's goal of attacking Iraq. Bush resolved this conflict eight months later by simply lying, declaring in a major speech in Cincinnati in October 2002 that "we've learned that Iraq has trained al Qaeda members in bomb making and poisons and gases." Colin Powell repeated the lie in his infamous prewar speech to the UN in February 2003, when he described "the story of a senior terrorist operative telling how Iraq provided training in these weapons to al Qaeda."

It's a simple story, really: how torture led to lies, which were the pretext for the Bush administration's Big Lies, that led to war, that led to the deaths of thousands of Iraqi citizens and U.S. soldiers.

An Innocent Man

Khaled El-Masri needed a break. It was New Year's Eve 2003, and the 42-year-old unemployed car salesman from Germany and father of five had just had a spat with his wife. He decided to get on a bus to Macedonia to cool off for a few days. Little did he know that his innocent getaway would end up as a five-month odyssey of torture, starvation, and prison—courtesy of the Bush administration.

At the Macedonian border, Masri was ordered off the bus. It turns out that his name, which means "Khaled the Egyptian," was similar to the name of an associate of one of the 9/11 hijackers.[27] El-Masri was born in Kuwait in 1963 to Lebanese parents. He moved to Germany in 1985 to escape the Lebanese war, became a German citizen in 1995, and married in 1996. But the Macedonian border guards suspected that his German passport was a fake. They drove El-Masri to Skopje, the Macedonian capital, for further questioning.

Unbeknownst to the unwitting German citizen, the Macedonian police contacted the CIA station in Skopje. The station chief was away for the holidays, so the deputy CIA station chief handled the case. She was excited about her chance to be a player in the global war on terror. "The Skopje station really wanted a scalp because everyone wanted a part of the game," a CIA officer told the *Washington Post*.[28] Since a number of mid-level CIA officials were away for the holidays, the junior officer in Skopje got to deal directly with the head of the al Qaeda unit at the CIA Counterterrorist Center (CTC) in Virginia. This was a big score for her.

The CTC was "the Camelot of counterterrorism," said a former official. It was a place teeming with aggressive agents eager to make their mark, a shadowy underworld where laws could be ignored or flouted. "We didn't have to mess with others—and it was fun," said the official.[29]

El-Masri was about to be sucked up in a global dragnet. There was no evidence that El-Masri was not who he insisted he was: a

German citizen of Lebanese descent. But the CTC al Qaeda unit chief "didn't really know—she just had a hunch" that El-Masri was probably a terrorist, according to another CIA official.[30] She ordered that he be sent to a CIA prison in Afghanistan and interrogated immediately.

An extraordinary rendition was set in motion. The Macedonian police handed El-Masri over to a CIA rendition group. They followed their standard procedure, according to the *Post*:

> Dressed head to toe in black, including masks, they blindfold and cut the clothes off their new captives, then administer an enema and sleeping drugs. They outfit detainees in a diaper and jumpsuit for what can be a day-long trip. Their destinations: either a detention facility operated by cooperative countries in the Middle East and Central Asia, including Afghanistan, or one of the CIA's own covert prisons—referred to in classified documents as "black sites."[31]

Khaled El-Masri recounted what happened to him after he was detained at the Macedonian border: "Eventually, I was transferred to a hotel in Macedonia where I was held for twenty-three days. I was guarded at all times, the curtains were always drawn, I was never permitted to leave the room, I was threatened with guns, and I was not allowed to contact anyone. At the hotel, I was repeatedly questioned about my activities in Ulm [Germany], my associates, my mosque, meetings with people that had never occurred, or associations with people I had never met. I answered all of their questions truthfully, emphatically denying their accusations. After thirteen days I went on a hunger strike to protest my confinement."[32]

On January 23, 2004, El-Masri recounts that he was beaten, thrown in a car, and taken to a waiting airplane in Macedonia. There, his clothing was cut off, and he was forcibly given an enema and drugged. He woke up surrounded by American soldiers—in

Afghanistan. The innocent man's ordeal was just beginning. He recounted to ACLU lawyers:

> Once off the plane, I was shoved into the back of a vehicle. After a short drive, I was dragged out of the car, pushed roughly into a building, thrown to the floor, and kicked and beaten on the head, the soles of my feet, and the small of my back. I was left in a small, dirty, cold concrete cell. There was no bed and one dirty, military-style blanket and some old, torn clothes bundled into a thin pillow. I was extremely thirsty, but there was only a bottle of putrid water in the cell. I was refused fresh water.
>
> That first night I was interrogated by six or eight men dressed in the same black clothing and ski masks, as well as a masked American doctor and a translator. They stripped me of my clothes, photographed me, and took blood and urine samples. I was returned to my cell, where I would remain in solitary confinement, with no reading or writing materials, and without once being permitted outside to breathe fresh air, for more than four months.
>
> In March, I, along with several other inmates, commenced a hunger strike to protest our confinement without charges. . . . On day 37 of my hunger strike I was dragged into an interrogation room, tied to a chair, and a feeding tube was forced through my nose to my stomach. After the force-feeding, I became extremely ill and suffered the worst pain of my life.
>
> Near the beginning of May, I was brought into the interrogation room to meet an American who identified himself as a psychologist. He told me he had traveled from Washington, D.C., to check on me, and promised I would soon be released. Soon thereafter, I was interrogated again by a native German speaker named "Sam," the American prison director, and an American translator. I was warned at one point that as a condition of my release, I was never to mention

what had happened to me, because the Americans were determined to keep the affair a secret.[33]

On May 28, 2004, Khaled El-Masri was led out of his cell in Afghanistan, blindfolded and handcuffed, and put on a plane to Europe. He was told that he would not be flown directly to Germany, because the Americans wanted to keep secret their involvement in his ordeal. When his plane landed, he was driven blindfolded for several hours up winding mountain roads. Finally, his captors handed him his passport, removed his blindfold, sliced off his handcuffs, and dumped him on the side of a deserted road. They told him not to look back. After all he'd been through, El-Masri assumed this was the final moment, that he would now be shot. But the car sped away, and the German citizen was soon confronted by local police, who informed him he was in Albania. When he finally flew home to Germany, he discovered that his wife and family were gone. El-Masri eventually located his wife—in Lebanon. For five months, she thought her husband had abandoned her. So she uprooted her five children from Germany and moved to be closer to family.

The CIA confirmed in March 2004—three months after Khaled El-Masri was illegally detained—that his German passport was authentic; they had gotten the wrong man. But it took over two more months of jail and torture for him to be dumped, a free man, in Albania.

El-Masri's story is far from unique. The CIA has captured an estimated three thousand people in its roundup of alleged terrorist leaders.[34] It is impossible to know how many of these people are innocent. The CIA acts as judge, jury, and executioner: Its agents decide on their own who to arrest, and the CIA decides if and when a mistake has been made. If the CIA isn't getting the information it wants from a suspect—or if officials want to cover up an embarrassing mistake—the agency can simply "disappear" someone by transferring that prisoner to Guantánamo Bay or Bagram,

Afghanistan. Out of sight and beyond the reach of the media, it can take years for a suspect's case to be reviewed by the military. One senior official describes Guantánamo Bay as "a dumping ground" for CIA mistakes.[35] Indeed, nearly 300 prisoners have been released without charges from Guantánamo, having been illegally detained and after suffering years of isolation and abuse.

As a German citizen, Khaled El-Masri could not be so easily silenced—but the United States would try its best. In May 2004, U.S. ambassador to Germany Daniel R. Coats met with the German interior minister to inform him that the CIA was about to release a German citizen who had been wrongfully imprisoned for five months. Coats asked the Germans not to disclose what it knew about El-Masri's ordeal—even if El-Masri went public. The United States feared exposure of its shadowy rendition program, and was afraid of possible legal action by El-Masri and others.

The CIA was right about one thing in the El-Masri case: the backlash. In December 2005, the ACLU filed suit on behalf of El-Masri against former CIA director George Tenet. The unprecedented lawsuit charged that Tenet and other CIA officials broke U.S. and international human rights laws when they kidnapped El-Masri, and that his unlawful abduction and treatment were the direct result of the illegal CIA policy of extraordinary rendition. A federal judge dismissed the lawsuit five months later, declaring that El-Masri's rights must yield to "the national interest in preserving state secrets."[36]

With its cover blown for its illegal global roundup, the Bush administration has been reduced to barnstorming through skeptical foreign capitals and lying about what it's done before furious audiences. An irritated Secretary of State Condoleezza Rice declared in Europe in December 2005, "The United States does not transport and has not transported detainees from one country to another for the purpose of interrogations using torture."[37] But just four months later, investigators for the European Parliament revealed that the CIA had flown one thousand secret flights over Europe since 2001, sometimes ferrying terrorism suspects to countries that torture.

The United States has a product to sell, but no one is buying. "It's clear that the text of [Rice's] speech was drafted by lawyers with the intention of misleading an audience," said Andrew Tyrie, a Conservative member of the British parliament. Reporting on Rice's calamitous "we never torture" European tour in December 2005, a *New York Times* correspondent observed dryly, "It would be hard to imagine a more sudden and thorough tarnishing of the Bush administration's credibility than the one taking place here right now."[38]

It turns out that Germany may have been a silent partner to the United States in El-Masri's abduction. El-Masri has insisted that during his detention in Afghanistan, a fluent German-speaker participated in his interrogations. In February 2006, El-Masri picked a senior German police official out of a lineup of ten people and identified him as the man who interrogated him. The *New York Times* reported the story but astonishingly declined to identify the German official "at the request of Germany's intelligence services because he often does undercover intelligence work."[39]

The innocent victims of the war on terror, such as Khaled El-Masri, are piling up too high to be ignored. "I don't think I'm the human being I used to be," he said in announcing his lawsuit.[40] He is vowing to continue his fight.

He said, "I'm filing this lawsuit because I believe in the American system of justice. What happened to me was outside the bounds of any legal framework, and should never be allowed to happen to anyone else."[41]

Hiding the Hidden Prisons

"The CIA has been hiding and interrogating some of its most important al Qaeda captives at a Soviet-era compound in Eastern

Europe, according to U.S. and foreign officials familiar with the arrangement," began a startling Pultizer Prize–winning exposé by *Washington Post* reporter Dana Priest on November 2, 2005. "The secret facility is part of a covert prison system set up by the CIA nearly four years ago that at various times has included sites in eight countries, including Thailand, Afghanistan and several democracies in Eastern Europe, as well as a small center at the Guantánamo Bay prison in Cuba, according to current and former intelligence officials and diplomats from three continents."

The article continued, "Virtually nothing is known about who is kept in the facilities, what interrogation methods are employed with them, or how decisions are made about whether they should be detained or for how long. While the Defense Department has produced volumes of public reports and testimony about its detention practices and rules after the abuse scandals at Iraq's Abu Ghraib prison and at Guantánamo Bay, the CIA has not even acknowledged the existence of its black sites. To do so, say officials familiar with the program, could open the U.S. government to legal challenges, particularly in foreign courts, and increase the risk of political condemnation at home and abroad."

Yes, the free flow of information in a democracy carries certain political risks. But the obligation of America's press is to inform its readers without concern for "political condemnation." Right? Well, not quite. The article adds a bombshell: "The *Washington Post* is not publishing the names of the Eastern European countries involved in the covert program, at the request of senior U.S. officials. They argued that the disclosure might disrupt counterterrorism efforts in those countries and elsewhere and could make them targets of possible terrorist retaliation."

The single most important piece of information—where the CIA is illegally warehousing prisoners—is being withheld, because the Bush administration, so trustworthy when it comes to the treatment of detainees, wants it that way.

Human Rights Watch quickly stepped in to say that the prisons were likely in Poland or Romania. The group based this on records it obtained of military flights from Afghanistan. Officials from both Poland and Romania denied the allegations. Maintaining secret prisons would violate European human rights treaties.

Post executive editor Len Downie responded to the furor about the withheld information. Speaking on CNN, he said, "In this case, we agreed to keep the names of those particular countries out, because we were told, and it seems reasonable to us, that there could be terrorist retaliation against those countries, or more importantly, disruption of other very important intelligence activities, antiterrorist activities."

Commenting on the *Post*'s excuses, the media watch group Fairness and Accuracy in Reporting said, "The possibility that illegal, unpopular government actions might be disrupted is not a consequence to be feared."[42] Indeed, isn't exposing abuse exactly what a free press is for?

In an environment where journalists acknowledge that widespread abuse is taking place, lives hang in the balance when the media withholds information. As Peter Kornbluh, a senior analyst at the National Security Archive, told *Democracy Now!*, "I think that the *Post* bears a responsibility for the continuation of these abuses that we know have taken place in the past and probably are taking place in the present."[43]

To say that revealing the locations of probable torture centers somehow endangers American security is to tacitly endorse the legitimacy of the terror inflicted in these dungeons. As Kornbluh argued, "What is at stake is these secret detention centers. And the Romanians, the Poles, and other Eastern European citizens have been building a civil society focused on the abuses of the past—museums, monuments, efforts to say 'Never again!' And here the poetic irony is that the CIA appears to be using actual Soviet gulags that were in place in these countries when the Soviet Union was running them."

Yet when Amnesty International secretary general Irene Khan described Guantánamo Bay in May 2005 as "the gulag of our times," there was a furious backlash.

"Absurd," hit back President Bush.

"Offensive," declared Vice President Dick Cheney.

"Reprehensible," fumed Defense Secretary Donald Rumsfeld. "To try to equate the military's record on detainee treatment to some of the worst atrocities of the past century is a disservice to those who have sacrificed so much to bring freedom to others."[44]

"Dramatic, overwrought and, yes, outrageous," chimed in liberal pundit E. J. Dionne Jr.[45]

Khan shot back that her critics "overlooked U.S. operation of a worldwide network of prisons beyond Guantánamo Bay—extending from Afghanistan to Diego Garcia, from Pakistan to Iraq to Jordan—even to U.S. ships. . . . To the more than 70,000 prisoners—none yet tried, many tortured or ill-treated, enduring years of detention and interrogation—the prisons are far from 'ad hoc.' The United States should recommit to respecting the rule of law and human rights, actions that could begin to repair damaged U.S. credibility."[46]

British journalist Stephen Grey was among the first to report on the secret prisons and clandestine CIA flights that transported people to be tortured, in his article "America's Gulag," which appeared in May 2004 in *The New Statesman*. He explained on *Democracy Now!*, "The phrase 'gulag' is relevant, not because of the numbers involved. Clearly there were tens of thousands, if not hundreds of thousands, of prisoners in the Soviet gulag. But the interesting parallel is to look at how Solzhenitsyn described the Soviet gulag [in his 1973 classic, *The Gulag Archipelago*], which was a chain of islands of secret detention centers that existed hidden beneath normal society.

"And what you have here are these flights moving around from very normal airports, but inside are prisoners in the war on terror. Likewise, these jails are scattered around the world and no one sees them. They're connected by these flights. And the numbers are probably a few dozen in the CIA's own prisons, but thousands more in the jails of allied countries, such as Egypt and Morocco and Jordan."[47]

The *Washington Post,* instead of revealing the key detail that could throw open the doors of the gulags to international view, instead helped cover it up. Months after the *Post* broke the story about the prisons in Eastern Europe, human rights investigators were still unable to confirm their exact whereabouts because of government stonewalling. "The entire continent is involved," said Swiss senator Dick Marty, who was investigating the secret prisons for the Council of Europe's parliamentary assembly, a body comprising several hundred national lawmakers. "It is highly unlikely that European governments, or at least their intelligence services, were unaware."[48]

When the major media and the government collude to cover up a politically embarrassing story, democracy is undermined. Press freedom is mocked. And lives are lost.

Deception and Death

Consider what happened in the run-up to the disastrous Bay of Pigs invasion. In early 1961, *The New Republic* was about to publish an article about the CIA's covert effort to recruit Cuban refugees in Florida to attack Cuba and overthrow Fidel Castro. In a last-minute panic, *New Republic* publisher Gilbert Harrison sent the galley proofs of the story to Arthur Schlesinger Jr., then an assistant to President John F. Kennedy. Schlesinger has written that the article was a "careful, accurate and devastating account of CIA activities among the [Cuban] refugees [in Florida]."[49] Schlesinger showed the article to JFK, and at the president's request, the *New Republic* killed the story.

New York Times reporter Tad Szulc also filed a story with his newspaper on the imminent invasion of Cuba. It was slated to run on the front page under a four-column headline. At the eleventh hour, *Times* publisher Orvil Dryfoos told managing editor Turner Catledge that he was "troubled" by the security implications of exposing the secret invasion. Washington editor James Reston was consulted, and the story was gutted, stripped of references to an imminent invasion, and pushed down to a smaller below-the-fold placement. The news editor and assistant managing editor protested, but to no avail.

On April 17, 1961, a ragtag group of fifteen hundred Cuban exiles attacked Cuba at the Bay of Pigs with CIA backing. It was a disaster for the Kennedy administration: One hundred fourteen of the invaders died, and nearly twelve hundred were taken prisoner.

Ten days later, JFK met with *Times* managing editor Turner Catledge. "If you had printed more about the operation," scolded the president, "you would have saved us from a colossal mistake."

A year later, JFK sounded the same theme to Orvil Dryfoos: "I wish you had run everything on Cuba. I am just sorry you didn't tell it at the time."[50]

Reston, who acquiesced in the cover-up, later wrote, "If the press had used its freedom during this period to protest, it might have been influential even in the White House, where instead it was being encouraged to put out false information and was actually putting it out."

A month after the failed invasion—and the *Times* role in it—the newspaper ran a stinging editorial titled "The Right Not to Be Lied To": "A democracy—our democracy—cannot be lied to. . . . The basic principle involved is that of confidence. A dictatorship can get along without an informed public opinion. A democracy cannot."[51]

The problem is not just that governments lie. It's that the media, then as now, actively participates in the deception. A half century after the Bay of Pigs, the corporate media is still covering for power, with similar disastrous results for democracy.

2. Watching You

The president was a liar. America was bogged down in an unpopular, immoral foreign war. Americans were coming home by the score in body bags. The specter of a foreign menace was invoked to justify every new assault on civil liberties. Government critics were being spied on, harassed, and arrested. Congress was a paper tiger. The American media was largely silent about the abuses.

The year was 1971. The president: Richard Nixon. Concerned citizens in a suburb of Philadelphia decided something had to be done. They were about to change the course of history.

On March 8, 1971, anonymous activists used a crowbar to force their way into the two-man office of the FBI in Media, Pennsylvania, in the middle of the night. FBI agents arriving at work in the morning found only empty file cabinets; more than a thousand documents had been taken. The Citizens' Commission to Investigate the FBI, as the activists dubbed themselves, had pulled off its first and only action. The impact of that break-in is still being felt today.

Over the next few weeks, manila envelopes with no return addresses began arriving in newsrooms around the country. Inside each one was a collection of stolen FBI documents. Reporters at the *Washington Post, New York Times, Los Angeles Times,* and *Village Voice* all received copies. A statement of purpose from the Citizens' Commission accompanied some of the documents: "We believe that citizens have the right to scrutinize and control their own government. . . . The FBI has betrayed its democratic trust, and we wish to present evidence for this claim to the open and public judgment of our fellow citizens."[1]

Attorney General John Mitchell asked *Washington Post* executive editor Ben Bradlee not to publish the information because it could "endanger the lives" of government investigators.[2] The *Post* responded by being the first to break the story on March 24, 1971. The newspaper reported on how the FBI recruited a local police chief, mail carriers, and a telephone operator at Swarthmore College to spy on campus and black activist groups in the Philadelphia area.

The *Post* wrote that it was publishing the stolen files "in the public interest. . . . We believe the American public . . . needs to think long and hard about whether internal security rests essentially upon official surveillance and the suppression of dissent or upon the traditional freedom of every citizen to speak his mind on any subject, whether others consider what he says wise or foolish, patriotic or subversive."[3]

Buried in the stolen documents was a new term: COINTELPRO. It stood for the FBI's "counterintelligence program." The documents revealed that the super-secret program began in 1956, "in part because of frustration with Supreme Court rulings limiting the Government's power to proceed overtly against dissident groups," according to the Church Committee reports issued later.[4] As one stolen memo put it, the FBI used COINTELPRO to "enhance the paranoia endemic in these circles to get the point across there is an FBI agent behind every mailbox."[5]

The stolen documents and subsequent revelations shined a light on one of America's darkest chapters. The FBI was not simply gathering intelligence. COINTELPRO was a program aimed at aggressively destabilizing, provoking, smearing, and destroying organizations and individuals, many of whom were doing nothing more than exercising their free speech rights. Often, the only transgression of these groups and individuals was that FBI Director

J. Edgar Hoover disagreed with them. The groups that were targeted included the Black Panthers, the American Indian Movement, Students for a Democratic Society, and many antiwar, civil rights, and religious groups. Students, celebrities, professors, and concerned citizens were all targeted in the FBI's covert program. One stolen memo captured the vicious mentality of COINTELPRO: "Neutralize them in the same manner they are trying to destroy and neutralize the U.S."[6]

COINTELPRO operations often took a devastating toll. As Allan Jalon recounted in the *Los Angeles Times,* agents tried to blackmail Martin Luther King Jr. into killing himself. Actress Jean Seberg was targeted for having made a donation to the Black Panther Party; she ended up committing suicide after spurious gossip about her, based on an FBI wiretap, was leaked and published in the *Los Angeles Times.*

No one has ever claimed responsibility for the 1971 break-in in Pennsylvania. The FBI concluded a six-year, 33,000-page investigation, but couldn't solve the "crime."

The explosive contents of the COINTELPRO memos shocked the nation. Congress members were outraged at having been in the dark about the FBI's rogue operations. The exposés led to hearings by Sen. Frank Church of Idaho on abuses by the intelligence agencies (see Chapter 5, "The Mighty Wurlitzer," for more on this). The torrent of government abuse was slowly stemmed— but only temporarily.

They're back. Three decades after the FBI COINTELPRO program was exposed and supposedly dismantled, the federal government is once again spying on Americans. The targets of this illegal spying usually share one thing in common: They are innocent Americans who are exercising their right to speak freely.

Sarah Bardwell, an intern at the American Friends Service Committee in Denver, discovered that the Bush administration has another name for free speech: terrorism. She learned this when heavily armed police dressed in SWAT gear showed up at her door in July 2004. She recounted on *Democracy Now!*:

> It was Thursday on July 22, there were four FBI agents and two Denver police officers who came to our house in the afternoon. We asked them to stay on the front porch. They told us that they were doing preemptive investigations into suspected terrorists about actions planned at the RNC and the DNC [the 2004 Republican and Democratic presidential conventions]. Then they proceeded to ask us if we were planning any criminal activity or if we knew anybody who was planning any criminal activity for the convention.
>
> Myself and several of my roommates told them that [we] were choosing not to answer those questions. . . . They spent a lot of time sort of looking into our house, taking notes on the things that were on the walls in the living room, asking us about what our house was, and who we all were, and they asked us what our names were, which we also told them that [we] wouldn't give. Finally, they did say that since we weren't giving them the information that they wanted, they were taking that as noncooperation and they were going to have to therefore take more intrusive effort in the future to find out what they needed to know. But they wouldn't specify what they needed to know specifically or what those more intrusive efforts were.

Bardwell didn't know it at the time, but she was one of numerous activists being targeted by the FBI in a nationwide campaign of spying and political intimidation. See, in the aftermath of being attacked by Saudi-born terrorists, the Bush administration vowed to make us safer . . . by illegally spying on critics at home.

In the months before the 2004 Democratic and Republican national conventions, the FBI visited political activists in at least six states to question them about their involvement in protests. FBI officials described the questioning as part of a larger effort to track any planned disruptions related to the conventions, the presidential debates, or the November election.

An FBI spokesman said that the individuals visited were "people that we identified that could reasonably be expected to have knowledge of such plans and plots if they existed."[7] But civil rights groups say the forty to fifty documented cases of FBI questioning before the conventions amounted to harassment with the intent of chilling free speech. "The FBI is unjustifiably regarding demonstrations and public dissent as potential terrorism," said Mark Silverstein, legal director of the ACLU of Colorado.[8]

Silverstein told *Democracy Now!,* "I'm very, very skeptical that these visits are what the FBI claims them to be. They don't sound like a good faith investigation of reasonably suspected criminal activity. They sound much more like visits designed to intimidate these young people from engaging in protest activity or from associating with people who are engaging in such activities. The questions the FBI asked are not the kind of questions that would be asked if they were really trying to investigate suspected criminal activity."[9]

Silverstein charged that the FBI visits send a clear message "that if you participate in actions critical of the government or government policies, you might wind up with an FBI file. The danger, of course, is that these kinds of actions on the part of the FBI could deter people from joining a protest, from signing a petition, from writing a letter to the editor if they feel that that's going to prompt FBI scrutiny and maybe an FBI file."

That is exactly the effect that FBI surveillance had in Missouri. In 2004, a student and two former students at Truman State University in Kirksville, Missouri, were questioned by the FBI about their plans to go to the Democratic convention. For good measure, they were also subpoenaed by a grand jury, and they were under twenty-four-hour FBI surveillance for nearly a week. The students were never charged with a crime. "The subpoenas and surveillance were not to get information, but to harass and intimidate them," said Denise Lieberman, former ACLU legal director in eastern Missouri, in *The Nation*. The students ended up not attending the convention. Lieberman observed, "It worked. It was very frightening."[10]

In 2005, the American Civil Liberties Union filed Freedom of Information Act (FOIA) lawsuits in twenty states to obtain information about who the FBI was spying on and why. State by state, the answers have been trickling in, and a chilling national pattern has come into sharper focus: The Bush administration has unleashed the FBI to silence its political opponents. A few examples:

- In December 2005, the Colorado ACLU released secret FBI documents that showed that the Joint Terrorism Task Force (JTTF) in Denver monitored environmental activists involved in nonviolent protests against a 2002 convention of the North American Wholesale Lumber Association. The documents show that the names and license plates of several dozen activists are in an FBI file marked "counterterrorism." This case was especially surprising because the Denver Police had reached an agreement to rein in such tactics after the Colorado ACLU revealed that in 2003, the department maintained files on some three thousand people and two hundred groups involved in protests.
- Members of the organization Peace Fresno were shocked when they found out that one of their participants, Aaron Stokes, died in a motorcycle accident. An obituary published in the local newspaper in August 2003 showed Aaron's picture. But the name under the picture was not Aaron Stokes. It was Aaron Kilner—an undercover detective who was working for the Fresno County Sheriff's Department. He was also a member of the local anti-terrorism unit. Peace Fresno member Nicholas DeGraff told *Democracy Now!*, "If you have law enforcement equating dissent with terrorism, people are less likely to [express] their views."[11]

- In March 2006, the Colorado ACLU revealed that as part of a "domestic terrorism" investigation, the FBI's JTTF spied on a Denver bookstore, Breakdown Books (since closed) on February 15, 2003. Agents spent two hours monitoring forty people who gathered there to carpool to an antiwar demonstration in Colorado Springs later that day. The FBI recorded the descriptions and license plate numbers of a dozen cars "in the vicinity" of the bookstore.

- In December 2005, the ACLU released more than 2,300 pages of FBI documents revealing how counterterrorism agents have been monitoring domestic organizations active in causes as diverse as peace, the environment, animal cruelty, and poverty relief. The groups under FBI surveillance included Greenpeace, People for the Ethical Treatment of Animals, the Muslim Public Affairs Council, the American-Arab Anti-Discrimination Committee, Ancient Forest Rescue, the American Friends Service Committee, Code Pink, the National Lawyers Guild, and the Catholic Worker. The documents revealed that the FBI had monitored protests and used confidential informants inside the organizations to gain intelligence. One document indicated that FBI agents in Indianapolis planned to conduct surveillance of a "Vegan Community Project." Another document talked of the Catholic Workers' "semi-communistic ideology." A third indicated the Bureau's interest in determining the location of a protest over llama fur planned by People for the Ethical Treatment of Animals. Many of the investigative documents turned over by the Bureau are heavily edited, making it difficult or impossible to determine the full context of the references and why the FBI may have been discussing events such as a PETA protest.

The Joint Terrorism Task Forces are on the front lines of domestic spying. The JTTFs are teams of state, local, and federal agents that are led by the FBI. There are currently sixty-six JTTFs around the country, according to the ACLU.[12] Among the institutions that work closely with the JTTFs are "just about every university in the country," says the FBI. Many of the JTTFs have campus police officers assigned full-time to the FBI, funneling information about students and campus organizations to the Bureau. When reporter John Friedman of *The Nation* cold-called a number of universities to inquire whether they had officers assigned to the FBI, about one-third confirmed that they did— including the University of Illinois, Champaign/Urbana; the University of Texas, Austin; the University of Massachusetts, Amherst; the University of Florida, Gainesville; Michigan State; and Yale.[13]

With campus police now serving as the eyes and ears of the federal government, it's little wonder that students feel an icy wind blowing through their dorms. At North Carolina State University, the FBI went door-knocking and interrogating students following a protest at a nearby Republican headquarters shortly after the 2004 election. Campus police also increased their presence at campus antiwar protests. It "definitely had a chilling effect," said recent NCSU graduate Elena Everett, chair of the North Carolina Green Party. "People, especially international students, didn't feel comfortable speaking out anymore."[14]

In February 2005, federal prosecutors subpoenaed Drake University in Iowa for information about the sponsor of a campus antiwar forum. The demand was dropped after community protest.

"They don't know where Osama bin Laden is, but they're spending money watching people like me," said an incredulous Kirsten Atkins, an environmental activist whose license plate number turned up in an FBI terrorism file after she participated in a protest against the lumber industry in Colorado Springs in 2002.[15]

Around Denver, where numerous cases of spying have been exposed, activists report that people are avoiding protests out of fear that they will be investigated by the FBI.

"We've kind of gathered up our skirts and pulled in," peace activist Sarah Bardwell told the *Los Angeles Times* in March 2006, nearly two years after her visit from the authorities. "In our house, we don't talk about politics anymore. There's been a toning down of everything we do."[16]

"They Spied on Us"

In 1972, the Thomas Merton Center was founded in Pittsburgh to "find common ground in the nonviolent struggle to bring about a more peaceful and just society."

In 2002, a year after George W. Bush became president, the Center's activities made it a target of an international terrorism investigation.

According to secret FBI files obtained by the ACLU in March 2006, the Pittsburgh JTTF conducted a secret investigation into the activities of the Thomas Merton Center beginning as early as November 2002 because of its opposition to the war in Iraq. The ACLU said that these documents were the first to show conclusively that the rationale for FBI targeting was a group's opposition to the war.

One memo describes the Merton Center as a "left-wing organization advocating, among many political causes, pacifism." It notes that the center hands out leaflets on a daily basis opposing the war in Iraq. The FBI files also note that one of the peace activists observed handing out fliers "appeared to be of Middle Easter (sic) descent." Another file on the peace center is titled "International Terrorism Matters," and it includes information on a series of antiwar rallies taking place in Pittsburgh and around the country. Yet another FBI document said the Pittsburgh Joint Terrorism Task Force had learned that "The Thomas Merton Center . . . has been determined to be an organization which is opposed to the United States' war with Iraq."

Tim Vining, former director of the Thomas Merton Center, told *Democracy Now!*, "The activity that we were cited for was simply leafleting in Market Square. It was Buy Nothing Day, the day after Thanksgiving in November 2002, and we went out just simply to hand out leaflets about a variety of issues—transit advocacy, antiwar, global justice. And for that, we were targeted."

Vining suspects that the peace center's effort to work with the local Muslim community drew special attention from the FBI. "Because we tried to build relationships that cross the lines of religion that are used to divide people, because of that, we were spied on by our government. Now, at a time when religious misunderstandings and differences lead to so much terrorism and violence in the world today, you would think our government would applaud us for seeking peace and trying to understand one another. Instead, they spied on us."

William J. Crowley, a spokesman for the FBI in Pittsburgh, said, "We have to be able to go out and look at things. We have to be able to conduct an investigation."[17]

Increasingly, Americans are being given a new label by the government: suspect. The *Washington Post* reported that the National Counterterrorism Center now has a central repository of 325,000 names of international terrorism suspects or people who allegedly aid them—a number that has more than quadrupled since the fall of 2003.[18]

Tim Vining insisted, "I think what's important is that we not allow this to get us to not trust one another or to live in fear and paranoia. You know, for years, since the Thomas Merton Center was formed in 1972, we have always stood with people who have been targeted or have been scapegoated, whether that be African-Americans, gays and lesbians, immigrants, workers, youth, and we're not about to stop now. And if that makes us a threat to this government, then so be it. But we're not going be deterred. In fact, this Saturday, we're going back out into the streets of Pittsburgh, and we're going to have another huge protest in the thousands to defend our rights and to speak out against this war."

Spying for the Pentagon

When a group of activists got together at the Quaker Meeting House in Lake Worth, Florida, in 2004 to plan a protest against military recruiters in local high schools, there was a secret uninvited guest: a Pentagon spy, who reported the planned protest as a "threat." The activists only learned this in December 2005, when NBC News and journalist William Arkin exposed the existence of a secret Pentagon database to track intelligence gathered inside the United States. The database included information on dozens of antiwar protests and rallies, particularly actions targeting military recruiting.

The Department of Defense has strict guidelines, established in 1982, that restrict the information it is allowed to collect and retain on U.S. citizens. These guidelines may now be being either bent or violated. The Pentagon database obtained by NBC included 1,519 "threats" that were reported between July 2004 and May 2005, including:

- Countermilitary recruiting meetings held at the Quaker Meeting House in Lake Worth, Florida
- Antinuclear protests staged in Nebraska on the anniversary of the U.S. atomic bombing of Nagasaki
- An antiwar protest organized by military families outside Fort Bragg in North Carolina
- A rally in San Diego to support war resister Pablo Paredes

In all, the Pentagon "threat" list included four dozen antiwar meetings, including some that took place far from any military facility or recruitment office.[19] All were entirely legal gatherings.

The documents also indicate that the Pentagon is now conducting surveillance at protests and possibly monitoring Internet traffic. One Pentagon briefing document stamped "secret" concluded: "We have noted increased communication and encouragement between protest groups using the Internet." The same document indicated that the military is tracking who is attending protests in part by keeping records on cars seen at demonstrations.

The Pentagon's domestic intelligence gathering has been done through a secretive program that allows military bases and other defense installations to file Threat and Local Observation Notices (TALON) of suspicious activity into a consolidated database. The program, established in 2003 by then deputy secretary of defense Paul Wolfowitz, is so secret that even the number of reports in the database is classified. Also classified is the size and budget of the new agency overseeing the database, Counter-Intelligence Field Activity (CIFA).

Marie Zwicker works with the Truth Project, the counter-recruiting group in Lake Worth, Florida, that was spied upon. She told *Democracy Now!*, "We hold open meetings, and our work, as other counter-recruiting groups do, is in the high schools to counter and balance the effects of the military recruiting."

Zwicker said that she and other members of her organization were "outraged that our government would be spying on groups like this. Freedom to dissent is not only a right guaranteed to us in the Bill of Rights and by our Constitution. It is an absolute responsibility of people who see that and believe that their government is acting and going in the wrong direction. It is our responsibility to stand up and speak out. This is what we feel that we were doing."

Bill Dobbs, a spokesperson for United for Peace and Justice, a coalition of some fifteen hundred groups that has sponsored national antiwar demonstrations, observed on *Democracy Now!*, "The crackdowns on dissent come in many different forms. What's alarming about the surveillance, of course, is that we don't know what sort of infiltration is going on, what sort of covert action may be taking place, and we may never know."

Even top officials are being kept in the dark about the extent of the spying. When the activities of two Vermont peace groups were listed as "threats" by the Pentagon, Vermont senator Patrick

Leahy sent three letters over two months to Defense Secretary Donald Rumsfeld demanding information about the surveillance. At a Senate hearing in March 2006, an exasperated Leahy confronted Rumsfeld: "I worry that we're getting back into the COINTELPRO days of Vietnam. My letters ask for specific things that, one, should have been very easy to answer: Is the press right that there was surveillance of citizens in my home state of Vermont? I would think that senators that have been here for 31 years ought to be able to get an answer to a simple question like that. For months, everybody's refused to answer my question."[20]

Following a testy exchange with Rumsfeld, Leahy finally received a letter from the Defense Department that afternoon conceding that the Vermont groups should not have been included in the TALON database, since the system was only supposed to report "suspicious incidents related to possible foreign terrorist threats" to the Defense Department. There was no indication that the spying on domestic groups would stop; the letter simply noted that the reports on the Vermont groups were filed in the wrong database.

Warrantless Spying

The most breathtaking and far-reaching of all the Bush administration spy programs that have been revealed so far has been the warrantless eavesdropping by the National Security Agency. The program was first exposed in an article in the *New York Times* in December 2005—after the story was withheld by *Times* editors for over a year at the request of the White House (see Introduction). The *Times* revealed that President Bush had authorized the NSA to eavesdrop—without warrants—on calls and e-mails of people suspected of having links to terrorists. Then, in May 2006, *USA Today* exposed how the National Security Agency has been secretly collecting the phone call records of millions of Americans with the help of AT&T, Verizon, and BellSouth (the latter two companies have denied the charge). One source told the paper that the NSA is attempting to create the world's largest database—big enough to include "every call ever made" within the United States. An AT&T whistle-blower, Mark Klein, has revealed that the telecom company has built secret eavesdropping rooms in their main switching centers where calls are monitored. The Electronic Frontier Foundation filed suit against AT&T in January 2006, demanding that the company stop illegally spying on its customers.

Soon after the *Times* exposed the existence of the program, an NSA whistle-blower, Russell Tice, spoke about it on *Democracy Now!* "I believe I have seen some things that are illegal," he began. "This is probably the number one commandment of the Ten Commandments as a SIGINT [signals intelligence] officer: You will not spy on Americans. . . . Apparently the leaders of NSA have decided that they were just going to go against the tenets of something that's a gospel."

There has long been a legal way to monitor the electronic communications of Americans: Obtain a warrant from the secret court authorized by the Foreign Intelligence Surveillance Act (FISA). The warrants are readily given, as Tice explained: "I kinda liken the FISA court to a monkey with a rubber stamp. . . . It just stamps 'affirmed' . . . and a banana chip rolls out, and then the next paper rolls in front of the monkey. When you have like twenty thousand [eavesdropping] requests and only, I think, four were turned down, you can't look at the FISA court as anything different."

He continued, "So, you have to ask yourself the question: Why would someone want to go around the FISA court in something like this? I would think the answer could be that this thing is a lot bigger than even the president has been told it is, and that ultimately a vacuum cleaner approach may have been used. . . . That's ultimately why you wouldn't go to the FISA court."

The Bush administration has justified the illegal spying in a time-honored fashion: through fear and deceit. Vice President Dick Cheney told CNN in December 2005 that warrantless eavesdropping "has saved thousands of lives." President Bush refers to the program as "terrorist surveillance" and said, "If you're talking to a member of al Qaeda, we want to know why."

The reality of the program is that in the months after 9/11, thousands of Americans were spied on by the NSA, sending a flood of phone numbers, e-mails, and names to the FBI. Of these tips, "virtually all of them, current and former officials say, led to dead ends or innocent Americans," according to the *New York Times*. Meanwhile, intelligence resources have been swamped with the glut of useless information. FBI agents joke that new domestic terrorism tips from the NSA meant more "calls to Pizza Hut," according to an FBI supervisor.[21]

The result is that these massive and illegal spy programs undertaken by the FBI and NSA have made us less safe. While police spy on peace activists and other innocent Americans, real national security needs go unaddressed: A Senate panel was told in March 2006 that congressional investigators testing U.S. port security smuggled enough radioactive material into the United States last year to make two radiological "dirty" bombs.[22]

So much for homeland security.

The real threat to America's security now comes from within. As Russell Tice, a lifelong Republican who voted for George W. Bush, said in a letter to Congress, "The freedom of the American people cannot be protected when our constitutional liberties are ignored and our nation has decayed into a police state."

This warning was echoed by retired Supreme Court justice Sandra Day O'Connor in March 2006. "We must be ever-vigilant against those who would strong-arm the judiciary into adopting their preferred policies," she declared just two months after stepping down from the bench. "It takes a lot of degeneration before a country falls into dictatorship, but we should avoid these ends by avoiding these beginnings."[23]

Today's war on terror themes are familiar ones: A foreign threat requires curbs on civil liberties. Innocent people have nothing to fear. The end justifies the means. But as we learn of how innocent people are being swept up in the government dragnet, memories of those earlier abuses are recalled. The Bush administration is attempting to cover its lies with the blunt instrument of government power—from Iraq to Denver—turned against its own citizens. Perhaps the abuse is not surprising, when we see that key players from the Nixon era—Donald Rumsfeld (a former member of Nixon's cabinet) and Dick Cheney (former deputy assistant to Nixon)—have risen again from the swamp of COINTELPRO to grab the levers of power.

In 1971, the media, giving voice to dissenters, played a crucial role in exposing and halting the government abuse. Today, journalists are a last line of defense against a government that has arrogated to itself unprecedented powers. Is our modern media up to the challenge? Early signs are not reassuring. In contrast to the principled stand taken by the *Washington Post* in 1971, the *New York Times* in 2005 chose to hide the truth about NSA's warrantless spying for over a year. We may never know the cost of that shocking betrayal of its journalistic and moral duty.

The Citizens' Commission to Investigate the FBI were patriots and heroes. By defying a corrupt and lawless government, they, and the newspapers who published the FBI documents, held America's leaders accountable to democracy's highest ideals. Now, as then, America staggers under the yoke of lying leaders, an immoral war, illegal government actions against innocent citizens, and a media that is alternately cowed and complicit. Now, as then, America sorely needs such patriots and heroes.

All governments lie, but disaster lies in wait for countries whose officials smoke the
same hashish they give out. **—I. F. Stone (1907–1989), muckraking journalist**

By 2006, President Bush was presiding over a continuous string of
scandals, policy failures, and public relations fiascoes. His pet war
had become a bloody quagmire. Hurricane Katrina had laid waste
to the Gulf Coast, and laid bare the incompetence of his appointed
cronies. Bush's signature program for his second term—privatizing
Social Security—hit a wall of public opposition and sank in a few
short months. The economy was in the toilet, his party's key
enforcer—House majority leader Tom "The Hammer" DeLay—
was indicted and quit Congress, his vice president's chief of staff
was indicted, as was Republican über-lobbyist Jack Abramoff, White
House domestic policy advisor Claude Allen, and the administration's chief procurement officer, David Safavian. The Abramoff
scandal was threatening to bring down a slew of top Republicans. By
mid-2006, 70 percent of Americans disapproved of their president.

For Bush, none of this was a problem that propaganda couldn't
solve. Bush had used deception and disinformation to get us into a
war; he would do the same to bail himself out of political trouble.
The administration that claimed it could not afford Medicare,
school lunches, or adequate body armor for its soldiers spared no
expense when it came to burnishing the president's image. For a
government based on illusion, carnage could simply vanish with
the banning of cameras or the stroke of a pen.

Since coming to power, the Bush administration has engaged in
a systematic campaign of covert propaganda aimed at subverting

both domestic and foreign media. The Government Accountability Office estimates that between 2003 and 2005, the administration spent $1.6 billion on advertising and public relations to promote its policies.[1] The subterfuge against the U.S. media has been remarkable for its breadth—and for how similar the propaganda has been to standard media coverage.

In Iraq, the challenge for the Bush administration was not how to rebuild the country—a task that the United States has largely abandoned. No, the challenge was to get Iraqis to cheer up. Iraqis just needed to believe that the U.S. occupation was a boon to their devastated country, and overlook the fact that in Baghdad, electricity was on for four hours per day, down from sixteen to twenty-four hours per day before the U.S. invasion. And ignore the fact that by 2006, virtually every service sector in Iraq—including oil, electricity, water, and sewerage—had fallen below pre-invasion levels.[2] Iraqis just shouldn't worry that insurgent attacks were spiking to record highs, that thousands of innocent Iraqis were being abused in American-run prisons, and that they risked getting killed by a car bomb each time they went to the market.

All this was wished away. In its place, good news started to appear in Iraqi newspapers in mid-2005. MORE MONEY GOES TO IRAQ'S DEVELOPMENT, blared one headline. THE SANDS ARE BLOWING TOWARD A DEMOCRATIC IRAQ, gushed another. One article reported cheerily, "As the people and the [Iraqi security forces] work together, Iraq will finally drive terrorism out of Iraq for good."[3]

The stories, made to appear as if they were written by independent Iraqi journalists, were in fact written by American "information operations" troops as part of a multimillion-dollar covert Pentagon operation to plant propaganda in the Iraqi media. Cash-strapped Iraqi newspapers were paid from $50 to $2,000 to run a story. In addition, Iraqi journalists were paid stipends of up to $500 per month, depending on how many pro-American pieces they published.[4]

This secret program is run by a relatively unknown defense

contractor called the Lincoln Group, which in 2005 landed a multi-year $100 million contract to produce pro-American, anti-insurgent TV, radio, and print messages. The Lincoln Group was founded in 2003 by Paige Craig, a 31-year-old West Point dropout and former Marine who served in Iraq, and Christian Bailey, 30, an Oxford-educated Briton who moved to the United States and headed Lead 21, a networking group for young Republicans. Bailey and Craig realized there was a killing to be made in Iraq—in "reconstruction." In 2004, they formed Iraqex, which partnered briefly with the Rendon Group, the PR firm that promoted the pro-war Iraqi exiles (more on this later). In mid-2004, Iraqex won a $6 million Pentagon contract to design and execute "an aggressive advertising and PR campaign that will accurately inform the Iraqi people of the Coalition's goals and gain their support."[5] The Rendon Group dropped out weeks after Iraqex got the contract. One of the Iraqex projects was to persuade people in Iraq and the United States of the "strength, integrity and reliability of Iraqi forces during the fight for Fallujah" in 2004. Most accounts suggest that Iraqi troops played a minor role in Fallujah.

Iraqex changed its name to the Lincoln Group and, despite the fact that Bailey and Craig had no background in media or communications, bid on a military public affairs contract in 2004 that called for a "full service advertising and public relations firm." They landed a three-year $18-million contract.[6] In 2005, the Lincoln Group scored a $20 million two-month contract to influence public opinion in Iraq's Al Anbar province, an insurgent hotbed. The big payoff came in the summer of 2005, when Lincoln won a $100 million contract, which was part of a $300 million global stealth PR campaign by the Pentagon.[7]

By December 2005, the Lincoln Group had placed over one thousand articles in fifteen to seventeen Iraqi and Arab newspapers. It also paid Islamic clerics for advice on how to persuade Sunnis to participate in elections and oppose the Iraqi insurgency. The Lincoln Group also proposed an Arab sitcom based on the Three

Stooges, featuring bumbling terrorists as the main characters; the Pentagon rejected the idea.[8]

Current and former Lincoln Group employees told the *Los Angeles Times* that the Al Anbar PR campaign "was unnecessarily costly, poorly run and largely ineffective at improving America's image in Iraq."

"In my own estimation, this stuff has absolutely no effect, and it's a total waste of money," said a former employee. "Every Iraqi can read right through it."[9]

But the propaganda was useful—not in Iraq, but in the United States. In the absence of real progress in Iraq, the illusion would do fine for the Bush administration. And so Defense Secretary Donald Rumsfeld hailed the thriving, independent pro-American Iraqi media as one of the great by-products of the Iraqi invasion. In November 2005, Rumsfeld declared that Iraq's "free media" offered a "relief valve" for the Iraqi public to debate current issues.

Among the "free media" that ran the U.S.-planted stories was *Al Mutamar*, a Baghdad daily run by associates of Iraqi deputy prime minister Ahmad Chalabi. Prior to the invasion of Iraq, Chalabi was paid by the United States to head the Iraqi National Congress and was the darling of Pentagon neoconservatives. He was a key source for the bogus stories about Iraq's alleged WMDs that President Bush invoked to make his case for war.

Now Chalabi is a key source for bogus stories about the U.S. occupation that Bush invokes to make his case for having triumphed. As Luay Baldawi, editor in chief of *Al Mutamar*, explained about the newspaper's stringent criteria for publishing a story: "We are pro-American. Everything that supports America we will publish."[10]

The Pentagon propaganda campaign is being waged as the State Department is offering programs in basic journalism skills and media ethics to Iraqi journalists. One workshop was titled "The Role of Press in a Democratic Society."[11]

"Here we are trying to create the principles of democracy in

Iraq," said a senior Pentagon official who opposes planting stories in the Iraqi media. "Every speech we give in that country is about democracy. And we're breaking all the first principles of democracy when we're doing it."[12]

Iraq's Free Fake Media

Creating the illusion of a free Iraqi media was a high priority for President Bush. Shortly after the invasion, the U.S.-led Coalition Provisional Authority awarded defense contractor Science Applications International Corporation (SAIC) a no-bid $82 million contract to create the Iraqi Media Network.

SAIC hired longtime TV producers such as Don North to set up the network of thirty TV and radio transmitters, three broadcast studios, and twelve bureaus around Iraq. With the ouster of the Iraqi dictator, North thought that he was establishing Iraq's first independent journalism centers. How naïve of him.

"We immediately started clashing with the Coalition Provisional Authority, who wanted control—they just couldn't resist controlling the message," North told *Democracy Now!* "Our aim [was] to sort of make a PBS, a public broadcast radio and TV for the Iraqis. But instead, it just became a mouthpiece for the Coalition, and the Iraqis didn't find it credible. They just thought of it as another Voice of America, and turned to other satellite broadcasters like Al Jazeera."[13] The Voice of America is a U.S. government-funded broadcast service that airs in foreign countries; the secretary of state is a member of its oversight board, and it is widely viewed as a U.S. propaganda outlet.

At times it was hard to tell where the Coalition Provisional Authority ended and where the "free" Iraqi Media Network began. One foreign official told the *Washington Post* in 2003 that Margaret Tutwiler, who was later tapped to head the State Department's Office of Public Diplomacy, and CPA spokesman Dan Senor were "effectively acting like the station manager and the news director."

Senor once interviewed his boss, Paul Bremer, on camera after he determined that an inexperienced staff member of the Iraqi Media Network was unprepared.

One well-placed reconstruction agency advisor said that Tutwiler and Senor had achieved "what the White House has been dreaming of for years: . . . controlling the evening news."[14]

The network also tried to cut many corners. Salary for the news anchors started at $60 a month, and the network offered a small clothing allowance—but only for clothes from the waist up. There was money to buy a TelePrompTer—not for the network's Iraqi anchors, but for Paul Bremer.[15]

None of this should have come as a surprise. SAIC did not have media experience—just deep ties to the Pentagon. SAIC's former CEO, Admiral William Owens, served as vice chair of the Joint Chiefs of Staff and on the Pentagon's Defense Policy Board. SAIC board member Wayne Downing is a retired Army general and former lobbyist for the Iraqi National Congress. Downing was also on the board of the pro-war Committee for the Liberation of Iraq.[16]

The Iraqi Media Network was such a failure that its top Iraqi anchor, Ahmad Rikabi, quit after three months and the United States ended its contract with SAIC after only one year.

But less than two years later, in June 2005, the Pentagon's Special Operations Command selected SAIC and two other firms—the Lincoln Group and SYColeman—to oversee a new five-year, $300 million media campaign in "areas such as Iraq and Lebanon." Coordinating the campaign is something called the Joint Psychological Operations Support Element. Under the contract, the three companies will "conduct media campaigns to garner support for U.S. government policies and objectives in foreign countries among foreign audiences." The *San Diego Union-Tribune* reported, "The campaign will include radio broadcasts, video programs, news articles, printed material and even novelty items such as T-shirts, balls and bumper stickers."[17]

SAIC wasn't the only U.S. contractor with no journalism experience to win a no-bid Iraqi media contract. In January 2004, the United States handed $96 million to the Florida-based Harris Corporation to pick up where SAIC failed. Months later, the main U.S.-run newspaper, *Al-Sabah*, nearly fell apart. On April 25, 2004, its editor, Ismail Zaher, and about twenty staffers walked out in protest over its lack of editorial independence under Harris and the United States. In an open letter explaining their walkout, the staff of *Al-Sabah* accused a Harris subcontractor of "turning the building into a fortress, as if this is going to provide better security than independence of *Al-Sabah*."

Iraqi reporters discovered that working for a U.S. propaganda organ was a dangerous business. The newspaper staff wrote: "The battles in Fallujah and other Iraqi cities have changed the situation. The newspaper's journalists and even drivers and printers cannot cope any longer with the numerous death threats they have been receiving. They fear for their lives. Five times attempts to bomb the newspaper's building in Al-Qahera have been foiled, but what will happen the next time?" The staffers concluded, "Although we were a patriotic, even-handed newspaper, we have to take into account the reality that *Al-Sabah* is regarded, rightly, as a U.S.-funded newspaper, and wrongly, as the voice of the CPA and/or the Governing Council."[18]

After the staff of *Al-Sabah* walked out, the U.S.-backed paper continued publication under the editorship of one Maher Faisal. "We don't need the independence [former editor Ismail] Zayer talks about," Faisal told the *Washington Post*. "We only have to publish credible information. These exiles have nothing to teach Iraqis. We can work without them."

Faisal was well versed in the rules of state media—he used to work for one of Saddam Hussein's official newspapers, *al-Jumhuriya*.

So how did Harris land a huge no-bid media contract with little journalism experience? It's easy: To the Pentagon, media is just another weapon. "The primary goal of the U.S. government's media expansion in Iraq always has been a military and political one: to quell unrest, win the minds of the people and combat anti-American propaganda from other sources," said Sherrie Gossett of the right-wing group Accuracy in Media. "The fact that the U.S. started the job with a defense contractor . . . and then chose Harris—a media technology company with no journalism experience—underscores those priorities."[19]

It also helps to have ties to the Pentagon and the Republican Party. During the 2004 election cycle, Harris donated $263,570 to GOP political action committees and candidates—thirty-two times what it gave to Democrats. And the senior vice president of Harris, Robert K. Henry, spent eight years with the U.S. Army Communications Command and the Defense Communications Agency.[20]

The U.S. propaganda campaign is not only undermining Iraqi democracy. It is undermining U.S. democracy as well. A secret 2003 Pentagon directive on information operations policy prohibits U.S. troops from conducting psychological operations targeting the U.S. media. The order was signed by Rumsfeld.[21] Part of the intent of the order was to keep propaganda that was planted in foreign publications from being picked up by U.S. media—which is forbidden by law. But clearly, Americans are part of the target audience for the propaganda.

The military has already been caught planting false stories in the U.S. press. In October 2004, a Marine spokesperson appeared on CNN to declare that U.S. forces had started a major operation to take the Iraqi city of Fallujah. "Troops crossed the line of departure," said 1st Lt. Lyle Gilbert. "It's going to be a long night."

In fact, the invasion of Fallujah wouldn't begin for another three weeks.

The *Los Angeles Times* reported, "Gilbert's carefully worded announcement was an elaborate psychological operation—or 'psy-op'—intended to dupe insurgents in Fallujah and allow U.S.

commanders to see how guerrillas would react if they believed U.S. troops were entering the city."[22]

That isn't the only time the military has used the domestic press in its psy-ops campaigns. Shortly after September 11, a military officer admitted to the *Washington Post*, "This is the most information-intensive war you can imagine. . . . We're going to lie about things."[23]

Ahmad Chalabi's Iraqi National Congress was paid lavishly to deceive Americans. The INC was established after the first Gulf War under a CIA contract with the Rendon Group, the PR firm. The plan was for the INC, with the help of the Rendon Group, to place stories in the British press about atrocities committed by Saddam Hussein. "The aim was for the stories to then be picked up by the American media, thereby bypassing U.S. laws that prevented government funding of domestic propaganda," wrote Jack Fairweather, former Baghdad bureau chief for the London *Daily Telegraph*, in an article for *Mother Jones*.[24] This "legal end run caused some unease" at the CIA, Fairweather reported, but not enough to keep the Agency from backing the effort. Nabeel Musawi, the political liaison of the INC, said of his U.S. patrons, "What did they expect? We were committed to overthrowing Saddam Hussein, not holding a tea party. We had to take some risks to achieve that."

In 1998, the Republican-led Congress approved the Iraq Liberation Act. The INC received $17.3 million for the "collection and dissemination of information" to the media about Saddam Hussein's crimes.[25] By 2002, the Defense Department was paying the INC $340,000 a month for its "intelligence," although by that time the CIA had determined that the INC's information was unreliable.

The INC put the American money to work doing what the group did best—lying and fabricating stories. The INC planted bogus stories about nonexistent weapons of mass destruction, and concocted tales of a meeting between Saddam Hussein and Osama bin Laden. It planted these stories through a network of credulous

American journalists, notably Judith Miller of the *New York Times*. And its fakery went further: In November 2001, the INC presented a supposed Iraqi general, Jamal al-Ghurairy, to be interviewed by a *New York Times* reporter. The subsequent front page *Times* story quoted the general describing how foreign Arab fighters were being trained to hijack planes at Salman Pak, a military facility south of Baghdad. "We were training these people to attack installations important to the United States," he said. Versions of this remarkable charge were repeated in numerous publications, including the *Washington Post, Vanity Fair,* and the London *Observer.* In a final coup de grâce, the White House included the Salman Pak story in the background paper "Decade of Deception and Defiance," prepared for President Bush's September 12, 2002, speech to the UN General Assembly.

But it turns out the real Iraqi Lieutenant General al-Ghurairy has never left Iraq. The INC "general" was an imposter, as Jack Fairweather revealed later in *Mother Jones.*

The circle of deception was complete. The Bush administration bankrolled the preparation and dissemination of bogus stories to the American media, then cited the bogus accounts as a justification to launch a war. With American journalists only too eager to sacrifice truth for access, reality never had a chance.

Even the "experts" are bought off. In a December 2005 article about the covert Iraq propaganda program, the *New York Times* quoted Michael Rubin, a Middle East expert at the American Enterprise Institute, as saying, "I'm not surprised this goes on. Especially in an atmosphere where terrorists and insurgents—replete with oil boom cash—do the same. We need an even playing field, but cannot fight with both hands tied behind our backs."[26]

The Bush administration couldn't have scripted a better defense—because it was already paying Rubin for his scripting help. A month after this article ran, the *Times* revealed that Rubin had worked for the Lincoln Group—covertly, of course.[27] Rubin refused to reveal how much he had been paid by the group.

And why should he? He's just another member of the Bush and Rumsfeld "free media" offering his opinions . . . to the highest bidder.

As for results, the Iraq propaganda campaign has failed to win over many Iraqis. In a poll done by the University of Maryland in January 2006, half of Iraqis—including nine out of ten Sunnis—said they approve of attacks on U.S.-led forces. Eighty percent of Iraqis think the United States plans to have permanent bases in Iraq, while 70 percent support a timetable for withdrawal of U.S. troops. Two-thirds of Iraqis believe their security and the availability of public services will both improve if U.S. forces leave in six months.[28]

Looks like reality trumps spin in Iraq. But President Bush is determined not to let that happen in the United States.

The truth is the mortal enemy of the lie, and thus by extension, the truth is the greatest
enemy of the State.   —**Joseph Goebbels (1897–1945), Nazi Propaganda Minister**

Reporter Karen Ryan delivered the good news: George W. Bush's
controversial Medicare plan was going to be a huge success. "All
people with Medicare will be able to get coverage that will lower
their prescription drug spending," declared Ryan. She then interviewed Tommy G. Thompson, secretary of Health and Human
Services, who stated, "This is going to be the same Medicare system only with new benefits, more choices, more opportunities for
enhanced benefits."

Forty TV stations around the country carried the news segment
in 2004, revealed a March 2005 *New York Times* exposé. There was
no mention of the scandals surrounding the Medicare law, including how it was passed in November 2003 when Republican leaders
in Congress kept the vote open until almost 6 A.M. as they threatened, bribed, and cajoled reluctant opponents into changing their
votes. Nor was there any mention of criticism that the Medicare
law, which bars the federal government from seeking competitive
bids on drugs, was slammed by critics as a giveaway to pharma-
ceutical companies.[1]

Then there was the glowing report about the oft-criticized
Transportation Security Administration. Reporter Jennifer Morrow explained how the TSA's "top-notch work force"—roundly
criticized elsewhere for security lapses, including missing one out
of four fake bombs in a test at Newark Airport[2]—had led "one of
the most remarkable campaigns in aviation history." With a

bustling airport security system humming smoothly for the camera, Morrow intoned, "Thousands leaving impressive careers and good jobs to take up the front lines in the war against terrorism."[3]

As for the war on terror, it's going great, thanks to President Bush. We know, because we saw an ecstatic Iraqi-American man on the evening news responding to the fall of Baghdad: "Thank you, Bush! Thank you, USA! I love Bush, I love USA, because they do that for Iraqi people's freedom."

Remarkable testimonials, compelling narratives—and all of them fake. These stories, which aired on American news programs, were each produced by the U.S. government. The "reporters" were public relations professionals hired by the government, often using pseudonyms, the *Times* reported.

This is the Bush administration's version of "reality TV": When they don't like reality, they simply create an alternate reality. We call this propaganda when we hear about it in other countries. Here, TV networks pass along these fantasies as news.

Under the Bush administration, at least twenty federal agencies have spent $250 million creating hundreds of fake television news segments that are sent to local stations.[4] State Department official Patricia Harrison (she became president of the Corporation for Public Broadcasting in 2005) told Congress in 2003 that the Bush administration considers its "good news" segments to be "powerful strategic tools" for influencing public opinion.[5]

The Government Accountability Office, the investigative arm of Congress, had a different term for it: "covert propaganda."[6] In four different reports issued in 2005, the GAO detailed how the Bush administration had broken the law. The administration's response: The White House instructed the heads of all government agencies in a March 2005 letter to disregard the GAO findings on covert propaganda.[7]

The Bush administration intensified its efforts to disseminate domestic propaganda after 9/11. At that time, White House officials wanted positive news coverage of its so-called war on terror.

When the U.S. media wasn't sounding sufficiently enthusiastic, Bush operatives decided to create their own news. Officially, they said they wanted, according to the *Times*, "to counter charges of American imperialism by generating accounts that emphasized American efforts to liberate and rebuild Afghanistan and Iraq."[8]

The State Department knew just where to turn: It already had an Office of BS (officially, the Office of Broadcast Services). Starting in early 2002, working closely with the White House, about thirty editors at the Office of BS—who previously spent their time distributing videos from press conferences—began churning out feature news reports promoting the Bush administration's accomplishments in Iraq and Afghanistan, and promoting the case for war. The videos cleverly disguised their origins, offering journalist-like narration and sign-offs. In one case, a Memphis Fox affiliate ran an entire segment about Afghanistan, using a local news reporter to read the State Department script so it sounded like it had been produced locally. "After living for decades in fear," reporter Tish Clark said on station WHBQ, Afghan women "are now receiving assistance—and building trust—with their coalition liberators."[9]

The State Department has distributed these videos around the United States and the world. By early 2005, the Office of BS had produced fifty-nine such fake news segments. The Pentagon's Army and Air Force Hometown News Service is also in the business of manufacturing news. In 2004, it created fifty stories that were broadcast 236 times, reaching 41 million American households.[10]

Numerous other government agencies have also been getting into the propaganda business. Fortunately for the Bush administration, many U.S. news organizations are eager to act as its mouthpiece. The aptly named television station WCIA in Champaign, Illinois, ran more than two dozen news segments made by the U.S. Department of Agriculture in one three-month period in 2005. In one fawning piece about the government's role in hurricane cleanup in Florida, a local official crowed about the USDA, "They've done a fantastic job." Another quoted Agriculture Secretary Mike Johanns describing President Bush as "the best envoy in the world."[11]

Jim Gee, the news director at WCIA, defended having his station become a pipeline for government-produced "news" stories, telling the *New York Times*, "We don't think they're propaganda. They meet our journalistic standards. They're informative. They're balanced."[12]

The GAO disagrees. In one of its investigations into the government's fake news program, it concluded that video news releases from the Office of National Drug Control and Policy "constitute covert propaganda and violated the publicity or propaganda prohibition."

That's because the U.S. government is barred from using taxpayer funds to do its own PR. According to a federal statute cited by the GAO, "No part of any appropriation contained in this or any other Act shall be used for publicity or propaganda purposes within the United States not heretofore authorized by the Congress."[13]

Another federal law governing propaganda dates to 1948. The Smith-Mundt Act forbids the government from disseminating propaganda within the United States, only permitting it abroad through such outlets as the Voice of America. Congress passed the law to ensure that a U.S. government agency could not brainwash citizens as Adolf Hitler had done in Germany.[14] American citizens have no idea that their local TV stations are now fulfilling the same role.

Confronted with a public outcry following the fake news revelations, President Bush defended the practice. "This has been a longstanding practice of the federal government to use these types of videos," he declared in March 2005. He suggested that it would be "helpful if local stations then disclosed to their viewers" that they were watching "news" produced by the government, but he added that "evidently, in some cases, that's not the case."

When not passing off government propaganda as news, many TV stations are repackaging corporate PR as news. The Center for Media and Democracy tracked how television newsrooms used thirty-six video news releases (VNRs) that were produced by three PR firms for a variety of corporations, including General Motors, Pfizer, and Capital One. Seventy-seven stations aired the VNRs ninety-eight times without disclosing to viewers that the material was produced by the companies. The VNRs typically promoted products in the course of the segment. According to the research, "Without exception, television stations actively disguised the sponsored content as their own reporting. In almost all cases, stations failed to balance the clients' messages with independently gathered footage or basic journalistic research. More than one-third of the time, stations aired the prepackaged VNR in its entirety."[15]

Robin Raskin, the "Queen of VNRs," knows firsthand about how television stations use corporate-sponsored video news releases. Hired by companies such as Panasonic, Namco, and Techno Source, Raskin has appeared in numerous TV spots promoting their products while also attacking the competition. In one VNR on holiday gifts, Raskin, appearing as a technology expert, warned how an iPod (made by Apple, a competitor of Panasonic) could show what she called "iPorn."

During an interview on *Democracy Now!*, Raskin defended her work but admitted that television stations need to disclose who is funding her segments. "I certainly do the best I can to inform the stations," Raskin said.

But do the stations inform the viewers that she is a hired gun?

"It's a hotly debated subject. . . . Nobody's made a clear decision."[16]

With media outlets prostituting their airwaves to special interest groups, it's little wonder that some journalists are also dabbling in the world's oldest profession. In an environment where the airwaves and front pages are sold to the highest silent bidder, government propagandists have had easy pickings from the Fourth Estate.

Paid-Off Pundits

Creating an alternate reality is a painstaking job that requires more than simply manufacturing news. Ideally, independent pundits should wax eloquent about a government program in order to lend it some street cred. This sleight of hand requires journalists to do some of the dirty work. For the Bush administration, finding shills-for-hire has not been difficult.

In January 2005, *USA Today* revealed that conservative columnist Armstrong Williams had been paid $240,000 by the Department of Education to tout the virtues of the No Child Left Behind Act. The deal stipulated that Williams "would regularly comment on NCLB during the course of his broadcasts and would work with African-American newspapers to place stories and commentary on NCLB." Williams would also provide "department officials with the option to appear as studio guests to discuss NCLB and other important education reform issues." The conservative commentator would also use "his long-term working relationship with America's Black Forum [an African-American news program] to encourage the producers to periodically address NCLB."[17] He would also produce two TV ads promoting NCLB.

In short, Armstrong Williams offered to use his cover as a journalist to be a one-stop propaganda shop for the Bush administration. In his come-on to the Department of Education, he promised to "win the battle for media space [through] favorable commentaries [that] will amount to passive endorsements from the media outlets that carry them."[18]

Williams delivered on his promise to prostitute himself. He penned sycophantic articles gushing that the No Child Left Behind Act "has provided more funds to poor children than any other education bill in this country's history," and that Education Secretary

Rod Paige "has long been at the forefront of the movement to increase educational options for underprivileged students."[19]

The GAO investigated the Williams case and once again determined that the Education Department violated the law by disseminating "covert propaganda."[20] Williams claimed to have performed
"168 activities other than ads . . . promoting NCLB." But the Department of Education could provide the GAO with only one of
his columns as evidence.[21]

Another hack for hire is Maggie Gallagher, a syndicated columnist who backed President Bush's $300 million initiative promoting
marriage as a way of strengthening families. She wrote in *National
Review Online*, "The Bush marriage initiative would . . . educate
teens on the value of delaying childbearing until marriage." She
added that this could "carry big payoffs down the road for taxpayers and children."[22] But there was one other big payoff of the marriage initiative that Gallagher failed to mention: the one she
received from Bush's Department of Health and Human Services.
It turns out that in 2002, Gallagher was paid $21,500 to promote
the president's policy. She was paid another $20,000 by the Justice
Department the following year to write the report "Can Government Strengthen Marriage?" for the National Fatherhood Initiative, a private organization founded by Wade Horn, who became
HHS assistant secretary for children and families under Bush.[23]

Following the disclosure of her government contracts by the
Washington Post, Gallagher, whose syndicated column runs in
seventy-five newspapers, wrote a column saying she "had no special obligation to disclose this information" but would have done
so anyway, "if I had remembered."[24]

While news of Gallagher's government payoff caused Tribune
Media Services to drop her column, it did not trouble some media
outlets. "This is what we hired Maggie to write about," said Kathie
Kerr, spokeswoman for United Press Syndicate, which continues
to distribute Gallagher's column. "It probably wouldn't have
changed our mind to distribute it." *National Review* editor Rich

Lowry said, "We would have preferred that she told us, and we would have disclosed it in her bio."[25]

Leaving nothing to chance, the Bush regime also paid off conservative columnist Mike McManus. As Salon.com revealed, McManus, founder of the group Marriage Savers and author of a syndicated column called "Ethics and Religion" that ran in more than fifty newspapers, received $10,000 from HHS to train marriage counselors as part of the agency's marriage promotion initiative.[26] The revelation came a day after Bush ordered a stop to hiring commentators to promote administration initiatives.

These were merely the high-profile cases. The Bush administration's covert propaganda campaign has been pervasive. An Education Department investigation in 2005 revealed that at least eleven newspapers had run op-ed pieces written by education advocacy groups that were paid for by the federal government, but never identified their government funding.[27]

Rep. George Miller (D-Calif.), who demanded the Education Department investigation, declared, "People looking at advertisements or reading their local newspapers would have had no idea that what they were reading was bought and paid for with their tax dollars. No matter which way you slice it, that is propaganda."[28]

The corporate media has been in high dudgeon over the fake news scandal. Their leaders professed to being shocked, shocked by the government's covert propaganda campaign. As the *New York Times* editorialized, "Only sophisticated viewers would easily recognize that these videos are actually unpaid commercial announcements for the White House or some other part of the government."[29]

The *Times* is right, but the media has only itself to blame for the fact that most people—including TV news managers—can't distinguish journalism from propaganda. It is because media organizations have reached an all-time low in how they cover the powerful. Instead of confronting those in power, news establishments have acted as an echo chamber. Rather than challenge the fraudulent claims of the Bush administration, we have media that have acted as a conveyor belt for the government's lies.

Government propaganda would be ludicrously obvious if the media were doing their job as a watchdog of our democracy. Instead, nothing about official feel-good news seems out of the ordinary.

Fake Journalists

In Bush's alternate reality, there's no need to persuade reporters to give good press. The Bush administration simply turns to fake journalists to carry its water.

That was the case with Jeff Gannon, who attended White House press conferences as a reporter for an outfit called Talon News/GOPUSA. At a rare presidential press conference in the White House in January 2005 (during his first term Bush held fifteen solo news conferences, fewer than any president since records were kept[30]), Bush was getting hounded by reporters over the Armstrong Williams scandal. For a lifeline, he called on the guy in the fourth row with the shaved head. Gannon stood up and lobbed the president a softball question: "Senate Democratic leaders have painted a very bleak picture of the U.S. economy. Harry Reid was talking about soup lines, and Hillary Clinton was talking about the economy being on the verge of collapse. Yet, in the same breath, they say that Social Security is rock solid, and there's no crisis there. How are you going to work—you said you're going to reach out to these people—how are you going to work with people who seem to have divorced themselves from reality?"

At least Gannon had the part right about being divorced from reality. Turns out this "journalist" was in fact one James Guckert, a male escort, webmaster of gay porn sites (including Hotmilitary stud.com and Militaryescorts4m.com), and the rising star for a faux news Web site sponsored by Texas Republican activist Bobby Eberle.[31]

Guckert was the perfect complement to the Bush administration's world of fake news and covert propaganda. Now they had their own puppet reporter to turn to for Republican good news when real reporters strayed off message.

The White House has yet to fully explain how Guckert obtained White House press credentials before he published his first article, or why he was allowed access to the White House 196 times since 2003.

Other journalists, such as *New York Times* columnist Maureen Dowd, haven't been as fortunate. "I was rejected for a White House press pass at the start of the Bush administration, but someone with an alias, a tax evasion problem and Internet pictures where he posed like the 'Barberini Faun' [a nude male statue] is credentialed to cover a White House that won a second term by mining homophobia and preaching family values?" Dowd wrote.

She added, "At first when I tried to complain about not getting my pass renewed, even though I'd been covering presidents and first ladies since 1986, no one called me back. Finally, when Mr. McClellan replaced Ari Fleischer, he said he'd renew the pass—after a new Secret Service background check that would last several months."[32]

Then there is the case of Helen Thomas, the dean of the White House press corps. Thomas has covered every president since Kennedy and has worked in journalism since 1943. She has long occupied a seat in the front row at presidential press conferences—until 2003, when she was unceremoniously moved farther back. "They don't like me," she explained about why the Bush administration has tried to banish her. "I ask too [many] mean questions."[33]

Conservative commentator Ann Coulter, in her syndicated column, questioned why Thomas even had press credentials: "Press passes can't be that hard to come by if the White House allows that old Arab Helen Thomas to sit within yards of the president."[34]

It wasn't just Thomas's Syrian heritage that angered Coulter, but her insistence on demanding actual answers. Here is an ex-

change between Thomas and White House press spokesperson
Ari Fleischer on January 6, 2003:

HELEN THOMAS: Ari, you said that the president deplored the taking of innocent lives. Does that apply to all innocent lives in the
world? And I have a follow-up.

ARI FLEISCHER: I refer specifically to a horrible terrorist attack on
Tel Aviv that killed scores and wounded hundreds. And the
president, as he said in his statement yesterday, deplores in the
strongest terms the taking of those lives and the wounding of
those people, innocents in Israel.

THOMAS: My follow-up is, why does he want to drop bombs on innocent Iraqis?

FLEISCHER: Helen, the question is how to protect Americans, and
our allies and friends—

THOMAS: They're not attacking you.

FLEISCHER: —from a country—

THOMAS: Have they laid a glove on you or on the United States, the
Iraqis, in eleven years?

FLEISCHER: I guess you have forgotten about the Americans who
were killed in the first Gulf War as a result of Saddam Hussein's
aggression then.

THOMAS: Is this revenge, eleven years of revenge?

FLEISCHER: Helen, I think you know very well that the president's
position is that he wants to avert war, and that the president has
asked the United Nations to go into Iraq to help with the purpose of averting war.

THOMAS: Would the president attack innocent Iraqi lives?

FLEISCHER: The president wants to make certain that he can defend our country, defend our interests, defend the region, and
make certain that American lives are not lost.

THOMAS: And he thinks they are a threat to us?

FLEISCHER: There is no question that the president thinks that Iraq
is a threat to the United States.

THOMAS: The Iraqi people?

FLEISCHER: The Iraqi people are represented by their government. If there was regime change, the Iraqi—

THOMAS: So they will be vulnerable?

FLEISCHER: Actually, the president has made it very clear that he has no dispute with the people of Iraq. That's why the American policy remains a policy of regime change. There is no question the people of Iraq—

THOMAS: That's a decision for them to make, isn't it? It's their country.

FLEISCHER: Helen, if you think that the people of Iraq are in a position to dictate who their dictator is, I don't think that has been what history has shown.

THOMAS: I think many countries don't have—people don't have the decision—including us.[35]

White House officials have never revoked Thomas's press badge, but they have silenced her in another way: She is no longer called on to ask questions. On March 21, 2006, President Bush finally called on her—for the first time in three years. Thomas picked up right where she left off, asking the president: "Your decision to invade Iraq has caused the deaths of thousands of Americans and Iraqis, wounds of Americans and Iraqis for a lifetime. Every reason given, publicly at least, has turned out not to be true. My question is, why did you really want to go to war?"

In a testy exchange, a flustered Bush shot back, "In all due respect to your question and to you as a lifelong journalist . . . I didn't want war. To assume I wanted war is just flat wrong, Helen."

Then there is Russell Mokhiber, editor of the *Corporate Crime Reporter*. He frequently attends the White House press briefings but is seldom given a chance to ask questions. (Like Thomas, Mokhiber is Arab-American.) But he has been involved in some of the more memorable exchanges with White House Press Secretary Scott McClellan, such as this one from September 2, 2003:

RUSSELL MOKHIBER: Scott, two things. First, does the president know how many people have been killed and wounded in Iraq since the beginning of the war?

SCOTT MCCLELLAN: Those numbers are made available, publicly.

MOKHIBER: Does the president know how many—

MCCLELLAN: He's very well aware of the sacrifices that are made in Iraq.

MOKHIBER: Well, how many—how many people have been killed in Iraq? Not just Americans—total people killed and wounded in Iraq since the beginning of the war?

MCCLELLAN: . . . I don't know that you can keep track of all the numbers. I mean those are issues you need to address to the Coalition Provisional Authority . . .

MOKHIBER: Does the president know how many people have been killed—

MCCLELLAN: The president knows that what we are doing in Iraq is central to winning the war on terrorism.

MOKHIBER: That wasn't my question.

MCCLELLAN: It is central—

MOKHIBER: Does he know how many people have been killed and wounded?

MCCLELLAN: It is central to bringing about—

MOKHIBER: I know that. But does he know how many—

MCCLELLAN: —a more peaceful and more secure—

MOKHIBER: —have been killed and wounded.

MCCLELLAN: —which means a safer world.

MOKHIBER: That's not the question, Scott. The question I had was, does the president know how many—

MCCLELLAN: Again, I've answered the question. I told you he's well aware of the sacrifices that our troops have made and the sacrifices that their families are making with our troops over there in Iraq.[36]

Throughout the Iraq War, Mokhiber has had difficulty getting press access to the White House. At one point he even had a lawyer call to threaten the White House press office. But he did make it back in on February 1, 2005:

MOKHIBER: Scott, last night in an amicus brief filed before the U.S. Supreme Court, the Justice Department came down in favor of displaying the Ten Commandments at courthouses and state houses around the country. My question is: Does the president believe in commandment number six, "Thou shalt not kill," as it applies to the U.S. invasion of Iraq?

MCCLELLAN: Go ahead. Next question.[37]

An Army of Cheerleaders

Cocooned in his virtual fantasyland of fake journalists, counterfeit news, and hired hacks, you'd think President Bush could rest secure in the knowledge that he was getting his message across. But an image-obsessed leader can never be too careful.

In October 2005, President Bush held what the White House billed as an impromptu conversation with the troops. The nationally televised videoconference came a few days before Iraqis were to vote on a new constitution. "This is an important time," Allison Barber, deputy assistant defense secretary, said to the soldiers before Bush appeared on screen. "The president is looking forward to having just a conversation with you."[38]

This was to be a freewheeling discussion—with the soldiers saying exactly what they were told to say.

Barber proceeded to coach the ten handpicked U.S. soldiers from the Army's 42nd Infantry and one Iraqi in their answers. She stood at the White House podium where Bush would later stand, read part of his opening remarks, and then outlined the questions Bush would ask. At times, she suggested phrasing for the soldiers' responses. With all hell breaking loose in the cities of Iraq, the White House clearly wanted this event to give the impression that the U.S. plan in Iraq was moving ahead just as Bush intended.

The videoconference was set in Saddam Hussein's hometown of Tikrit, which Bush lightly acknowledged he could not safely visit. Interestingly, Tikrit was the backdrop for many of Saddam Hussein's propaganda videos.

During the brief videoconference, the soldiers appeared to fawn over the president. At one point, one told him, "We began our fight against terrorism in the wake of 9/11, and we're proud to continue it here." But a telling moment came when Bush asked the soldiers to comment about their interactions with Iraqi civilians. Captain David Williams could cite only a secondhand account: "Sir, I was with my Iraqi counterpart in the city of Tikrit last week, and he was going around talking to the locals. And from what he told me that the locals told him, the Iraqi people are ready and eager to vote in this referendum."

There was one Iraqi present for the videoconference, Sgt. Maj. Akeel Shaker Nassir, who was in charge of the Iraqi army training facility in Tikrit. His contribution was brief, but gushing: "Thank you very much for everything. I like you."

When it emerged that the event was staged, reporters grilled White House spokesperson Scott McClellan about the coaching:

SCOTT MCCLELLAN: I'm sorry, are you suggesting that what our troops were saying was not sincere, or what they said was not their own thoughts?

REPORTER: Nothing at all. I'm just asking why it was necessary to coach them.

MCCLELLAN: Well, in terms of the event earlier today, the event was set up to highlight an important milestone in Iraq's history, and to give the president an opportunity to, once again, express our appreciation for all that our troops are doing when it comes to defending freedom, and their courage and their sacrifice.[39]

The news story about the event in the *Washington Post* described it as "one of the stranger and most awkwardly staged publicity events of the Bush presidency."[40]

President Bush could only be baffled by the flap. He actually thought he was making news—just like always.

———

The Bush administration's covert propaganda programs have had their intended effect: The public is woefully confused. Karl Rove and George Bush must have been delighted to learn that as late as December 2005, a Harris poll revealed that American adults still believed in the following discredited justifications for invading Iraq:

- 41 percent of U.S. adults believe that Saddam Hussein had "strong links to al Qaeda."
- 22 percent of adults believe that Saddam Hussein "helped plan and support the hijackers who attacked the United States on September 11."
- 26 percent of adults believe that Iraq "had weapons of mass destruction when the U.S. invaded."
- 24 percent of all adults believe that "several of the hijackers who attacked the United States on September 11 were Iraqis."[41]

The one hopeful sign is that far fewer people believe in these hoaxes than they once did: Just ten months earlier, twice as many people in the Harris Poll believed Saddam Hussein was involved in planning 9/11.

Among America's soldiers, the confusion is even greater: According to a first-ever poll of U.S. troops in February 2006, nearly nine of every ten said the U.S. mission is "to retaliate for Saddam's role in the 9/11 attacks," while 77 percent said they believe the main or a major reason for the war was "to stop Saddam from protecting al Qaeda in Iraq."[42]

Americans believe these lies not because they are stupid, but because they are good media consumers. They trust the media to report without fear or favor and act as good-faith referees of democracy. Sadly, this trust is often betrayed.

We need media in this country that are fiercely independent, that ask the hard questions and hold those in power accountable. Only then will government propaganda be seen for what it is, and citizens can begin making choices informed by reality, not self-serving misinformation. Anything less is a disservice to the servicemen and -women of this country, and a disservice to a democratic society.

> The media's the most powerful entity on earth. They have the power to make the innocent guilty and to make the guilty innocent, and that's power. Because they control the minds of the masses.
>
> **—Malcolm X (1925–1965)**

The cozy relationship between the corporate media and the U.S. government has not been left to chance. America's top journalists once worked closely and unapologetically with the Central Intelligence Agency (CIA), with some even on the spy agency's payroll.

Frank Wisner, head of the CIA's covert action division in the early 1950s, called it his "Mighty Wurlitzer": "Almost at the push of a button," as the *New York Times* described it, "the Wurlitzer became the means for orchestrating, in almost any language anywhere in the world, whatever tune the CIA was in the mood to hear."[1] A Wurlitzer was a large pipe organ used in movie theaters in the 1920s and 1930s that could mimic thunderstorms and car horns, as well as play music.

Wisner's Mighty Wurlitzer was backed by a large orchestra of journalists. From the 1950s to the 1970s, more than 400 American journalists secretly carried out assignments for the CIA.[2] This program, referred to as Operation Mockingbird in some accounts, reached its peak in the 1960s when the CIA's propaganda network included more than 800 news and public information organizations and individuals, according to a 1977 investigative series in the *Times*.[3] The United States was in the grip of the Cold War, and the top managers of the leading news organizations enlisted as soldiers in battle. While American politicians ridiculed the notion of state-sponsored media in places such as the Soviet Union, American journalists became willing agents of their own government. Until the early 1970s, hardly a peep of surprise or protest was uttered about these arrangements.

In an article in *Rolling Stone* in 1977, reporter Carl Bernstein, who with Bob Woodward had exposed for the *Washington Post* the Watergate scandal that brought down President Nixon, detailed decades of close cooperation between the CIA and the media. Among the chief executives who helped the CIA were William Paley of CBS, Henry Luce of *Time,* Arthur Sulzberger of the *New York Times*, Barry Bingham Sr. of the *Louisville Courier-Journal,* and James Copley of the Copley News Service. The leading TV networks, including ABC and NBC, and the wire services—AP, UPI, Reuters—along with Hearst Newspapers, Scripps Howard, *Newsweek,* the *Miami Herald,* and the *Saturday Evening Post* all had dealings with the spy agency. The CIA's most valuable associations were with the *New York Times,* CBS, and Time Inc.[4]

"Some of these journalists' relationships with the Agency were tacit; some were explicit," wrote Bernstein. "There was cooperation, accommodation and overlap. Journalists provided a full range of clandestine services—from simple intelligence gathering to serving as go-betweens with spies in Communist countries. Reporters shared their notebooks with the CIA. Editors shared their staffs. Some of the journalists were Pulitzer Prize winners, distinguished reporters who considered themselves ambassadors without portfolio for their country. Most were less exalted: foreign correspondents who found that their association with the Agency helped their work; stringers and freelancers who were as interested in the derring-do of the spy business as in filing articles; and, the smallest category, full-time CIA employees masquerading as journalists abroad. In many instances, CIA documents show, journalists were engaged to perform tasks for the CIA with the consent of the managements of America's leading news organizations."

The CIA was intensely interested in cultivating these arrangements. "One journalist is worth twenty agents," a high-level CIA official explained to *Rolling Stone*. "He has access, the ability to ask questions without arousing suspicion."

One of the early reporters to work with the CIA was Joseph Alsop, a leading syndicated columnist in the fifties. In 1953, he traveled to the Philippines to report—at the request of the CIA. "I'm proud they asked me and proud to have done it," said Alsop, who did clandestine work for the Agency. "The notion that a newspaperman doesn't have a duty to his country is perfect balls."[5]

Media organizations were largely enthusiastic partners in this deceit. As CIA director William Colby exclaimed at one point to investigators for the Church Committee, the Senate committee that was investigating CIA and FBI abuses in the mid-seventies, "Let's not pick on some poor reporters, for God's sake. . . . Let's go to the managements. They were witting."[6]

New York Times publisher Arthur Hays Sulzberger went so far as to sign a secrecy agreement, promising not to divulge his newspaper's cooperation with the Agency. But usually the arrangements were more informal so as to maintain "plausible deniability" for everyone involved.

Collaboration with the CIA was so pervasive and routine that many reporters just figured it was part of their job. CIA director Allen Dulles instituted a "debriefing" procedure for American foreign correspondents. Upon return to the United States, correspondents would routinely offer their notes and impressions to CIA officials—who would often meet reporters at the ship docks. "There would be these guys from the CIA flashing ID cards and looking like they belonged at the Yale Club," said Hugh Morrow, a *Saturday Evening Post* correspondent who later became press secretary to Vice President Nelson Rockefeller. "It got to be so routine that you felt a little miffed if you weren't asked."[7]

The relationship that reporters had with the CIA was mutually beneficial. The reporter might get some inside contacts and even some cash. The Agency would get favorable coverage, or a forum

for its point of view. Bernstein noted that *New York Times* columnist C. L. Sulzberger (the publisher's nephew) was a particularly
useful asset:

> According to a senior CIA official, "Young Cy Sulzberger had
> some uses. . . . He signed a secrecy agreement because we
> gave him classified information. . . . There was sharing, give
> and take. We'd say, 'We'd like to know this; if we tell you this
> will it help you get access to so-and-so?' Because of his access
> in Europe he had an Open Sesame. We'd ask him to just re-
> port: 'What did so-and-so say, what did he look like, is he
> healthy?' He was very eager, he loved to cooperate." On one
> occasion, according to several CIA officials, Sulzberger was
> given a briefing paper by the Agency which ran almost verba-
> tim under the columnist's byline in the *Times*. "Cy came out
> and said, 'I'm thinking of doing a piece, can you give me
> some background?'" a CIA officer said. "We gave it to Cy as a
> background piece and Cy gave it to the printers and put his
> name on it." Sulzberger denies that any incident occurred. "A
> lot of baloney," he said.[8]

Sulzberger protested to Bernstein that he was friendly with several CIA directors and even "used to play golf with" former CIA
director John McCone. "But they'd have had to be awfully subtle
to have used me," he said.

Such were—and are—the cozy relationships between the titans
of media, government, and industry. It is why muckraking journalist I. F. Stone felt compelled to argue that a reporter's job is not
to socialize with the powerful, but to challenge and expose them.

CBS was the CIA's preferred TV network. In the fifties and sixties, CBS correspondents would join the CIA's top brass for annual
private dinners and briefings. CBS owner William S. Paley and CIA
director Allen Dulles personally established the close cooperation
between the network and the Agency. Among the arrangements

was that CBS provided the CIA with news film, including outtakes. In addition, Frank Kearns, a reporter for CBS-TV from 1958 to 1971, and CBS stringer Austin Goodrich were both undercover CIA employees who were hired in arrangements approved by Paley.[9] In 1976, when CBS correspondent Daniel Schorr leaked the contents of a suppressed congressional report about CIA and FBI activities in the media and subsequently refused to reveal his source, Paley was furious and reportedly wanted him fired; Schorr ultimately resigned from CBS.

Newsweek was also a shill for the government. The magazine had several stringers who it knew were CIA contract employees, and the CIA "occasionally used the magazine for cover purposes." As Harry Kern, *Newsweek* foreign editor from 1945 to 1956, told *Rolling Stone:*

> The informal relationship [between *Newsweek* and the CIA] was there. Why have anybody sign anything? What we knew we told them [the CIA] and the State Department. . . . When I went to Washington, I would talk to Foster or Allen Dulles [Secretary of State and CIA Director, respectively] about what was going on. . . . We thought it was admirable at the time. We were all on the same side.

In 1973, CIA director William Colby revealed that he had "some three dozen" American journalists "on the CIA payroll," including five working for "general-circulation news organizations." In 1976, an unpublished report of the House Select Committee on Intelligence chaired by Rep. Otis Pike revealed that at least fifteen news organizations were still providing cover for CIA operatives.[10]

CIA, Inc.

Not content to cajole and bribe American journalists to do its bidding, the CIA created an entire parallel universe of Agency-backed media around the world. From the 1950s to the 1970s, the CIA owned or subsidized more than fifty newspapers, radio stations, news services, periodicals, and other media, mostly overseas. Some of these were set up to disseminate propaganda, while others were intended to provide a journalistic cover for covert operations. At least a dozen full-time CIA agents were employed by American news organizations, often with the knowledge of their top management. Another dozen or so foreign news organizations were infiltrated by paid CIA agents, and at least twenty-two American news organizations had employed American journalists who were also working for the CIA. About a dozen American publishing houses printed more than one thousand books that were produced or subsidized by the CIA.[11]

When asked in 1976 whether the CIA had ever told foreign journalists, working as its paid agents, what to write, former CIA director William Colby replied, "Oh, sure, all the time."[12]

The CIA is prohibited by law from disseminating propaganda in the United States. But even before the Internet age, the CIA knew that the sheer breadth of its disinformation operations would mean that false or planted stories would appear in U.S. media outlets. This was hardly a deterrent, as the *Times* revealed in 1977:

The CIA accepts, as an unavoidable casualty of its propaganda battles, the fact that some of the news that reaches American readers and viewers is tainted with what the Russians call "disinformation." The agency has even coined terms to describe the phenomenon: blowback, or replay, or domestic fallout. . . .

A 1967 CIA directive stated simply that "fallout in the United States from a foreign publication which we support is inevitable and consequently permissible." Or as one succinct former CIA man put it, "It hits where it hits."

Some former agency employees said in interviews, however, that they believed that apart from unintended blowback, some CIA propaganda efforts, especially during the Vietnam War, had been carried out with a view toward their eventual impact in the United States.

And although nearly all of the American journalists employed by the CIA in years past appear to have been used for the collection of intelligence or the support of existing intelligence-gathering operations, a few cases emerged in which such agents became, knowingly or otherwise, channels of disinformation to the American public.[13]

One way that the CIA would knowingly route propaganda back to the United States was when it placed stories on the wire services, which were picked up all over the world, including the United States. The Associated Press estimated that in 1977 its material reached half the world's population. The CIA was actively placing false information through the AP, UPI, and Reuters. During the Vietnam War, one CIA officer summed up his job as spreading news that "whatever bad happened in Vietnam had to be the enemy's fault," which he figured was intended for an American audience. The CIA also mounted major propaganda efforts to undermine Cuban president Fidel Castro and Chilean president Salvador Allende; these efforts were also aimed at American audiences.

The CIA tried hard to suppress news that it didn't like. In 1964, journalists David Wise and Thomas B. Ross published *The Invisible Government*, the first major exposé about CIA covert operations around the world. A top CIA official visited Random House, proposing that the Agency would buy the entire press run. The publisher said the Agency was welcome to buy as many copies as it liked, but that Random House would simply issue another printing. The idea was shelved, but the CIA launched a smear campaign to encourage reviewers to trash the book.

Another unsuccessful CIA smear effort was mounted against *The Politics of Heroin in Southeast Asia,* a 1972 book by Alfred McCoy and Cathleen Read. Now a professor of history at the University of Wisconsin-Madison, McCoy had researched the book in the mountains of Laos, where he discovered that CIA-backed soldiers were buying opium and shipping it to a CIA compound, where it was turned into heroin, which was then sold in South Vietnam. McCoy recounted what happened to the book on *Democracy Now!*: "When the book was in press, the head of covert operations for the CIA called up my publisher in New York and suggested that the publisher suppress the book." Harper & Row allowed the CIA to review the manuscript, but then published the book with "not a word changed."[14]

In 1976, the U.S. Senate Church Committee investigated the covert operations of the CIA. Its multivolume final report detailed covert assassinations, support for coups, and the like. But there were only nine pages devoted to the Agency's use of journalists, and crucial details—including the names of journalists who worked with the CIA—were kept from the Senate committee and omitted from the final report. It was a sign of how closely the CIA guarded this prized program: The CIA was willing to divulge its poison-pen killings of foreign leaders, but it would not give up one of its most productive, valued, and secret operations—the use of journalists.

The Church Committee report on the media "hardly reflects what we found," stated former senator Gary Hart, a member of the committee. "There was a prolonged and elaborate negotiation [with the CIA] over what would be said."[15]

In 1976, CIA director George H.W. Bush seemed to promise a new era when he declared, "Effective immediately, the CIA will not enter into any paid or contract relationship with any full-time or part-time news correspondent accredited by any U.S. news service, newspaper, periodical, radio or television network or station." But there were crucial caveats: This rule could be waived by the CIA director; many stringers are not accredited reporters; and the CIA would continue to accept the voluntary cooperation of journalists. It was clear that the CIA had no intention of ending its covert work in the newsrooms.

The Wurlitzer's New Tune

The Mighty Wurlitzer is alive and well. These days, the CIA doesn't need to rely on covertly placed and paid reporters. It has people such as former *New York Times* national security reporter Judith Miller, who will do the government's bidding for free. Miller gave two years of front-page play in the *Times* to the Pentagon-backed Iraqi National Congress and its leader, Ahmad Chalabi. To help her, Miller—like *Times* reporter C. L. Sulzberger decades earlier—received a "government security clearance" that gave her access to secret documents but barred her from reporting freely on what she saw.

"During the Iraq war, the Pentagon had given me clearance to see secret information as part of my assignment 'embedded' with a special military unit hunting for unconventional weapons," Miller revealed on October 16, 2005, years after she first began reporting on Iraq's alleged weapons of mass destruction. "I was not permitted to discuss with editors some of the more sensitive information about Iraq."[16]

Miller's secret arrangement with the Pentagon was widely criticized. "This is as close as one can get to government licensing of journalists," wrote Bill Lynch, a veteran CBS correspondent.[17]

Turns out Miller, whose apocalyptic—and bogus—missives about Iraq's WMDs were given top billing in America's most influential media outlet, has a track record for being a government mouthpiece. Craig Pyes, a former contract writer for the *Times* who worked with Miller for a series on al Qaeda, complained about her in a December 2000 memo to *Times* editors, in which he demanded that his byline be removed from a piece: "I'm not willing to work further on this project with Judy Miller," wrote Pyes, now at the *Los Angeles Times*. "I do not trust her work, her judgment, or her conduct. She is an advocate, and her actions threaten the integrity of the enterprise, and of everyone who works with her. . . . She has turned in a draft of a story of a collective enterprise that is little more than dictation from government sources over several days, filled with unproven assertions and factual inaccuracies . . . [and] tried to stampede it into the paper."[18]

The bogus stories by Miller and other leading journalists had their intended effect. One could hear the well-worn pipes of the Mighty Wurlitzer chiming in perfect harmony as America's tanks rolled into Baghdad.

As a senior CIA official concluded presciently in 1977: "The pendulum will swing, and someday we'll be recruiting journalists again." When that day comes, he added confidently, "I will have no problem recruiting. I see a lot of them, and I know they're ripe for the plucking."[19]

6. Hijacking Public Media

In public broadcasting we need to get back to the revolutionary spirit of dissent and courage that brought us into existence in the first place, and this country does, too.
—Bill Moyers[1]

There is a war on, but it's not just in Iraq. The Bush administration has launched a full-scale assault on independent journalism. This regime has bribed journalists, manufactured news, blocked reporters' access to battlefronts and disasters, punished reporters who ask uncomfortable questions, helped ever bigger corporations consolidate control over the airwaves, and been complicit in the killings of more reporters in Iraq than have died in any other U.S. conflict.

In this global attack, one area has come under especially heavy fire: public broadcasting. The Corporation for Public Broadcasting (CPB), which disburses about $400 million per year for public television and public radio networks such as National Public Radio (NPR) and the Public Broadcasting System (PBS), was established in 1967. "In authorizing CPB, Congress clearly intended that noncommercial television and radio in America, even though supported by Federal funds, must be absolutely free from any Federal Government interference beyond mandates in the legislation,"[2] according to the CPB Inspector General.

CPB is often described as the "heat shield" designed to insulate public broadcasting from political interference. This posed a problem for the Bush administration, which wanted to turn *up* the heat on public broadcasting. Instead of a shield, they installed a right-wing blowtorch to run the CPB: Kenneth Tomlinson. His mission as CPB chairman, until he was forced to resign in scandal in November 2005, was to transform public broadcasting into an extension of the White House propaganda machine. What Fox News is to TV and the *Washington Times* is to newspapers, the Bush regime has hoped to make of public broadcasting: just another outlet for government spin.

Tomlinson was perfect for this job. His bona fides as a professional propagandist were impeccable: He worked for the Voice of America in the 1980s, was editor in chief of the right-wing *Reader's Digest*, and then under Bush, he became head of the Broadcast Board of Governors, a position he still holds. The BBG oversees all nonmilitary U.S. government broadcasting to foreign countries. This includes the Voice of America and a variety of U.S. foreign propaganda outlets, including the anti-Castro Radio and TV Marti, the Arabic satellite TV station Alhurra, and the Farsi-language Radio Farda. It is illegal for these networks to broadcast inside the United States because of prohibitions against disseminating domestic propaganda. The secretary of state is a member of the BBG board, confirming the essential purpose of these outlets as instruments of U.S. foreign policy.

Tomlinson saw little difference between his roles overseeing journalism at CPB and managing propaganda for BBG. For this White House, it's all propaganda, all the time. Upon becoming CPB chair in September 2003, Tomlinson, with guidance from the Bush administration, set about packing the staff with political hacks and State Department officials. Tomlinson insisted he had "absolutely no contact" with White House partisans as he carried out this task. But an investigation by the CPB inspector general in November 2005 revealed that he exchanged "cryptic" e-mails with Bush's top political advisor, Karl Rove, that showed Tomlinson's hiring decisions at CPB were "strongly motivated by political considerations." Rove and Tomlinson have known each other since the 1990s when they served together on the Board for International Broadcasting, the predecessor agency to the BBG.[3]

After President Bush took office, the CPB began to look like a cross between the State Department and the Republican National Committee:

- Tomlinson handpicked Patricia Harrison to run the CPB. Harrison was a high-ranking official at the State Department overseeing public affairs who praised efforts to place government-produced news segments on TV stations. Most important, she was co-chair of the Republican National Committee, raising money for Republican candidates, including George W. Bush.
- In September 2005, longtime Republican fund-raiser Cheryl Halpern was elected to be the new CPB chair. Halpern, who was appointed to the CPB by President Bush in 2002, has overseen a diverse range of government propaganda programs, including Voice of America, Radio Marti, and Radio Free Iraq. She has accused National Public Radio of having an anti-Israel bias.
- The CPB also elected Gay Hart Gaines, a member of the conservative Heritage Foundation, as vice chair. Gaines was president of the Palm Beach Republican Club and is a former chairwoman of Newt Gingrich's GOPAC, the political action committee that raised millions of dollars for Republican candidates across the country. An interior designer by training, she has no background in broadcasting.
- Tomlinson hired Mary Catherine Andrews, director of the White House Office of Global Communications, to be senior advisor to the CPB president. Tomlinson also hired her, while she was still on the White House's payroll, to advise him on creating an ombudsman to bring "balance" to public broadcasting.
- Tim Isgitt (vice president, government affairs) served in the Bush State Department promoting the Shared Values campaign, which placed pro-American propaganda in Arabic media worldwide.

In addition to stacking the CPB with Republican operatives and propagandists, Kenneth Tomlinson was also criticized for trying to reshape PBS programming. CPB's inspector general accused him of violating federal law by promoting a $4 million deal for conservative editorial writers from the *Wall Street Journal* to have a PBS show as a "balancing program." The show aired on PBS for fifteen months and then moved to Fox News. As for "balance," *Variety* described the *WSJ* show as "four co-workers who sat around agreeing with each other—no debate, no conflict, no nothing."[4]

The Crusades

President Bush famously warned the world in September 2001, "Either you are with us, or with the terrorists." In this simple frame, journalists, whose job it is to be skeptical (well, at least that's the theory), are a natural enemy. And in Tomlinson's eye public enemy number one at PBS was Bill Moyers, who hosted the popular PBS show *NOW with Bill Moyers*, a weekly public affairs and investigative news hour.

Tomlinson secretly paid more than $14,000 to an outside consultant to monitor and rate the political leanings of the guests on thirty-eight episodes of *NOW*. The consultant, one Fred Mann, also monitored National Public Radio's *The Diane Rehm Show* fifteen times, and the PBS talk shows *Tucker Carlson: Unfiltered* (twice) and *Tavis Smiley* (twenty-three times).

Mann wrote a secret report for Tomlinson in which he classified the political views of the guests. Any guest who questioned the Bush presidency was labeled "anti-administration," and others were rated L for liberal or C for conservative. There were subcategories too, such as "anti-DeLay." It didn't take much to get pigeonholed: Republican senator Chuck Hagel was branded with a scarlet L for expressing doubts about the Iraq policy. Hagel is so liberal that the conservative Christian Coalition and the Eagle

Forum both gave him a 100 percent rating in 2004. Former Republican congressman Bob Barr, who helped lead the effort to impeach President Clinton, was labeled "anti-administration."[5]

"[Mann's report] appears to have been cobbled together by an armchair analyst with little or no professional preparation for the task," said Senator Byron Dorgan (D-N. Dak.). "The report is itself steeped in deep political bias."[6] The report was also widely ridiculed because it was filled with typos and faxed from a Hallmark card store in Indianapolis.

It turns out that before Fred Mann was tapped to be an arbiter of objective journalism, he worked for the American Conservative Union and for a right-wing group called the National Journalism Center. At the Center, Mann didn't work as a journalist—he helped students find employment (including placing interns at *Reader's Digest*) and set up networking social events. The Center's director, M. Stanton Evans, wrote a book, *Blacklisted by History: The Real Story of Joe McCarthy and His Fight Against America's Enemies,* to burnish the reputation of that unfairly pilloried former senator from Wisconsin.

The parallels to McCarthy's witch hunts are eerily appropriate. Eric Boehlert revealed in Salon.com that Tomlinson and William Schulz, an ex–*Reader's Digest* editor, both once worked for Fulton Lewis Jr., a well-known radio personality who was an infamous ally of McCarthy.[7] Lewis's son, who took over his father's radio broadcast, recalls Tomlinson as "a very good journalist, a hard worker, and as someone who was very responsibly conservative."[8]

As Tomlinson marshaled his witch-hunters and assembled his blacklists, he consulted with the White House about who to hire to fill key positions at CPB. Turns out it was illegal for him to do this, but he had a mission to rout out liberals, and laws were not going to get in his way.

By mid-2005, with Tomlinson sniffing for liberal bias in the back alleys of *Sesame Street*, CPB was in turmoil. At a Senate hearing in

July 2005, Sen. Dick Durbin (D-Ill.) confronted Tomlinson about his "crusade":

SEN. RICHARD DURBIN: It strikes me as odd, Mr. Tomlinson, that we're on this crusade of a sort here, this mission to change what's going on. I don't quite get it, understand what your agenda is here and what you're trying to achieve. . . . I think Bill Moyers's program *NOW* was a balanced program. And I think most people would agree with it. Now, Mr. Mann that you hired, or someone hired, to monitor this program came up with some rather strange conclusions about who's a liberal and who's a conservative and who's a friend of the President and who isn't.

. . . It's been reported that you have championed the addition of *Wall Street Journal Editorial Report* to the PBS lineup and that you've raised money for that purpose. . . . What was your purpose in bringing in the *Wall Street Journal*, which has been noted is a publication owned by a company that's been very profitable and would not appear to need a subsidy to put on a show?

KENNETH TOMLINSON: I think Senator Stevens hit the nail on the head. No bias—no bias from the left, no bias from the right. If we have programs like the Moyers program that tilt clearly to the left, then I think it's to—according to the law, we need to have a program that goes along with it that tilts to the right and lets the people decide.

DURBIN: Let me ask you about this "clearly to the left" bias on the Moyers show. How did you reach that conclusion? Did you watch a lot of those shows?

TOMLINSON: I watched a lot of those shows, and I think Mr. Mann's research demonstrates that the program was clearly liberal advocacy journalism. . . .

DURBIN: You have perceived a problem here which the American people obviously don't perceive.

. . . Can we expect you to do the same for *The Nation* magazine? Are you going to raise $5 million to make sure they have a show?[9]

In November 2005, a damning report from the CPB inspector general charged Tomlinson with breaking federal laws and violating ethics rules. The White House's hatchet man at CPB resigned under a cloud of scandal. But the apparatchiks he left behind in the top positions at CPB ensure that loyal Republican soldiers will continue to wage war on independent journalism, while hiding behind the smokescreen of "balance."

"We Are in Danger of Losing Our Democracy"

It's a pretty good bet that a journalist loathed by the Bush White House must be doing his job well. Bill Moyers has been an icon of American journalism for the last three decades. He was one of the organizers of the Peace Corps, was special assistant to Lyndon Johnson, a publisher of *Newsday*, senior correspondent for CBS News, produced numerous groundbreaking shows on public television, has won more than thirty Emmys, nine Peabodys, three George Polk Awards, and is the author of three best-selling books.

Since retiring from *NOW with Bill Moyers* in 2005, Moyers has been speaking out forcefully in defense of journalism in general, and public broadcasting in particular. He challenged Kenneth Tomlinson to debate him on PBS; the former CPB head declined. In June 2005, in the thick of the right-wing attacks against him, Bill Moyers spoke on *Democracy Now!*

Moyers observed that packing the Corporation for Public Broadcasting with partisans is both mistaken and unprecedented. "All the attacks on public broadcasting in the past have come from outside," he said. "They've come from the Nixon White House, from Newt Gingrich when he was Speaker of the House, and they've been rebuffed because the Corporation for Public Broadcasting was led by principled Democrats and Republicans who took seriously their job of resisting pressure from Congress and the White House to influence public broadcasting.

"Now this is an inside job. Kenneth Tomlinson is there as an ally of Karl Rove to help make sure that public broadcasting doesn't report the news that they don't want reported."

Moyers noted that CPB president Patricia Harrison and Kenneth Tomlinson "both would like to see public broadcasting be an arm of government propaganda—in particular, the administration's propaganda." The veteran newsman accused Republican operatives of having "intimidated the mainstream media so that you don't get much reporting of what is contrary to the official view of reality." Their dream is to have "state-manipulated media: media that may not be owned by the state, but is responsive to the state." He says that Tomlinson, as overseer of the U.S. government–backed Voice of America, "thinks like a propagandist."

Moyers was appalled at the revelation that Tomlinson had secretly hired a conservative "consultant" to monitor his show. Tomlinson "could have just watched the broadcast. He could have called me and asked me who was on. He did not tell his board he was doing this. He did not tell his staff he was doing this. He did it arbitrarily on his own."

In an interview with the *Washington Post,* Tomlinson said that the turning point for him came while watching a show that *NOW* did about a town in Pennsylvania:

It was November 2003, and [Tomlinson] was watching Bill Moyers, host of the Public Broadcasting Service show "Now," talk about how free-trade policies had harmed small-town America. Tomlinson knows small-town America—he grew up outside tiny Galax, Va., in the Blue Ridge Mountains—and Moyers's presentation of the issues struck him as superficial and one-sided. Indeed, it struck him as "liberal advocacy journalism." Right then, Tomlinson said, he decided it was time to bring some "balance" to the public TV and radio airwaves.[10]

Moyers explained that the show Tomlinson watched was done by journalist Peter Bull. He traveled to Tamaqua, Pennsylvania, "looking at what was happening economically in this town as a result of downsizing, outsourcing, loss of jobs, people losing $20-an-hour jobs for $9- or $6-an-hour jobs. It was really good reporting about the losers in the class war.

"And Kenneth Tomlinson, a right-wing Republican, couldn't take that because it was contrary to the party line. The party line is: Globalization, NAFTA, CAFTA—all of this is really good for people, and if we just have the patience, we'll see that. Well, we were reporting from the front lines of what's happening on globalization to American workers, and he became furious. . . . Why? Because we were reporting what was contrary to the official view of reality."

Moyers mused, "It's not my opinions he opposes. It's journalism that is beholden to nothing but getting as close as possible to the verifiable truth."

One problem for Tomlinson as he tried to recast PBS into a house organ for the Bush administration was that Moyers was one of the founding fathers of public broadcasting. Moyers has pushed back against partisan operatives by invoking the original mission of public media.

"I was a young policy assistant in the White House of Lyndon Johnson. I attended my first meeting to discuss the future of educational television in 1964 when I was 30 years old. I was present at the creation," Moyers recounted.

"We established public broadcasting back in the 1960s because we believed there should be an alternative to commercial television and to commercials on television. We thought commercial television was doing pretty well at what it was doing, but it was even then beginning to dumb down its programming to satisfy the largest common denominator. It had made its peace with the little lies and fantasies of merchandising. It treated Americans as consumers, not as citizens. Congress approved public broadcasting as an alternative to corporate and commercial broadcasting."

Moyers concedes now, "Public broadcasting has failed in many respects. We've not been enough of an alternative. We need a greater variety of voices on public broadcasting: conservative, liberal, and beyond conservative and liberal. But it's still the best alternative we have for providing the American people with something other than what is driven by commercials, corporations, and the desire constantly to sell, sell, sell."

But public broadcasting is more closely tied than ever to traditional corporate backers. Public radio stations now get 18 percent of their revenues from businesses, and 11 percent comes from government. That's a sharp reversal from 1980, when nearly one-third of funding for public radio stations came from the federal government, and just 8 percent came from businesses. The shift toward corporate underwriting is often dramatic: for example, KPCC, a public radio station in Pasadena, California, has seen its business-underwriting budget increase nearly sixfold, from $561,000 in 2001 to $3 million in 2005.[11]

As public broadcasting has added more and more time for commercial-like plugs from its sponsors, it sounds, well, more and more like commercial media. Moyers acknowledged the point after hearing the news summary at the start of *Democracy Now!* just before his interview. "You cannot get anywhere in the public broadcasting universe the kind of information that you provided in the opening of your broadcast. That's not the news summary you're going to get on CNN tonight or Fox News tonight or ABC or CBS. Public broadcasting—still unfulfilled, still flawed, still imperfect—my message is to remind people what's at stake if we allow it to go under."

Moyers is not particularly hopeful right now. "I feel more pessimistic at the moment about the future of public broadcasting than I ever have in my thirty-five years—despite the Nixon attacks, despite Newt Gingrich's attack—because these right-wingers are organized. . . . They're taking over the governance of public broadcasting at that level, and they don't pay any attention to opposition or to protest or to pressure. They are actually dogmatic and determined in their agenda. So it will take a bipartisan response to what is happening by the right wing. But I'm not optimistic about that because the Republicans, for the first time, have given up on public broadcasting."

The stakes in the public broadcasting fight are high, says Moyers: freedom of expression itself is under fire. "There is a desire to silence any dissent in this country by the [Bush] administration. They practice extraordinary media manipulation. They're the most secretive administration in my seventy years. And this whole attack on me is indicative of how when anyone rises up to speak an alternative truth, an alternative vision of reality, they try to discredit them. . . . They have been trying to discredit the mainstream journalists for a long time so that their own right-wing media can be accepted by their constituency, in particular, as *the* media. So I'm targeted because my reporting on *NOW* was telling the stories that they didn't want told about secrecy in government, about Cheney's energy task forces, about a cover-up at the Department of Interior, about the relationship between business, corporations, and the administration. We were reporting what good muckraking journalism always reports, and they don't like that."

Instead, news is increasingly presented and sponsored by the very corporations that are the subject of the news. ExxonMobil, for example, has pumped more than $8 million into forty think tanks—which then provide "experts" to the media to dismiss problems such as global warming.[12] These corporate Trojan horses are a staple of American broadcasting, both public and private. That helps explain the reluctance of the U.S. media to even cover global warming: The topic gets three times as much coverage in British newspapers as it does in American papers.[13] When global warming—about which there is overwhelming scientific consensus—does get coverage by the American press, it is presented in false balance with the views of industry-sponsored skeptics. A 2003 study by Maxwell and Jules Boykoff of major newspaper reporting on global warming showed that most articles gave the handful of "experts"—many of them funded by ExxonMobil—roughly the same amount of attention as the thousands of independent scientists who concur on global warming.[14]

Moyers has seen this dynamic in action on public broadcasting. When Congress passed a tax bill in late 2004 that included a huge giveaway to corporations to move their operations offshore, "which we all know hurts American workers and the American economy," he says, he turned to PBS's *NewsHour* for some discussion. "And that night, on our premier broadcast on public broadcasting, the only person who was called on that show to talk about what was in that bill was a representative of the American Enterprise Institute, which is corporate-supported. And not one word was said about the entrails of that bill, about what was really in it. . . . But nobody said the American Enterprise Institute is paid for by many of the corporations that are benefiting from this legislation." AEI has received $960,000 in funding from ExxonMobil, to name just one of its corporate backers.[15]

"There were two major scholarly studies in the 1990s that show that 90 percent of all the people who appear on public broadcasting represent elites: elite corporations, political elites, and journalistic elites," said Moyers. "They do not represent consumers, environmentalists, ordinary people, people of color out across the country. Public broadcasting, which I believe in deeply, including the *NewsHour,* nonetheless reflects the official view of reality more than we should."

Which may explain why public broadcasting has become so vulnerable to attack: It has deserted the very constituency that would defend it. Moyers concedes, "I think it has lost the public. Too many of us consider our audiences to be audiences, and not a public. We, too, look out on the country and see a society of passive spectators instead of potential activists. The American Revolution came about because independent voices like Thomas Paine rallied people to the cause of independence. We have settled in public broadcasting into a comfortable, complacent niche where we provide information that isn't necessarily the truth.

"I think we're at a moment in American history that is unique. I think we are in danger of losing our democracy because of the domination, the monopoly of power being exercised by huge economic interests, both directly and indirectly." Moyers implores, "In public broadcasting, we need to get back to the revolutionary spirit of dissent and courage that brought us into existence in the first place. And this country does, too.

"A student once asked my colleague Richard Reeves, the great journalist and historian, 'What do you mean by real news?' And Reeves said, 'Real news is the news we need to keep our freedom.' We are not getting that kind of news from the American press today. . . . There are exceptions, like *Democracy Now!* and other independent voices in the country. But we're not getting from the mainstream press or the right-wing press the news we need to keep our freedoms. And we better think about that, because it's easy to fall into a kind of anesthetized complacency thinking that democracy—since it is 'the worst form of government, except all others'—that we can take it for granted. We can't take it for granted."

I spent most of my time as a high class muscle man for Big Business, for Wall Street and the bankers. In short, I was a racketeer, a gangster for capitalism. . . . I helped make Haiti and Cuba a decent place for the National City Bank boys to collect revenues in. I helped in the raping of half a dozen Central American republics for the benefit of Wall Street.

—**Maj. Gen. Smedley Butler (1881–1940), leader of the 1915 Marine invasion of Haiti, and one of the most decorated Marines in U.S. history**

Haiti was in crisis. It was March 1, 2004, and the political situation in Haiti had been rapidly deteriorating. For a month, *Democracy Now!* had reported numerous stories about the growing evidence that the United States was secretly supporting armed rebels intent on overthrowing the democratically elected government of President Jean-Bertrand Aristide. Then, in the early hours of Sunday, February 29, the State Department and the mainstream media announced that Aristide had "resigned" the presidency and fled Haiti. His whereabouts were unknown.

On Monday morning, just after *Democracy Now!* finished broadcasting, a phone call came in from Rep. Maxine Waters, the California congresswoman who has long championed Haitian rights. Waters had stunning news: She said Aristide told her that he had been forcibly taken by U.S. soldiers to the Central African Republic. She stated, "He's surrounded by military. It's like he is in jail. He says he was kidnapped. He said that he was forced to leave Haiti." According to Representative Waters, Aristide said that diplomats from the American Embassy in Port-au-Prince had told him that Guy Philippe, a former Haitian police chief and coup plotter, was coming to Port-au-Prince and that "[Aristide] will be killed, many Haitians will be killed, that they would not stop until they did what they wanted to do."

Next, an urgent call came in from Randall Robinson, the founder and former director of TransAfrica, a group that advocates the interests of the Caribbean and Africa. Robinson, a family friend of the Haitian president, said that Aristide had called him as well and "emphatically" denied that he had resigned. "He did not resign," Robinson said. "He was abducted by the United States in the commission of a coup."

Democracy Now! broke into normal programming to put Waters and Robinson on the air. Thus began a series of events that culminated two weeks later with Amy accompanying a small delegation to the remote Central African Republic to report on an unprecedented mission to defy the world's greatest power, challenge the corporate media's whitewash of what has been happening in Haiti, and bring the Aristides home.

The island of Hispaniola—home to Haiti on its western third and the Dominican Republic on the rest—lies six hundred miles off the coast of Florida. Haiti's 8 million people live in an area the size of Maryland. The country is distinguished by its extremes: With 80 percent of the population living below the poverty line (per capita income is $390 per year), Haiti is the poorest country in the Western Hemisphere, and one of the poorest in the world. About half the population is illiterate, nearly half of children are not in school, 6 percent of the population has HIV/AIDS, and life expectancy is 52 years. Most Haitians are involved in subsistence agriculture; sweatshops are one of the country's few export industries.

One would think Haiti's challenges were daunting enough, but for over two centuries, the United States has been intent on keeping Haiti under political and economic control, no matter the price.

Haiti, the oldest black republic in the world, was born of a slave uprising against French colonists in 1804. This fateful act of defiance against slaveowners has been punished in perpetuity. For decades after its establishment, the U.S. Congress wouldn't recognize the black republic, afraid it would inspire slaves in the United States to rise up. Shortly after independence, under threat of invasion by France, Haiti agreed to pay a crushing indemnity of about $500 million to the French government, in part to compensate the former colonial power for losing access to slave labor. The burden was devastating: It took Haiti until after World War II to pay off the debt.[1]

In 1915, with other nations distracted by World War I, the U.S. Marines, led by Maj. Smedley Butler, invaded Haiti, claiming to restore order. In reality, the United States was worried about French and German influence and determined to protect the Panama Canal. The U.S. occupation continued until 1934. One of its major legacies was the creation of the Haitian Army, accomplished by an act of the U.S. Congress. As the human rights activist and physician Paul Farmer writes, "From its founding during the U.S. occupation until it was demobilized by Aristide in 1995, the Haitian Army has never known a non-Haitian enemy. Internal enemies, however, it had aplenty."[2]

In 1957, François "Papa Doc" Duvalier came to power, starting three decades of iron-fisted rule. In 1961, Papa Doc dissolved the bicameral Haitian legislature, replacing it with a unicameral body stacked with his allies. His son Jean Claude "Baby Doc" Duvalier replaced him in 1971. The Duvaliers were propped up by both the Haitian Army and the Tonton Macoutes, a brutal armed militia established by Papa Doc and used by him and Baby Doc to crush all opposition. The Duvaliers and the Tonton Macoutes were responsible for murdering thousands of Haitians during their reign. Baby Doc fled the country in 1986 in the face of mounting political opposition.

It was against this backdrop of decades of government repression, backed by the United States, that Jean-Bertrand Aristide emerged as the hope of Haiti's long-suffering population.

Aristide was a fiery Catholic priest who won a landslide victory in Haiti's first internationally supervised democratic election in December 1990. Following his inauguration in February 1991, many thought that the wide grassroots support that he and his party, Lavalas ("the flood"), enjoyed—he won with 67 percent of the vote against eleven other candidates—would help immunize him against coups. Aristide moved quickly to purge the military of human rights abusers, democratize the government, and raise people's wages. He never got the chance.

The first coup against Aristide occurred in September 1991. The coup plotters were military leaders who had enjoyed unchecked power during the reign of the Duvaliers. When Aristide was elected president four years after Baby Doc Duvalier fled, Haiti's generals were restive. They and their henchmen had much to lose under a new president who was intent on delivering to Haiti some long-awaited civilian rule.

It turned out that the United States, despite publicly protesting the 1991 coup against Aristide, was funding it in private. Journalist Allan Nairn reported in *The Nation* that U.S. intelligence agencies had at least one of the coup leaders on its payroll. Emmanuel "Toto" Constant, head of the notorious right-wing paramilitary death squad FRAPH, the Haitian Front for Advancement and Progress, was on the payroll of the Defense Intelligence Agency. Other FRAPH members were trained by U.S. intelligence. The coup leader, Gen. Raoul Cedras, was trained by the U.S. military at the notorious School of the Americas, located at Fort Benning, Georgia.

In the three years that Aristide was in forced exile, the Haitian Armed Forces and FRAPH led a reign of terror against unarmed civilians. The toll of this rampage included at least 5,000 murders, 300,000 internal refugees, 40,000 boat people, and countless tortures, rapes, thefts, and beatings.

In 1994, Constant told Nairn that he was contacted by a U.S. military officer named Col. Patrick Collins, who served as defense attaché at the United States Embassy in Port-au-Prince. Constant says Collins pressed him to set up a group to "balance the Aristide movement" and do "intelligence" work against it. Constant admitted that, at the time, he was working with CIA operatives in Haiti. Constant is now residing freely in the United States. He is reportedly living in Queens, New York.

Shortly after Nairn revealed that Constant was on the U.S. government payroll, CIA director James Woolsey was forced out. The embarrassment wasn't that the United States was backing a death squad leader, just that this connection had been exposed.

Aristide's Return

Jean-Bertrand Aristide was reelected president in November 2000, following elections earlier in the year that had given his Lavalas party a majority of seats in the Haitian legislature. But Aristide's new term was once again cut short.

Throughout February 2004, *Democracy Now!* aired reports from Haiti about the growing violence and the threat of a coup. Armed gangs had been attacking poorly armed police stations and other government outposts around the country. At least forty people were killed in the battles. Aristide's official government forces, starved of funds and resources, were ill-equipped to defend against the violence. Aristide had dismantled the army in 1995, and the national police constituted an estimated three thousand men. Aristide supporters clashed regularly with the insurgents and other government opponents.

On February 16, 2004, Rep. Maxine Waters told us, "You have this opposition that is supported, I believe, by [Assistant Secretary of State for Western Hemisphere Affairs Roger P.] Noriega in the State Department, and others who have always had their hands in the politics of Haiti, who are trying to oust the president." Noriega had been a senior staff member of the Senate Foreign Relations Committee when it was chaired by former senator Jesse

Helms. Noriega and Helms were among a group of hardliners who, says Waters, "hated Haiti, and they have always worked against Haiti."

Waters said that the *New York Times* had quoted an anonymous State Department official as saying that "something was going to have to be done in Haiti, and it was possible that the State Department could support the ouster" of President Aristide.[3] In this and other not-so-subtle statements, U.S. officials hinted that they wanted Aristide gone. Secretary of State Colin Powell officially renounced this, but for anyone who has followed Haiti over the years, it came as no surprise that Washington was telegraphing its intentions.

On February 17, Haitian prime minister Yvon Neptune said, "We are witnessing the coup d'état machine in motion." The next day, *Democracy Now!* interviewed Kim Ives, the editor of the newspaper *Haiti Progres,* who described the situation on the ground in Haiti: "We see wealthy businessmen leading the rebellion against the government."[4]

What was particularly troubling to veteran Haiti observers was the fact that many of the leaders of the armed gangs also led the campaign of terror in the early 1990s that resulted in the overthrow of Aristide. According to *Haiti Progres*, Louis Jodel Chamblain, former vice president of the FRAPH paramilitary death squad, arrived in February 2004 in the Haitian city of Gonaives, where the armed gangs were largely based.

Attorney Ira Kurzban, general counsel to the Haitian government, charged that the United States had secretly armed the rebels. "These people came through the Dominican border after the United States had provided twenty thousand M-16s to the Dominican army," he said. "It is a military operation. It's not a ragtag group of liberators, as has often been put in the press in the last week or two.

"The question is," said Kurzban, "will the international community stand by and allow a democracy in this hemisphere to be terminated by a brutal military coup of persons who have a very, very sordid history of gross violations of human rights?"

Kurzban would soon have his answer. On February 27, 2004, White House press secretary Scott McClellan declared, "This long-simmering crisis is largely of Mr. Aristide's making."[5]

The Coup

Early Sunday morning, February 29, 2004, President Jean-Bertrand Aristide was forced from power and taken out of the country on an American plane.

The Bush administration claimed, and the U.S. media parroted, that Aristide fled the country of his own will. The *New York Times* article on the "Aristide resignation" was a blow-by-blow insider account comprised entirely of quotes from unnamed U.S. officials. It described the events in Haiti this way:

> [Aristide] made the decision to give up power on Saturday evening, hours after the White House in a statement questioned his fitness to rule.
>
> Mr. Aristide, signaling a disconnection from the violence engulfing his country and the appeals from world leaders to step aside, meekly asked the American ambassador [James B. Foley] in Haiti through an aide whether his resignation would help the country.
>
> "It was as if he was the last guy in the world to figure out that the country would be better off were he to relinquish power," the official said. . . .
>
> Mr. Aristide wanted to know . . . what were the choices of places that Mr. Aristide could go to in exile, the official said. . . . The American reply was: "Pick your destination; it's up to you."[6]

As Maxine Waters and Randall Robinson insisted in their calls to *Democracy Now!* on March 1, the official Bush administration/*New York Times* version of events in Haiti bore no resemblance to reality.

We put the transcripts of our conversations with Waters and Robinson on our Web site, and reporters took them to the White House and the Pentagon. A reporter asked Defense Secretary Donald Rumsfeld if our report was true that the United States was part of a coup that removed Aristide. Rumsfeld just laughed: "The idea that someone was abducted is just totally inconsistent with everything I heard or saw or am aware of. So I think that—that I do not believe he is saying what you are saying he is saying."

I've learned in my years as a reporter that when you get laughed at, you are probably on to something.

Secretary of State Colin Powell also spoke that day: "He was not kidnapped. We did not force him onto the airplane. He went onto the airplane willingly, and that's the truth."

And finally, White House Press Secretary Scott McClellan: "Conspiracy theories like that do nothing to help the Haitian people realize the future that they aspire to, which is a better future, a more free future and a more prosperous future. We took steps to protect Mr. Aristide. We took steps to protect his family as they departed Haiti. It was Mr. Aristide's decision to resign, and he spelled out his reasons why."

The Bush administration alibi had a basic flaw: Why would Aristide have willingly chosen to go to a place he'd never been—the Central African Republic—a remote African dictatorship with poor communications and minimal access to the outside world? Aristide said he was virtually banned from giving interviews, and the few that he did give were largely unintelligible.

A CNN reporter asked Rep. Maxine Waters about Aristide, "How can you believe him?"

That's a fair question. How can you believe anything the government says? That should be the attitude that journalists have about all government officials, beginning here at home.

On March 14, I received a surprise call from Randall Robinson: "We are chartering a plane to the Central African Republic and we are going to take the Aristides home. Can you come?"

Within twenty-four hours, I was at the airport in Miami, where I met up with Maxine Waters, Randall Robinson, and Sharon Hay Webster, a Jamaican member of parliament who had been sent to deliver a letter of invitation from then Jamaican prime minister P. J. Patterson, chair of the Caribbean Community and Common Market (CARICOM). I traveled as the only broadcast journalist to document this historic trip, along with Peter Eisner of the *Washington Post*.

We flew from Miami through Barbados to Dakar, Senegal, to the Central African Republic. Upon arriving, the delegation found itself in a delicate bind: It was the first anniversary of the military coup that brought to power the dictator of the Central African Republic, François Bozizé.

Yes, the Americans really turn to some wonderful allies in times of need.

The delegation did not want to appear in any way to be participating in the government "celebration" of its coup. So for the next seven hours, they negotiated inside the presidential palace with the dictator. When Bozizé would leave to "consider" a proposal, President Aristide told me the dictator was going to get his marching orders from France and the United States.

The Bush administration was now in a dilemma of its own making. Top officials had always insisted that Aristide had willingly left Haiti for a destination of his choosing. It wasn't their problem that Aristide chose the desolate, despotic Central African Republic. Now this small delegation had called the bluff of the most powerful country on Earth. The group insisted that if the Aristides had come freely, they should be able to leave freely. Finally, Bozizé announced that the Aristides could leave.

As Margaret Mead said, "Never doubt for a moment that a small group of committed, thoughtful people can make a difference. Indeed, it's the only thing that ever has."

And so the Aristides made their way back across the world toward their home. As we flew from C.A.R. to Senegal, to the Cape Verde Islands, then over the Atlantic, President Aristide described to me what had happened to him on his last day in Haiti: "They broke the constitutional order by using force . . . to take an elected president out of his country."

Aristide asserted that "there were U.S. military, and I suspect . . . other militaries from other countries."

One of the more disturbing details of his ouster was the refusal by the United States to allow the Steele Foundation, the American firm that utilized former U.S. Special Forces soldiers to provide Aristide's personal security, to bring in reinforcements as the security situation deteriorated. Aristide said that "U.S. officials ordered [the Steele Foundation] to leave and to leave immediately," and that twenty-five additional Steele agents who were supposed to arrive in Haiti on February 29 were prevented from leaving the United States. "That was a very strong message to them and to us," said Aristide. "It was obvious in my mind that was part of the global plan . . . to kidnap me through a coup d'état."

When I asked Steele Foundation CEO Kenneth Kurtz whether U.S. troops could have made a difference had they come before Aristide was ousted, instead of the day after, he replied, "I think that if international assistance would have arrived, it would have certainly stabilized the situation."

I also had a chance to speak with Franz Gabriel, Aristide's personal bodyguard, who was an eyewitness to the events of that night. I interviewed him inside the presidential palace in Bangui as the Aristides were meeting with the delegation. Gabriel recounted that at 5 A.M., personnel from the U.S. Embassy, including Deputy Chief of Mission Luis Moreno, arrived at Aristide's home. "They came in to tell the president that they were going to organize a press conference at the embassy, and for him to be ready to accompany them. The president called [his wife] Mildred, and we boarded the vehicles to go to the embassy." Gabriel understood

Aristide's press conference would be about "whether he would leave power."

But as the caravan drove toward the embassy, "We ended up making a right inside the airport. And that's when I realized that we were not going to the embassy.

"I saw a deployment of U.S. Marines everywhere," recounted Gabriel. "I saw a white plane with a U.S. flag at the tail of the aircraft, and it looked strange because there was no markings on it. And as the plane stopped, they had us board. Everybody boarded the plane. And all the Steele Foundation agents that were on contract with the government to give the president security boarded the plane also.

"We never knew where we were going," he said. "The president didn't even know where he was going. . . . I would say that it is a kidnapping."

Whose Country?

As our plane approached Barbados from Africa, we heard from the *Democracy Now!* newsroom that Defense Secretary Donald Rumsfeld, National Security Advisor Condoleezza Rice, and Secretary of State Colin Powell were threatening Aristide, saying that he was not to return to this hemisphere. U.S. Ambassador to Haiti James Foley said Aristide was not to return to within 150 miles of Haiti.

Whose hemisphere? Whose country?

Jamaican Prime Minister P. J. Patterson had invited the Aristides to stay in Jamaica. When we arrived there, I talked to CNN on the satellite phone. CNN correspondent Miles O'Brien asked me how much contact Aristide had with his supporters inside Haiti, as if the landslide of voters who backed Aristide were just a hard-core clique. The question reflected the way the Bush administration had framed the crisis: that there were two equal warring factions, and the United States was simply stepping in to restore order. I replied, "I'm not privy to his private communications with the people of Haiti. But I can only report that in the last election, he won overwhelmingly the democratic vote."

I pointed out, quoting U.S. Congressmember Maxine Waters, that "if people are concerned about violence in Haiti, they should be concerned about the so-called rebel leaders, people like Jodel Chamblain, who was convicted of murder in absentia" for the 1993 killing of Haiti's justice minister.

From reading and watching their media, Americans can only be hopelessly confused by what they learn about Haiti. Consider this whimsical analysis of the Haiti crisis by reporter Michael Wines that ran in the *New York Times* a week after Aristide was ousted:

> Jean-Bertrand Aristide, Haiti's latest strongman-in-exile, wants to lick his wounds in South Africa, a land of world-beating beauty. . . . Instead, he whiles his days away in the Central African Republic, a Texas-size nation of flat plains, Amazonian humidity . . . and cheap butterfly-wing art . . .
>
> . . . Perhaps he simply lacked the right stuff. Jean-Bedel Bokassa had the right stuff. . . . Idi Amin Dada had the right stuff. . . . History suggests that the more brutal the dictator, the more others are willing to cut him diplomatic slack in a headlong rush to end the brutality. . . .
>
> Despotism probably knows no nationality, and to some, accommodating tyrants in exile is arguably as much a humanitarian gesture as an amoral one. "Some of these people should be killed, obviously," said Michael Ledeen, a resident scholar at the American Enterprise Institute in Washington and an iconoclastic conservative on this and other subjects. "I am all for putting them on trial and recovering ill-gotten gains."[7]

The premise of the mocking *Times* article was wrong: South African foreign minister Zuma told Randall Robinson on March 1 that South Africa had never received an asylum request from Aristide. But the *Times* article was notable for what it revealed about the consequences of being out of favor with the Republican right wing and Haiti's conservative elite: You are equated with psycho-pathic mass murderers like Bokassa and Amin, and a right-wing American pundit suggests you should be executed.

The basic irritant to the U.S. government—and, by proxy, the American media—is that Aristide enjoys enormous grassroots support. He's just not supported by the small U.S.-backed Haitian elite. Yet the American media quotes and cites this elite (in part be-cause many of them speak English, while most Haitians speak French or Creole) to the near total exclusion of the masses of poor Haitians.

The story that most American media overlooked was how the United States has had a nearly unbroken record of sabotaging Haitian democracy. From backing Haitian death squads that over-threw Aristide in the 1990s, to blocking lifesaving development aid when Aristide was reelected in 2001, the United States has been obsessed with keeping Haiti in virtual serfdom. "You'd think this might be newsworthy: the world's most powerful nations joining forces to block aid and humanitarian assistance to one of the poor-est," wrote longtime Haiti advocate Paul Farmer. "But for three years this story was almost impossible to place in a mainstream journal of opinion. It was not until March 2004 that one could have read in a U.S. daily the news that the aid freeze might have contributed to the overthrow of the penniless Haitian govern-ment."[8] It was the *Boston Globe* that finally reported on March 7:

> For three years, the U.S. government, the European Union, and international banks have blocked $500 million in aid to Haiti's government, ravaging the economy of a nation al-ready twice as poor as any in the Western Hemisphere.
>
> The cutoff, intended to pressure the government to adopt political reforms, left Haiti struggling to meet even basic needs and weakened the authority of President Jean-Bertrand Aris-

tide, who went into exile one week ago. Today, Haiti's government, which serves 8 million people, has an annual budget of about $300 million—less than that of Cambridge [Massachusetts], a city of just over 100,000. . . .

Many of Aristide's supporters, in Haiti and abroad, angrily contend that the international community, particularly the United States, abandoned the fledgling democracy when it needed aid the most. Many believe that Aristide himself was the target of the de facto economic sanctions, just as Haiti was beginning to put its finances back in order.

"This is a case where the United States turned off the tap," said Jeffrey Sachs, an economist at Columbia University. "I believe they did that deliberately to bring down Aristide."[9]

The United States not only blocked aid, it demanded ransom from the impoverished nation: Aristide was forced to pay off the American loans to the Duvalier dictatorship and the subsequent military regimes. The result: In 2003, Haiti sent 90 percent of its foreign reserves to Washington to pay off these debts.[10]

Following the 2004 coup, more details emerged about how the United States worked to bring down the Aristide government. From before Aristide took office in 2001, the National Endowment for Democracy and one of its four core grantees, the International Republican Institute (which is led by powerful Republicans close to President George W. Bush), spent millions of dollars to create, arm, and organize an opposition. This was not about strengthening civil society. This was about making Haiti under Aristide ungovernable.

Since 1998, reported Max Blumenthal in Salon.com, "IRI, whose stated mission is to 'promote the practice of democracy' abroad, conducted a $3 million 'party-building' program in Haiti, training Aristide's political opponents, uniting them into a single bloc and, according to a former U.S. ambassador there, encouraging them to reject internationally sanctioned power-sharing agreements in order to heighten Haiti's political crisis."[11] The IRI point person in Haiti was Stanley Lucas, a former judo master who is closely associated with FRAPH and many of Haiti's most notorious human rights violators (Lucas is now working for the IRI's Afghanistan program[12]). Under the guise of party-building, Lucas brought together these ex–coup leaders into a sham grassroots opposition called the Democratic Convergence. Blumenthal explained on *Democracy Now!* that "the Democratic Convergence is not a traditional political party. It's more like the political wing of a coup, because the strategy that it took was to forgo the democratic process entirely."[13]

These facts are conveniently omitted, in favor of the official version of the Haiti story, which is simply that Aristide was a despot who had to go. Take the exchange I had with Colonel Lawrence Wilkerson, former chief of staff to Secretary of State Colin Powell, on *Democracy Now!* on November 22, 2005. I asked for his response to Aristide's charge that the United States pushed him out. Wilkerson replied:

COL. LAWRENCE WILKERSON: I can't imagine a man like Aristide, whose will to power is excessive, even obsessive, saying anything differently. Colin Powell, as you said, did know the situation in Haiti, probably as well as anyone in America. Colin Powell made the decision based on our ambassador in Haiti's very clear presentation of the circumstances, and the president made the decision ultimately, and it was a good decision, and I would stand by that decision.

Haiti is a situation that picks at all our hearts all the time. Haiti is right next to being a failed state. And because of its proximity to the United States, we know what that failure means. And Haiti is not apparently capable of coming out of that situation. It's a situation that, as I said, drags at all our hearts. But in this particular instance, I think a good decision was made, a decision that prevented further bloodshed that would have been widespread had it not been made.

AMY GOODMAN: Why say that the president, Aristide, had an obsession with power? This was a man who was the democratically
elected president of Haiti, certainly got a higher percentage of
the vote than President Bush got in this country.

WILKERSON: Please, don't refer to the percentage of vote as equatable to democracy, as equatable to the kinds of institutions we
have reflecting democracy in America. Hitler was elected by
popular vote.

Democracy Now! listeners and viewers inundated us with e-mail
to correct the colonel: Hitler, of course, did not come to power by
popular vote. He was appointed chancellor in a deal made with the
elderly German president Hindenburg in January 1933. But the
slip was telling. For the top State Department official, being
elected with overwhelming support from Haiti's poor masses
makes one a dictator. A president installed at gunpoint by the
United States is the real champion of democracy.

Two months after Aristide's overthrow, Assistant Secretary of
State Roger Noriega told the American Enterprise Institute, "The
Bush administration believes that if we all do our part and do it
right, Haiti will have the democracy it deserves."[14]

In place of Haiti's democratically elected government, the Bush
administration gave it bloodshed and misery. "Assassinations, mob
violence, torture and arbitrary arrests have created a 'catastrophic'
human rights problem," reported the *New York Times* in January
2006.[15] Following the coup, the Haitian leaders installed by the
Bush administration began a campaign of methodically hunting
down, arresting, and killing Aristide supporters. U.S. Marines
wouldn't intervene to help protect the elected president, but they
did arrive after he was deposed, to round up his supporters.
Among those picked up by the Marines was folk singer and community organizer So Ann Auguste. Aristide's former prime minister, Yvon Neptune, was jailed for a year without charge. After a
hunger strike and an international outcry, the government finally

accused him in 2005 of inciting a massacre—one that a UN investigation could not find any evidence ever took place. Father Gérard Jean-Juste, a prominent Aristide supporter who was considered a possible presidential candidate, was arrested; Amnesty International declared the priest "a prisoner of conscience."

In all, hundreds of Aristide supporters, from high-level officials to local activists, were put in filthy, overcrowded prisons. To oversee the jails, the United States brought in Terry Stewart, former head of the Arizona Department of Corrections. Before the Justice Department sent him to Haiti, Stewart was one of a team of consultants sent to Iraq to set up their prisons, including Abu Ghraib (see Chapter 10, "Exporting Abuse," for more on Stewart and globetrotting American prison consultants).

This, for the Bush administration, was the democracy that Haiti deserved.

Their Master's Voice

For some U.S. journalists, hewing closely to the government line isn't a coincidence; it's their job. Régine Alexandre was a freelance correspondent in Haiti for the Associated Press and the *New York Times*. From May 2004, her byline appeared on at least a dozen AP stories and on two stories in the *Times*. In December 2005 independent journalist Anthony Fenton revealed on Pacifica Radio's *Flashpoints* that Alexandre was wearing two hats: While working as a journalist, she also worked for the National Endowment for Democracy.[16]

The NED has played a controversial role in foreign elections. The organization is funded by the U.S. Congress and the State Department. While claiming a mission of "promoting democracy," the NED was involved in backing opposition groups in Venezuela, including funding leaders of the failed 2002 coup against President Hugo Chavez. The NED funds the International Republican Institute, which in turn backed anti-Aristide forces.

Indeed, the NED's Haiti operation bears remarkable similarities to its efforts to back the overthrow of Hugo Chavez. In both cases, U.S.-backed opposition groups staged violent protests against the elected government, which pro-U.S. media depicted as grassroots uprisings. Coup leaders then declared that the elected president had voluntarily resigned—claims that were trumpeted by State Department officials and that later turned out to be false. The main difference, of course, is that these U.S. efforts at subversion failed in Venezuela but succeeded in Haiti.

The NED acknowledged that Alexandre was working as a field representative for them in Haiti. When *Flashpoints* confronted Alexandre about this, she denied working for the NED. A day later, the AP announced it had severed ties to Alexandre; the *Times* followed suit a few days later.

In Haiti, the American media has been nothing if not reliable: It has done its master's bidding. For decades, it has championed some of the most repressive elements of Haitian society. With such compromised reporting appearing in the top American media outlets, it's going to take more than firing one stringer for the news out of Haiti to be fair and accurate anytime soon.

In February 2006, after months of delay and four postponements, Haiti held its first presidential elections since Aristide's victory in 2000. René Préval, a former president and an ally of Aristide, was declared the winner. Like Aristide, Préval was seen as a champion of the poor. He pledged to create jobs, improve education, and battle social inequalities in Haiti.

The American media—both those on and off the U.S. government payroll—chimed in with a chorus of skepticism. Shortly before Préval's victory was announced—and when it was already clear he had won roughly half the vote, out of thirty-two candidates—NPR ran a story, "Haitians Unsettled by the Prospect of a Préval Win." No doubt the coup plotters—and their backers in the Bush administration—were unsettled. Especially when Jean-

Bertrand Aristide announced shortly after the election that he would return home.

Father Gérard Jean-Juste captured the sentiments of the majority of Haitians about the election when he said on *Democracy Now!*: "I am happy, and I hope that from now on, nobody should stop the Haitian people from enjoying the right to vote. Also now, I hope that no one should try once more to go against the will of the people because that's created so much turmoil, such a chaotic situation that we have lived since February 29, 2004. So we hope that everyone from now on will have great respect for everyone. Particularly those poorest people who are trying hard to get off misery and to organize themselves. We have one more chance in history to regain our place as a nation and to contribute as our ancestors have contributed to freedom."[17]

I am wronged. It is a shameful thing that you should mind these folks that are out of their wits. —**Martha Carrier, tried for witchcraft in Salem, hanged August 19, 1692**

In February 1692, a group of young women near Salem, Massachusetts, became strangely ill. They complained of fever, dashed about, and became hysterical. Among the girls were the daughter and niece of the local minister. When questioned about their fainting and babbling, the girls claimed they were bewitched by other community members and possessed by the devil. Accusations followed quickly: The town beggar (a woman disliked by the Puritans) and a Native American slave were among the first to be charged with witchcraft. The notorious Salem Witch Trials began in June, and allowed for "spectral evidence"—testimony based on dreams or visions about actions done by the accused witch's spirit. By the time the witch hunt was finished in September, twenty innocent people had been executed. The royal governor of Massachusetts, Sir William Phips, finally ordered an end to the trials after his own wife was accused of being a witch.

Witch-hunting in America has taken different forms since the Salem Witch Trials. During World War II, the "Jap peril" resulted in 120,000 Japanese-Americans being rounded up, dispossessed, and dumped into internment camps. In the 1950s, there was the "Red Menace," in which Senator Joseph McCarthy led a crusade to rout out his political enemies from public life. Under the guise of anticommunism, the United States secretly backed wars in Southeast Asia and Central America from the 1960s through the 1980s. In the late 1990s, Chinese spying was briefly trumpeted. At the start of the twenty-first century, it is terrorism, especially from Muslims, that has become the new bogeyman.

The targets change, but the tactics have remained the same for centuries: Political leaders cite an external threat, the mass media inflates the charges and fans the flames of hysteria, and people, often ethnic minorities, are victimized. Civil liberties are trampled as the latter-day witches are brought to "justice."

Stealing the "Crown Jewels"

"A scientist suspected of spying for China improperly transferred huge amounts of secret data from a computer system at a Government laboratory, compromising virtually every nuclear weapon in the United States arsenal, Government and lab officials say."[1]

So began a terrifying article in the *New York Times* on April 28, 1999. Conjuring images of an impending Armageddon and reviving Cold War hysteria about marauding foreigners threatening the American way of life—all leavened with a dash of spy intrigue— the *Times* article had all the necessary ingredients for whipping the nation and lawmakers into a frenzy.

Every ingredient, that is, but one: the truth.

The *Times* article was one in a series of purported exposés of Taiwanese-born nuclear scientist Wen Ho Lee. Beginning on March 6, 1999, veteran *Times* reporters James Risen and Jeff Gerth revealed shocking details about lapses in security at the Los Alamos National Laboratory, the center of the American nuclear weapons program. The first article, "Breach at Los Alamos," referred darkly to "the main suspect, a Los Alamos computer scientist who is Chinese-American."[2] Two days later, Lee, a shy, 60-year-old man who had worked at the Los Alamos lab for over two decades, was fired from the lab on orders from U.S. Secretary of Energy Bill Richardson. In a wholesale violation of Lee's privacy, his identity was leaked and revealed in the *Times,* along with the news that he had been fired. Thus was launched the exhaustive smear campaign against him. In the course of the following year, Risen and Gerth penned dozens of articles for the *Times* about the Wen Ho Lee espionage case. With sensational *Times* articles, based on a steady stream of leaks about Lee's supposed criminality, stoking public hysteria about the case, and politicians in Washington fanning the flames about the threat of Chinese espionage, federal prosecutors ultimately threw Lee into pre-trial solitary confinement for nine months.

The case against Wen Ho Lee has come to represent what can go wrong when the media and government work together to target an individual. The gist of the *Times* articles was that Dr. Lee, a modest man who spoke in heavily accented English, had stolen blueprints for America's most advanced nuclear weapon and given or sold them to the Chinese. That would explain how China was able to copy the technology for miniaturized nuclear warheads, which are on the cutting edge of America's weapons technology.

The charges against Lee were being championed by the Department of Energy's director of intelligence, Notra Trulock III, a Soviet analyst during the Cold War.[3] He made his charges in a secret congressional investigation headed by California Republican Rep. Christopher Cox. The Cox Commission had been established in July 1998 at the urging of then House Speaker Newt Gingrich to investigate whether there was an illegal connection between contributions to President Clinton's 1996 reelection campaign and the export of military technology to China. The commission expanded its investigation to include Chinese espionage. The Cox Commission report was completed in January 1999 and was promptly leaked to the *Times*. The newspaper seized on Trulock's sensational charges and reported them as if they were fact.

From the very first *Times* exposé, a strange caveat was woven through the articles: In spite of Trulock's dark warnings, backed by countless column inches laying out the damning evidence of espionage against Wen Ho Lee, the FBI insisted that it didn't have enough evidence to arrest him. There were qualifiers such as these, which ran in the first story: "Investigators did not then have sufficient evidence to obtain a wiretap on the suspect, which made it difficult to build a strong criminal case."[4] This and other red flags (wiretaps require a relatively low legal threshold, yet authorities in this case could not clear it) were cited as proof for another hypothesis: that a cover-up of a major security breach was under way.

Early 1999 was no ordinary time in American politics. Republican rage against President Bill Clinton had culminated in his impeachment in December 1998 and his Senate trial two months later. Clinton's relations with China had become a focus of partisan ire. There were charges that China had funneled money into Democratic campaigns in 1996, and accusations that Clinton was trying to bolster political and economic ties to China in 1997.

In this politically poisonous atmosphere, the *Times* took sides by anointing a new hero right in its first article: "In personal terms, the handling of this case is very much the story of the Energy Department intelligence official who first raised questions about the Los Alamos case, Notra Trulock. Mr. Trulock became a secret star witness before a select Congressional committee last fall."[5]

Notra Trulock was an old Cold Warrior whose antipathy to Clinton and the Chinese was widely known among his colleagues. The *Times* championed his version of events, and took it further, imbuing it with an apocalyptic gloss: "At the dawn of the atomic age, a Soviet spy ring that included Julius Rosenberg had stolen the first nuclear secrets out of Los Alamos. Now, at the end of the cold war, the Chinese seemed to have succeeded in penetrating the same weapons lab. 'This is going to be just as bad as the Rosenbergs,' [CIA chief spy hunter Paul] Redmond recalled saying."[6]

What followed was a political and media witch hunt the likes of which hadn't been seen since, well, the Rosenbergs. After Lee was fired, he was interrogated relentlessly and repeatedly polygraphed. Finally, in December 1999, he was indicted on fifty-nine counts—but none of them were for spying. He was accused of having improperly downloaded classified information. A trial was set, but in a rare move, a federal judge agreed to the government's demand that Lee be kept locked up in solitary confinement. He lived in a cell with a light burning round the clock, and was allowed out to exercise for one hour per day, often in shackles.

The *Times* was doing a symbiotic dance with the government. The hysterical *Times* coverage drove the government investigation, and vice versa. David Kitchen, the head of the FBI's Albuquerque office, even suggested to agent Carol Covert (yes, that really is her name) that she bring up the Rosenberg case because the *Times* article had referred to it. Covert began her interrogation of the bewildered scientist by telling him—falsely—that he had failed a polygraph test. Covert then picked up where the newspaper left off:

> "Do you know who the Rosenbergs are?" Ms. Covert asked.
>
> "I heard them, yeah, I heard them mention," Dr. Lee said.
>
> "The Rosenbergs are the only people that never cooperated with the federal government in an espionage case," she said. "You know what happened to them? They electrocuted them, Wen Ho."[7]

The government and the press were in an echo chamber. There was no room for skepticism or questioning the fundamental assumptions of the case—namely, was Wen Ho Lee really a spy? Did the case have any merit?

As it turns out, the FBI had been winding down the investigation into Lee several months earlier. David Kitchen, now retired from the FBI, recounted in 2001 to the *Times,* "We couldn't understand how [DOE] came to the conclusion they came to, specifically about how Lee was the main suspect." Kitchen decided in late 1998 to close the Lee investigation. "We worked the case for quite a while, and what did we have to show for it?"[8]

The problems with the case were many. For one, the nuclear

"secrets" that China was alleged to have obtained were available from hundreds of sources, not just Los Alamos, and many of them were in the public domain. And despite Representative Cox charging that "the crown jewels of our nuclear arsenal" had been stolen, the theft, if it ever happened, occurred in the 1980s, and there was no evidence linking either Los Alamos or Lee to that case.[9]

In January 1999, the *Wall Street Journal* first published an article revealing that the FBI was investigating a leak of nuclear weapons secrets at Los Alamos. But it wasn't until the series of *Times* stories began two months later that the focus turned to Lee. Indeed, after the first *Times* article appeared, FBI agents confronted Lee and shoved the article at him. "Basically that is indicating that there is a person at the laboratory that's committed espionage, and that points to you," FBI Agent Covert told him.

"But do they have any proof, evidence?" Dr. Lee asked.

All the FBI had was a hunch—and the knowledge that the nation's most powerful newspaper had declared this flimsy case to be the most significant spy hunt in a half century. That was sufficient to plunge Lee into a long nightmare.

The *Times* extended the dark cloud of suspicion over Lee's wife, Sylvia, who worked as a secretary at the Los Alamos labs. On March 9, 1999, the *Times* reported, "Energy Department officials also said co-workers questioned why she frequently invited herself to gatherings at the lab with visiting Chinese delegations. FBI officials said she was not a target of their investigation, but said it is possible that others were involved in the theft of data. They have not yet identified any other suspects."[10]

What the *Times* didn't mention until six weeks later was that Sylvia Lee was an FBI informant from 1987 to 1992.[11]

Other newspapers, including the *Washington Post, Los Angeles Times,* and *Wall Street Journal,* reported on the case. But the *New York Times* pursued it as if it were prosecuting the case on its own. Which, in many ways, it was. In explaining the peculiarities of the case to its readers, the London *Independent* noted, "In government and political circles [the *Times*] wields a degree of influence that is unmatched in the U.S. media. When the *New York Times* names a suspected spy, it is not just another newspaper scare: the Establishment takes notice."[12]

Only a handful of reporters protested the newspaper's witch hunt at the beginning. Robert Scheer of the *Los Angeles Times* wrote a dozen columns decrying the miscarriage of justice in the case, including this view in October 1999: "It's a sad day for American journalism when the *New York Times,* one of the leading news organizations in the country, so uncritically publicizes inflammatory charges of spying against a U.S. citizen based on scandalous leaks from a congressional committee. But even worse was the behavior of the administration, which panicked in the face of these charges and fired Lee without a hearing in order to placate those calling for his scalp. Apologies to Lee are in order."

Instead of apologies, the government handed down its indictment in December 1999. The decision to prosecute was ultimately made at a meeting in the White House situation room on December 4, 1999. Among those attending the meeting were National Security Advisor Sandy Berger, Attorney General Janet Reno, FBI Director Louis Freeh, Energy Secretary Bill Richardson, and CIA Director George Tenet.[13]

It was a desperate face-saving move by the Justice Department and the FBI to cover for their failure to actually pin the crime—if indeed there had even been one—on someone, preferably a Chinese-born someone. The charges carried a life sentence.

Wen Ho Lee, a naturalized American citizen, charged that he was being targeted simply because he was ethnic Chinese. Asian-American groups decried his treatment and rallied to his defense. The Asian Pacific Americans in Higher Education and the Association of Asian American Studies passed resolutions urging all Asian-American scientists to boycott jobs at federal laboratories. But the government was unbowed. In early September 2000, in response to demands that the government justify Lee's continued solitary confinement, government lawyers declared that Lee's release would risk "hundreds of millions of lives."[14] The judge nevertheless demanded thousands of pages of documents from the government to assess whether it had prosecuted Lee based on his ethnicity.

Suddenly, the government's house of cards came tumbling down. The lead FBI agent recanted key testimony that he had given. In mid-September, the government abruptly dropped fifty-eight of the fifty-nine charges against Lee. The scientist pleaded guilty to a single count of mishandling secret information.

On September 13, 2000, after Lee had endured 278 days of solitary confinement, Judge James A. Parker, a conservative Reagan appointee, had had enough. Judge Parker released Wen Ho Lee from prison, and in an unusual statement from the bench, he rebuked the government and apologized to Wen Ho Lee. "I believe you were terribly wronged," began Judge Parker, describing Lee's imprisonment in "demeaning, unnecessarily punitive conditions. I am truly sorry that I was led by our Executive Branch of government to order your detention last December."

It is rare for a federal judge to criticize top elected officials, but Parker was unbowed. "Dr. Lee, I tell you with great sadness that I feel I was led astray last December by the Executive Branch of our government." The judge said that "top decision makers in the Executive Branch, especially the Department of Justice and the Department of Energy and locally . . . have embarrassed our entire nation and each of us who is a citizen of it."

Judge Parker concluded, "I might say that I am also sad and troubled because I do not know the real reasons why the Executive Branch has done all of this."[15]

As for Notra Trulock, the government spook who was obsessed with finding a fall guy for Chinese weapons advancements, he wound up being a key cause of the case's collapse. Wen Ho Lee's charge that he was the victim of racial profiling was borne out by testimony from Trulock's colleagues, who described him as a racist.

Robert Vrooman, the head of counterintelligence at Los Alamos, declared in a sworn statement, "The racial issue surfaced explicitly in comments made by Notra Trulock, the head of DOE's Office of Counterintelligence, who told me on November 20, 1996, that 'ethnic Chinese' should not be allowed to work on classified projects, including nuclear weapons."[16] Vrooman testified repeatedly in early 1999 in closed-door sessions before the House and Senate Intelligence committees, as well as to several investigative review boards, that no espionage had occurred. He insisted that Lee had been unfairly targeted because he was Chinese-American. In response, Energy Secretary Bill Richardson officially reprimanded Vrooman in August 1999 for failing to assist the FBI in its Chinese espionage investigation.[17]

Then there was the damning statement of Charles Washington, DOE's acting director of counterintelligence: "Based on my experience and my personal knowledge, I believe that Mr. Trulock improperly targeted Dr. Lee due to Dr. Lee's race and national origin."

In a final twist, Mr. Trulock himself became the subject of an FBI investigation for improperly disclosing classified information.[18] He went on to work as associate editor of the right-wing *Accuracy in Media Report*. (For an idea of AIM's political leanings, headlines from its Web site include: "Looney Clooney Smears Senator McCarthy," "Hollywood Surrenders to Terrorists," and "*New York Times* Aids al Qaeda.")

This was the man whom the *Times* dubbed a "star witness." The *Times* championed Trulock's view, delighting Republican leaders who were eager to club the Clinton administration for being lax on nuclear security.

The total collapse of the government's case against Wen Ho Lee forced public officials to explain their actions. President Clinton said that he was "quite troubled" by the fact that Lee had

been denied bail. Clinton said in September 2000, "It's very difficult to reconcile the two positions, that one day he's a terrible
risk to the national security, and the next day, they're making a
plea agreement for an offense far more modest than what had
been alleged."[19] Meanwhile, White House Press Secretary Joe
Lockhart blamed "near-hysterical investigative reporting" for
creating a crisis atmosphere around the issue of nuclear weapons
security.[20]

Two weeks after Lee was released from jail, the *New York Times*
published a sixteen-hundred-word editor's note, "The *Times* and
Wen Ho Lee." Now, finally, was the time to come clean. But the
Times blinked. "On the whole, we remain proud of work that
brought into the open a major national security problem of which
officials had been aware for months, even years," the editors
wrote. "But looking back, we also found some things we wish we
had done differently in the course of the coverage to give Dr. Lee
the full benefit of the doubt." The *Times* concluded that "the
blame lies principally with those who directed the coverage."[21]

Two days later, it was the turn of the *Times* editorial page to
search its soul. It largely defended its actions in running numerous
editorials that vilified Lee. It was a non-apology that merely allowed that "we too quickly accepted the government's theory that
espionage was the main reason for Chinese nuclear advances and
its view that Dr. Lee had been properly singled out as the prime
suspect."[22]

Wen Ho Lee has continued his crusade for justice. Asian-
American groups have demanded a presidential pardon for Lee.
And Lee sued the government, charging that top officials violated
his privacy by improperly disclosing information about him that
destroyed his reputation. As part of that suit, Lee demanded that
four journalists—James Risen of the *New York Times*, Bob Drogin
of the *Los Angeles Times,* H. Josef Hebert of the Associated Press,
and Pierre Thomas, formerly of CNN and now of ABC—reveal
who their confidential sources were that provided this informa-

tion. The journalists declined to reveal their sources, and were ruled to be in contempt of court.

Robert Scheer concluded appropriately, "Freedom of the press is presumably for the benefit of the readers in general and of victims of government abuse in particular. Yet the *Times*, like many media outlets these days, has perverted that freedom to justify its willful participation in government manipulation of the news."[23]

In arguing for the reporters to reveal their sources in both the Wen Ho Lee and Valerie Plame cases, the media watch group Fairness and Accuracy in Reporting (FAIR) declared, "The First Amendment exists so that the press can be a check on government abuse of power, not a handmaiden to it."[24]

In June 2006, Wen Ho Lee achieved victory: The federal government and five media organizations—AP, *New York Times, Washingon Post, Los Angeles Times,* and ABC—agreed to pay him $1.6 million to settle his privacy lawsuit, with the government paying $895,000 and the media groups paying $750,000. The unprecedented joint payment was fitting recognition of how the government and journalists had worked together to take down the scientist.

In September 2005, Bill Richardson, the former secretary of energy under Clinton who later became the Democratic governor of New Mexico, spoke to *Democracy Now!* He fired Wen Ho Lee in March 1999. In July 2005, Federal Judge David Sentelle stated that Richardson was the probable source of the leaks about Lee. Richardson has denied this. Has Richardson, who helped lead the crusade against Lee, learned anything from this sorry chapter? Clearly not. "I stand behind everything that I said and I did before in that case," he declared. "This was a man that was convicted on several counts of tampering with classified information. . . . I stand behind the very strong actions that I took to protect our nuclear secrets."

As for Judge Sentelle implicating Richardson in leaking Lee's name, Richardson was adamant. "He is totally wrong."

Richardson was also dismissive of Judge Parker's rebuke. "Well, that's his opinion. I believe that we acted properly in safeguarding our nuclear secrets. He was convicted on several counts. There were some mistakes in that case. It involved the entire federal government, and I stand behind everything that I did."[25]

Wen Ho Lee was not, as Richardson claimed, "convicted on several counts." He pleaded guilty to a lone charge of improperly downloading classified documents. Lee's attorney contrasted his treatment with that of former CIA director John Deutch, who downloaded far more sensitive national security secrets onto his home computer. The Pentagon inspector general described Deutch's action as "particularly egregious."[26] The Justice Department initially declined to prosecute Deutch, then opened an investigation. Deutch pleaded guilty to a misdemeanor in January 2001 and was pardoned by President Bill Clinton on his last day as president.

The New Bogeyman

In the aftermath of September 11, 2001, government witch-hunters are working overtime.

James Yee learned this the hard way. Yee, a third-generation Chinese-American, was born in New Jersey and graduated from West Point military academy in 1990. Shortly afterward, he converted from Christianity to Islam and underwent religious training in Syria. Yee was one of the first Muslim chaplains commissioned by the U.S. Army. After the 9/11 attacks, Yee became a frequent government spokesman, helping to educate soldiers about Islam and build greater religious tolerance in the military. In November 2002, he was selected to serve as Muslim chaplain at Guantánamo Bay. At that time, nearly 700 detainees were being held by the government for suspected terrorist activities. Yee's duties as chaplain gave him unrestricted access to the detainees.

Yee threw himself into his duties. As the only Muslim chaplain on the base for ten months, he led the detainees in daily prayer, tended to their dietary needs, and chastised guards for disrespecting the Koran and interfering in other Muslim rituals.

In the xenophobic and abusive environment of Guantánamo Bay, a place that President Bush has insisted is beyond the reach of regular laws, military colleagues began to question the loyalties of the Muslim chaplain. Their suspicions came to a head less than a year after Yee began serving there.

On September 10, 2003, Captain Yee stepped off a plane from Guantánamo Bay at a Florida naval base and was secretly arrested. He was supposedly in possession of classified documents, including a list of detainees and a drawing of where their cells were located. The implication was that Yee might be planning a massive jailbreak of terrorists from Guantánamo—or something like that.

Ten days after Yee's arrest, military officials leaked the story to the conservative *Washington Times,* which ran an article on September 20, 2003, about Yee. The newspaper revealed that Yee was being charged with sedition, aiding the enemy, spying, espionage, and failure to obey a general order.

"Captain Yee had almost unlimited private access to detainees as part of the Defense Department's program to provide the prisoners with religious counseling, as well as clothing and Islamic-approved meals," reported the *Washington Times.* The article hinted darkly, "The law-enforcement source declined to say how much damage Capt. Yee may have inflicted on the U.S. war against Osama bin Laden's global terror network. The source said the 'highest levels' of government made the decision to arrest Capt. Yee, who had been kept under surveillance for some time."[27]

A senior Bush administration official told the *Washington Times* the following day, "If the list of detainees got out, then you have a whole lot of al Qaeda cells go to ground." This source said both the Pentagon and the White House were involved in the decision to make the arrest.

It was a stunning fall from grace for an Army officer who had been held up as a poster boy of American patriotism ("When I go into the field," he told a reporter, "I have a copy of the Koran, and next to it, a copy of the U.S. Constitution"[28]) to being cast as a foreign-born traitor and threat to American security. The media went on a feeding frenzy. Chaplain Yee was vilified on the airwaves and on the Internet as a traitor and a mole inside the Army. All the important ingredients—foreign, Muslim, al Qaeda—were stirred together into a toxic brew to poison the atmosphere and ensure pretrial conviction.

"The government is engaging in overkill and is creating an atmosphere of hysteria around this case," said Yee's attorney, Eugene Fidell.[29] Indeed, hysteria was crucial to the case against Yee, since, as Fidell pointed out, the offenses with which he was charged—taking home classified material and carrying classified documents without proper coverings—were common infractions in the military that resulted in minimal penalties, if they were even prosecuted.

The witch hunt against Muslims at Guantánamo expanded. Following Yee's arrest, it was revealed that Ahmad Halabi, a Muslim and an Arabic translator in the U.S. Air Force who worked at Guantánamo, had been arrested in July and held secretly. Halabi was also charged with taking home classified documents and, like Yee, was accused by some Guantánamo colleagues of having "made statements criticizing U.S. policy with regard to the detainees and . . . the Middle East."

A month after Yee's arrest, the *Washington Post* reported:

Officials eventually suspected that Yee's allegiance shifted from the military to the 660 prisoners there as he complained that they had no release from the stress in their lives, which was partly created by the uncertainty over whether they will ever be released, numerous sources said.

"The fear was that he was in a quagmire as to how to handle this, and that he had started mixing his loyalties," one military official said. "It apparently was a challenge to him."

A second military official described Yee's belief that detainees were being treated too harshly as "ludicrous. . . . Yee was way out of line."[30]

Captain Yee was held for seventy-six days, much of it in solitary confinement in an eight-by-ten-foot cell, manacled and in leg irons. Yee was held in a Navy brig in South Carolina, along with Jose Padilla and Yasir Hamdi. At the time, the Bush administration had declared Padilla and Hamdi to be enemy combatants who could be held forever without trial.

The military postponed Yee's trial five times. Then, in March 2004, on a Friday evening, the Army announced that Yee was being released, and his charges reduced. The one-time superspy was now accused of adultery and downloading pornography on his computer. Yee denied the charges, and they were later thrown out.

"It was just a very shabby attack on Yee," said Gary Solis, a former Marine prosecutor who now teaches law of war at Georgetown University. "They said, 'Hey, our case has turned to crap, but oh wait, we have this.' They picked something to embarrass and humiliate him that was entirely unrelated."[31]

A few months later, Airman Ahmad Halabi, who had faced thirty espionage-related charges, was released after nine months in jail. The case against him also fell apart: Twenty-six charges were dropped, and the four that remained were relatively minor infractions. It was the third time the military had backed away from sensational allegations of spying against employees at Guantánamo in less than a year.[32]

As the real story has unfolded, James Yee infuriated his colleagues at Guantánamo Bay because he spoke out about the treatment of detainees. In October 2005, he described on *Democracy Now!* what he witnessed inside America's gulag:

"One of the most emotional things that I might say that I saw down there was the conditions and how they deteriorated within the time frame that I was there, the emotional and mental conditions of the prisoners themselves. I recall seeing, for example, two detainees permanently residing in the detainee hospital who had become so depressed, so despondent, that they no longer had an appetite and stopped eating. They had to be force-fed with a tube that is inserted through their nose medically into their stomach and force-fed in that manner. And I witnessed this tube in the hospital being put in the prisoner's nose—who didn't want it in his nose, of course. And it's a very painful experience. The prisoner had to be shackled down with handcuffs to both sides of the bed. A guard had to come back and hold the prisoner's head back, and then the medic or the nurse would come and put petroleum jelly on the end of this plastic tube, in his nose, so this tube slides down. As that happens, you hear the detainee scream out in pain."

The U.S. military has continued to use this method of force-feeding and has acknowledged that it is aimed at breaking hunger strikes. The number of hunger strikers at Guantánamo dropped dramatically from eighty-four in December 2005 to four in February 2006. UN human rights investigators declared in February 2006 that the force-feeding amounted to torture, and called for the closure of the Guantánamo prison.

The chief medical officer at Guantánamo, Capt. John S. Edmondson of the Navy, stated that his staff was not force-feeding any detainees but "providing nutritional supplementation on a voluntary basis to detainees who wish to protest their confinement by not taking oral nourishment." In January, Captain Edmondson left Guantánamo for a new post. Before he left, the Army awarded him a Legion of Merit Medal for "inspiring leadership and exemplary performance."[33]

Chaplain Yee, who has written about his ordeal in a book, *For God and Country: Faith and Patriotism Under Fire*, reflected on *Democracy Now!:* "If it could happen to me—a third-generation Chinese-American who graduated from West Point, patriotically serving his country, being praised and awarded and recognized for great contributions—[if I] could land in prison for seventy-six days with these huge death penalty charges, it could happen to any one of us. And this is why we have to stand up for justice."

The media should be a check against the abuse of government power. But too often, journalists' coziness with those in power make them instruments of the abuse. When the reflex of journalists is to simply trust those in power, justice can be long in coming.

It's been three centuries since the Salem Witch Trials. But as Wen Ho Lee and James Yee can attest, witch hunts are just as likely to spiral out of control today as they were when young girls claimed to be possessed by demons.

No President has ever done more for human rights than I have.
—President George W. Bush, January 2004[1]

"We do not torture," President Bush said in exasperation during a press conference in Panama at the end of a disastrous, riot-riddled Latin American tour. It was November 2005, and Bush was being harassed about his torture policies everywhere he went. So the president tried a technique that had served him so well in the run-up to the invasion of Iraq: Tell a big lie often enough, and people will start to believe it.

Problem was, Bush's "Vice President for Torture," as Dick Cheney was dubbed by the *Washington Post*,[2] was working overtime at that very moment trying to strong-arm the Senate into giving the CIA permission to torture. In spite of a 90–9 vote in favor of a bill sponsored by Sen. John McCain that would ban the "cruel, inhuman or degrading" treatment of prisoners, Cheney desperately wanted an exemption for the CIA that would keep them unfettered by squeamish restrictions.

The juxtaposition of the two leaders trying to pull off a carefully staged con job—with Cheney championing torture in the back rooms, while Bush smiled and denied it in front of the cameras—was farcical, were it not for the macabre story line. Throw in White House flak Scott McClellan trying to dance his way around the issue, and we were now in the realm of theater—a theater of war.

Indeed, a movie had already been made about this subject—in 1966. One of the most influential political films of all time, *The*

Battle of Algiers, by Italian filmmaker Gillo Pontecorvo, vividly depicts the Algerian struggle for independence against the French occupation in the 1950s and early '60s. There are striking parallels between the French use of torture against resistance fighters of Algeria's National Liberation Front (FLN) and the U.S. abuse of prisoners in Abu Ghraib and Guantánamo Bay.

The Battle of Algiers again made the news in 2003 after the Pentagon showed a screening of the film just months after Bush prematurely declared the Iraq War officially over. A flyer promoting the Pentagon screening stated: "How to win a battle against terrorism and lose the war of ideas. Children shoot soldiers at point-blank range. Women plant bombs in cafes. Soon the entire Arab population builds to a mad fervor. Sound familiar? The French have a plan. It succeeds tactically, but fails strategically. To understand why, come to a rare showing of this film."[3]

Democracy Now! contrasted how the Bush administration talks about torture today with how the French talked about it in the 1960s. In this scene from *The Battle of Algiers,* the ruthless leader of the French paratroopers, Colonel Mathieu, holds a news conference with reporters:

REPORTER: Colonel, there's been talk recently of the paras' [the French paratroopers in Algeria] successes and of the methods they are said to use. Could you say something on this?

COLONEL MATHIEU: The successes result from these methods. The one presupposes the other.

REPORTER: I feel that being excessively careful, my colleagues keep asking roundabout questions to which you can only reply in a roundabout way. It would be better to call a spade a spade. If it's torture, let's speak of torture.

MATHIEU: I understand. You have no questions?

REPORTER: The questions have been asked. We would like the answers.

MATHIEU: Let us be exact. The word "torture" does not appear in our orders. We ask questions as in any police operation against an unknown gang. The FLN asks its members to keep silent for twenty-four hours if they are captured. Then they can talk. That's the time required to render any information useless. How should we question suspects? Like the courts and take a few months over it? The legal way has its drawbacks. Is it legal to blow up public places? . . .

Our duty is to win; thus, to be quite clear, I'll ask you a question myself: Must France stay in Algeria? If the answer is still yes, you must accept all that this entails.[4]

Fast forward a half century to a news conference at the White House on November 8, 2005. President Bush's Press Secretary Scott McClellan was questioned by the tenacious veteran White House reporter Helen Thomas. On this day, Thomas was pressing McClellan about why the White House was asking for an exemption for the CIA from the proposed McCain amendment that would ban the "cruel, inhuman or degrading" treatment of prisoners:

THOMAS: I'm asking: Is the administration asking for an exemption?

MCCLELLAN: I am answering your question. The president has made it very clear that we are going to do—

THOMAS: You're not answering. Yes or no?

MCCLELLAN: No, you don't want the American people to hear what the facts are, Helen. And I'm going to tell them the facts.

THOMAS: [inaudible] the American people every day. I'm asking you: yes or no, did we ask for an exemption?

MCCLELLAN: And let me respond. You've had your opportunity to ask the question. Now I'm going to respond to it.

THOMAS: If you could answer in a straight way.

MCCLELLAN: And I'm going to answer it, just like the president—I just did. And the president has answered it numerous times.

THOMAS: Yes or no?

MCCLELLAN: Our most important responsibility is to protect the American people. We are engaged in a global war against Islamic radicals who are intent on spreading a hateful ideology and intent on killing innocent men, women, and children.

THOMAS: Did we ask for an exemption?

MCCLELLAN: We are going to do what is necessary to protect the American people.

THOMAS: Is that the answer?

MCCLELLAN: We are also going to do so in a way that adheres to our laws and to our values. We have made that very clear. The president directed everybody within this government that we do not engage in torture. We will not torture. He made that very clear.

THOMAS: Are you denying we asked for an exemption?

MCCLELLAN: Helen, we will continue to work with the Congress on the issue that you brought up. The way you characterize it, that we're asking for exemption from torture, is just flat-out false, because there are laws that are on the books that prohibit the use of torture. And we adhere to those laws.

THOMAS: We did ask for an exemption; is that right? I mean, be simple. This is a very simple question.

MCCLELLAN: I just answered your question. The president answered it last week.

DAVID GREGORY, NBC NEWS: What are we asking for? Would you characterize what we're asking for?

MCCLELLAN: We're asking to do what is necessary to protect the American people in a way that is consistent with our laws and our treaty obligations. And that's what we do.

GREGORY: Why does the CIA need an exemption . . . ?

MCCLELLAN: David, let's talk about people that you're talking about who have been brought to justice and captured. You're talking about people like Khalid Shaykh Muhammad; people like Abu Zubaydah.

REPORTER [UNIDENTIFIED]: I'm asking you—

MCCLELLAN: No, this is facts about what you're talking about.

REPORTER: Why does the CIA need an exemption from rules that would govern the conduct of our military in interrogation practices?

MCCLELLAN: There are already laws and rules that are on the books, and we follow those laws and rules. What we need to make sure is that we are able to carry out the war on terrorism as effectively as possible, not only—

REPORTER: What does that mean?

MCCLELLAN: That's what I'm telling you right now. Not only to protect Americans from an attack, but to prevent an attack from happening in the first place.[5]

This news conference was not fictional. Only the answers coming out of the White House were.

It turns out that the dramatic Oval Office handshake staged between President Bush and Sen. John McCain on December 15, 2005, was another fiction. President Bush declared that day that the legislation he was signing—after fighting it for months—made it "clear to the world that this government does not torture." But the Detainee Treatment Act of 2005 (the so-called McCain amendment) had been almost completely eviscerated by that point. At the insistence of Republican senator Lindsey Graham of South Carolina, with the acquiescence of Michigan Democrat Carl Levin, the bill stripped Guantánamo detainees of the right to challenge their detentions in U.S. courts, thereby reversing a landmark Supreme Court decision that explicitly affirmed these rights for the detainees. So while the act bans torture, Guantánamo detainees—who UN investigators, among others, confirm are being tortured by their American captors—have no way to enforce the law. If John McCain were still a prisoner of war in Vietnam, a law such as this would have elicited a hearty chuckle from his torturers, who then could have continued their brutality uninterrupted.

For the Bush administration, even this amount of legal oversight was too much. Two weeks later, at his Crawford estate, after signing a defense bill that included the McCain amendment, Bush issued a "signing statement." It was Friday evening, December 30, 2005, carefully timed to minimize attention from the press and the public. The statement declared: "The executive branch shall construe [the law] in a manner consistent with the constitutional authority of the president . . . as commander in chief."

In other words, Bush would do as he damn well pleased, because he's president.

The Justice Department got right to work—denying justice to torture victims. On January 3, 2006, the Justice Department, citing this new law, informed federal judges that it was seeking the immediate dismissal of all 160 habeas corpus cases already filed for 300 Guantánamo detainees. The solicitor general, citing the same new law, was close behind, informing the Supreme Court on January 12 that it no longer had jurisdiction over Guantánamo and asking the justices to dismiss *Hamdan v. Rumsfeld,* another potential landmark case involving "enemy combatants." As Professor Alfred McCoy summarized these events, "Then, putting the cherry atop the administration's many-layered legal confection, on January 24 the Army changed its standing orders to allow military executions at Guantánamo, thus keeping the U.S. courts from intervening in any drum-head death sentences for detainees."[6]

Bush's torture chambers, far from being dismantled, were getting a fresh coat of paint, and even some window blinds.

The Interrogator

America's interrogation dungeons have lately been spilling their secrets. As more soldiers are pressed into duty as tormentors, and more victims are telling their horrific tales of abuse at the hands of U.S. captors, we are learning daily the details about America's descent into the world of torture.

What we aren't hearing is that the United States has gained any useful intelligence from its medieval interrogation techniques.

Specialist Tony Lagouranis was in the U.S. Army from 2001 to 2005. He served a year in Iraq as an interrogator starting in January 2004. He first worked at Abu Ghraib months after the infamous torture photos taken at the prison had sparked international outrage. Then he was assigned to a mobile interrogation team that visited detention facilities around Iraq.

Lagouranis reluctantly went public with his allegations of torture. Moments before his live interview began on *Democracy Now!* on November 15, 2005, he said he didn't want to do it. At the last second, he agreed to speak.

Lagouranis explained that he joined the Army in May 2001 because he was looking for a way to pay off his student loans. He was also interested in learning Arabic; another ex-interrogator told him that the Army had taught him to speak Russian and German. "It just seemed like an attractive deal to me," said the earnest-looking young vet.

Lagouranis talked about some of the interrogation techniques that he used or witnessed in Iraq. His interrogations began innocuously, but he quickly learned that other interrogators were pushing the limits. "We would just talk to them, ask them questions, maybe, you know, use some psychological approaches, but nothing too serious. But I knew that some interrogators there were still, in January of 2004, using a little bit harsher techniques. Like, if a prisoner wasn't cooperating, they could adjust his diet. People were in deep, deep isolation for months there, which I believe is illegal, according to Army doctrine. [Interrogators] would also take their clothes and their mattress so they would be cold in their cells if they weren't cooperating.

"When the Navy SEALS would interrogate people, they were using ice water to lower the body temperature of the prisoner and they would take his rectal temperature in order to make sure that he didn't die."

Military interrogators discovered that using dogs was particularly effective in terrifying prisoners. At a detention facility at the

Mosul airport, "We would put the prisoner in a shipping container. We would keep him up all night with music and strobe lights, stress positions, and then we would bring in dogs. . . . The dog would be barking and jumping on the prisoner, and the prisoner wouldn't really understand what was going on.

"I knew that we were really walking the line," said Lagouranis. "I was going through the interrogation rules of engagement that were given to me by the unit that we were working with up there, trying to figure out what was legal and what wasn't legal. According to these interrogation rules of engagement, that was legal. So, when they ordered me to do it, I had to do it. You know, as far as whether I thought it was a good interrogation practice, I didn't think so at all, actually. We never produced any intelligence."

On April 28, 2004, the CBS show *60 Minutes II* aired the now iconic images of Iraqi detainees being tortured by their American captors at Abu Ghraib prison. Lagouranis recalled, "My initial reaction was that these were bad apples, like the White House line. But you know, it's funny, I didn't really tie it to what we were doing up there. We were using some pretty harsh methods on the prisoners. I had seen other units that were using, like, really severe methods. But I didn't tie it to the scandal."

Lagouranis said he began to question the interrogation techniques, but only to a point. "I was sort of pushing to back away from the harsh tactics, but at the same time I was—in a way, I sort of wanted to push, because we were frustrated by not getting intel. So I was on both sides of the fence. . . . I was still under the impression that we were getting prisoners who had intel to give us, and I still thought that these were bad guys. . . . Later it became clear to me that they were picking up just farmers. Like these guys were totally innocent and that's why we weren't getting intel. And it just made what we were doing seem even more cruel."

The exposure of what was happening at Abu Ghraib merely shifted the abuse from the prisons into the communities. From August to October of 2004, Lagouranis worked with a Marine reconnaissance unit in North Babel, just south of Baghdad. "They would go out and do a raid and stay in the detainees' homes, and torture them there," he said. "They were far worse than anything that I ever saw in a prison. They were breaking bones. They were smashing people's feet with the back of an axe head. They burned people.

"Every time Force Recon [Marines] went on a raid, they would bring back prisoners who were bruised, with broken bones, sometimes with burns. They were pretty brutal to these guys. And I would ask the prisoners what happened, how they received these wounds. And they would tell me that it was after their capture, while they were subdued, while they were handcuffed and they were being questioned by the Force Recon Marines. . . . One guy was forced to sit on an exhaust pipe of a Humvee. . . . He had a giant blister, third-degree burn on the back of his leg."

Lagouranis determined "that like 98 percent of these guys had not done anything. I mean, they were picking up people for the stupidest things. Like, there's one guy they picked up, they stopped him at a checkpoint, just a routine stop, and he had a shovel in his trunk, and he had a cell phone in his pocket. They said, 'Well, you can use the shovel to bury an IED [improvised explosive device, or roadside bomb], you can use the cell phone to detonate it.' He didn't have any explosives in his car. He had no weapons. Nothing. They had no reason to believe that he was setting IEDs other than the shovel and cell phone. That was the kind of prisoner they were bringing us."

A war based on fiction must continually conjure even greater fictions to perpetuate itself. So the fate of everyone that the Marines brought in was foreordained: "Basically everybody who came to the prison, they determined they were a terrorist, they were guilty, and they would send them to Abu Ghraib. When I would say they were innocent in my interrogation reports, they would send the prisoner up to Abu Ghraib without my interrogation report."

The young man who hoped to learn foreign languages and serve his country was revolted by the sadism and fraudulence that had become the central features of his mission. He began to make his objections known. "At that point, I was like so pissed at the military for what they were doing. And you know, I was yelling at the chief warrant officer Marine who was in charge of the defense facility. I was making an issue about it to the major of the Marines, and the lieutenant colonel who was the JAG guy [a military lawyer from the Judge Advocate General's Corps] who was in charge of release, who organized keeping the prisoners. But they just wouldn't listen, you know? They wanted numbers. They wanted numbers of terrorists apprehended . . . so they could brief that to the general."

Lagouranis filed abuse reports with the military. All of them mysteriously disappeared. It was only after he first spoke publicly about his experience on PBS *Frontline* that he was contacted by military investigators—who were investigating *him* about why he never reported the abuse.

At one point when Tony Lagouranis was deployed in Fallujah, he was tasked with bringing corpses back to a warehouse, and then searching their pockets to identify them and glean intel. He estimates that he searched 500 dead bodies. The military hadn't figured out what to do with the corpses, so they were just stacked up. At night, he slept in the warehouse alongside the dead bodies.

He explained about the body searches, "Initially, the reason that we were doing this was they were trying to prove that there were a lot of foreign fighters in Fallujah. So, mainly, that's what we were going for. . . . Maybe half of them had I.D.s. Very few of them had foreign I.D.s. There were people working with me who would, in an effort to sort of cook the books, you know, they would find a Koran on the guy and the Koran was printed in Algeria, and they would mark him down as an Algerian. Or you know guys would come in with a black shirt and khaki pants and they would say, 'Well, this is the Hezbollah uniform,' and they would mark him down as a Lebanese, which was ridiculous, but—you know." Of the 500 bodies Lagouranis searched—including many dead women and children—"about 20 percent of them actually had weapons on them."

For guidance on how to handle their mission, Lagouranis and his fellow soldiers followed the lead of their commander in chief, George W. Bush: In the absence of real evidence, just fake it. The grunts already knew the answers—Donald Rumsfeld had declared that foreign fighters were the cause of Iraq's problems—so their job was to manufacture some proof.

Interrogation sessions were largely unproductive. Lagouranis recounted, "I did more than three hundred interrogations in Iraq, and I'm guessing like twenty people I got any like real intel out of. And when I did it was when I would sort of form a rapport with the person and get them to trust me. Nothing ever came out of the harsh interrogation sessions."

On *Democracy Now!,* Tony Lagouranis spoke about what he wished he had done in Iraq. "We were trained to do interrogations according to the Geneva Conventions with enemy prisoners of war. . . . We weren't allowed to cross any lines. So, I don't know why I allowed the Army to order me to go against my training, and against my better judgment and against my own moral judgment. But I did. I should have just said no."

Lagouranis says that responsibility for encouraging and tolerating torture "obviously goes right up to the Pentagon, because they were issuing the interrogation rules of engagement [which] are not in accordance with the Army field manual and not in accordance with the Geneva Conventions." Prosecuting the abuse "should have gone all the way up the chain."

The Army interrogator reflects, "I think that using torture is the worst possible thing we could do. You cannot win a war against terrorism with bombs and force. It doesn't work. You have to win hearts and minds and we're really failing. Using torture is absolutely the wrong way to go. And we're not getting any intel out

of it, either. How many people did we get intel out of in Guantánamo? A small handful. And in Abu Ghraib . . . they got nothing.
They got no intel out of that place."

Lagouranis decided to speak out about what he saw. "I feel like
that's what my duty is right now.

"I'd like to apologize to Iraq, honestly, because I think we have
done so many things wrong over there. I think the military guys
wanted to go over there and really liberate Iraq, and we have just
really screwed it up. That's terrible. But to the military guys in
Iraq, I would say, follow your conscience. And don't do what
everybody else is doing just because it seems like that's the right
thing to do. It's not."

"The Cruel Science of Pain"

Far from being the work of a few "bad apples," as the White
House has insisted, the American style of torture used at Abu
Ghraib, Guantánamo Bay, and elsewhere has been secretly and sys-
tematically developed. For decades, the CIA has been perfecting
its interrogation methods and exporting them around the world.
The famous Abu Ghraib torture photos of hooded detainees and
naked men being sexually humiliated depict the culmination of a
half-century of American research into torture.

Alfred McCoy, professor of history at the University of
Wisconsin-Madison, is the author of *A Question of Torture: CIA Interrogation, From the Cold War to the War on Terror* (Metropolitan,
2006). He explained on *Democracy Now!* the madness behind the
methods.[7]

"If you look at the most famous of photographs from Abu
Ghraib—of the Iraqi standing on the box, arms extended with a
hood over his head and the fake electrical wires from his arms—in
that photograph you can see the entire fifty-year history of CIA
torture," McCoy noted. "It's very simple: He's hooded for sensory
disorientation, and his arms are extended for self-inflicted pain.

Those are the two very simple fundamental CIA techniques, developed at enormous cost.

"From 1950 to 1962, the CIA ran a massive research project, a veritable Manhattan Project of the mind, spending over $1 billion a year to crack the code of human consciousness, from both mass persuasion and the use of coercion in individual interrogation. They tried LSD, they tried mescaline, they tried all kinds of drugs. They tried electroshock, truth serum, sodium pentothal. None of it worked.

"What worked was very simple behavioral findings, outsourced to our leading universities—Harvard, Princeton, Yale, and McGill. The first breakthrough came at McGill. . . . Dr. Donald O. Hebb of McGill University, a brilliant psychologist, had a contract from the Canadian Defense Research Board, which was a partner with the CIA in this research. And he found that he could induce a state of psychosis in an individual within forty-eight hours. It didn't take electroshock, truth serum, beating, or pain. All he did was he had student volunteers sit in a cubicle with goggles, gloves, and headphones so that they were cut off from their senses. And within forty-eight hours, denied sensory stimulation, they would suffer—first hallucinations, then ultimately breakdown."

The Abu Ghraib images are simply a snapshot of the CIA method: "They show people with bags over their heads. If you look at the photographs of the Guantánamo detainees even today, they look exactly like those student volunteers in Dr. Hebb's original cubicle."

McCoy continued, "The second major breakthrough that the CIA had came in New York City at Cornell University Medical Center, where two eminent neurologists under contract from the CIA studied Soviet KGB torture techniques. They found that the most effective KGB technique was self-inflicted pain. You simply make somebody stand for a day or two. And as they stand—you're not beating them, they have no resentment—you tell them,

'You're doing this to yourself. Cooperate with us, and you can sit down.' As they stand, what happens is the fluids flow down to the legs, the legs swell, lesions form, they erupt, they separate, hallucinations start, the kidneys shut down."

Through a process of trial and error, the CIA refined its methods by experimenting with a variety of torture techniques, from beating, to secretly giving American soldiers hallucinogenic drugs. "LSD *certainly* didn't work—you scramble the brain. You got unreliable information," said McCoy. "But what did work was the combination of these two rather boring, rather mundane behavioral techniques: sensory disorientation and self-inflicted pain."

The CIA codified its findings in 1963 in the *KUBARK Counterintelligence Manual* (which can be found online). McCoy noted that *KUBARK* presented "a distinctively American form of torture, the first real revolution in the cruel science of pain in centuries—psychological torture. . . . It's proved to be a very resilient, quite adaptable, and an enormously destructive paradigm."

It is a mistake to consider psychological torture—sometimes referred to as "torture lite"—to be the lesser of evils. "People who are involved in treatment tell us [that psychological torture] is far more destructive, does far more lasting damage to the human psyche, than does physical torture," insisted McCoy. Even Sen. John McCain stated when he was advocating his torture prohibition in 2005 that he would rather be beaten than psychologically tortured.

The Abu Ghraib photographs provided important details on how the United States inflicts psychological torture. The key, said McCoy, is to attack "universal human sensory receptors: sight, sound, heat, cold, sense of time. That's why all of the detainees describe being put in dark rooms, being subjected to strobe lights, loud music. That's sensory deprivation, or sensory assault. That was sort of the Phase One of the CIA research."

Defense Secretary Donald Rumsfeld was determined to adapt

psychological torture techniques to be used in the war on terror. His torture point person was Maj. Gen. Geoffrey Miller, appointed in 2002 to be head of the Guantánamo Bay detention center—a.k.a., Gitmo. "General Miller turned Guantánamo into a de facto . . . torture research laboratory," explained McCoy. "Under General Miller at Guantánamo, [the U.S. military] perfected the CIA torture paradigm. They added two key techniques. They went beyond the universal sensory receptors of the original research. They added to it an attack on cultural sensitivity, particularly Arab male sensitivity to issues of gender and sexual identity.

"And then they went further still. Under General Miller, they created these things called BSCT (Biscuit) teams—behavioral science consultation teams—and they actually had qualified military psychologists participating in the ongoing interrogation. And these psychologists would identify individual phobias, like fear of dark or attachment to mother. And by the time we're done, by 2003, under General Miller, Guantánamo had perfected . . . a [multifaceted] assault on the human psyche: sensory receptors, self-inflicted pain, cultural sensitivity, and individual fears and phobia."

American-style torture, fine-tuned in offshore jails, was now ready to be unleashed on a larger stage. In mid-2003, Rumsfeld sent General Miller to Abu Ghraib prison in Iraq. Miller famously promised to "Gitmo-ize" Abu Ghraib. He carried through on his promise.

The insurgency was just beginning to take root in Iraq in mid-2003, and the Bush administration, believing its own propaganda that American troops "would be greeted as liberators," was completely unprepared. The response of the U.S. military to the insurgency was to round up thousands of Iraqi men and dump them in Saddam Hussein's notorious torture center, Abu Ghraib prison. General Miller arrived in August 2003 bearing a CD and a manual of his interrogation techniques. He distributed these to the military police and military intelligence officers at Abu Ghraib, and also gave copies to General Ricardo Sanchez, the U.S. commander in Iraq. Within a month, General Sanchez issued detailed new orders for expanded interrogation techniques beyond those allowed in the U.S. Army field manual.

The new methods bore the hallmarks of the CIA's signature torture techniques. "It was a combination of self-inflicted pain, stress positions, and sensory disorientation," Professor McCoy observed. "If you look at the 1963 CIA *KUBARK Counterintelligence Interrogation Manual,* you look at the 1983 CIA interrogation training manual that they used in Honduras for training Honduran officers in torture and interrogation, and then twenty years later, you look at General Sanchez's 2003 orders, there's a striking continuity across this forty-year span, in both of the general principles: this total assault on the existential platforms of human identity and existence, and the . . . way of achieving that, through the attack on these sensory receptors."

Rumsfeld, not content to leave the details to the grunts, has been an enthusiastic micro-manager of torture. *Newsweek* reported that when he read a report in November 2002 about new interrogation techniques at Guantánamo that called for standing for four hours straight, Rumsfeld scribbled in the margin, "Why is standing limited to 4 hours? . . . I stand for 8 hours a day." Perhaps if he were standing naked, with loud music blasting, bright lights shining, attack dogs lunging, and guards softening him up, Rumsfeld would understand why limits, even flimsy ones, were needed.

Nothing appears to diminish Rumsfeld's lust for torture. According to a December 2005 report by the Army inspector general obtained by Salon.com reporters Michael Scherer and Mark Benjamin, Rumsfeld "was personally involved" in the interrogation in late 2002 of Mohammed al-Kahtani, an al Qaeda detainee who was dubbed "the 20th hijacker." Rumsfeld communicated weekly with Maj. Gen. Geoffrey Miller about the interrogation sessions.[8]

According to Salon.com, al-Kahtani "suffered from what Army investigators have called 'degrading and abusive' treatment by soldiers who were following the interrogation plan Rumsfeld had approved. Kahtani was forced to stand naked in front of a female interrogator, was accused of being a homosexual, and was forced to wear women's underwear and to perform 'dog tricks' on a leash. He received 18-to-20-hour interrogations during 48 of 54 days."

Rumsfeld later "expressed puzzlement" at the charge that his policies led to abuses at Guantánamo. Lt. Gen. Randall M. Schmidt, an investigator who interviewed Rumsfeld twice in 2005 about the case, recounted Rumsfeld saying, "My God, you know, did I authorize putting a bra and underwear on this guy's head?"[9]

The defense secretary—with the strong backing of President Bush, who had declared that the Geneva Conventions didn't apply to "terrorists"—was signaling to the troops: Take off the gloves. Break the law. Torture.

The torture demons, once unleashed, do not easily retreat to their dungeons. "There's an absolute ban on torture for a very good reason: Torture taps into the deepest, unexplored recesses of human consciousness, where creation and destruction coexist, where the infinite human capacity for kindness and infinite human capacity for cruelty coexist," reflected Professor McCoy. "It has a powerful perverse appeal. Once it starts—both the perpetrators and the powerful who order them let it spread—it spreads out of control.

"So, when the Bush administration gave those orders for techniques tantamount to torture at the start of the war on terror, I think it was probably their intention that these be limited to top al Qaeda suspects. But within months, we were torturing hundreds of Afghanis at Bagram near Kabul. And a few months later in 2003, through these techniques, we were torturing literally thousands of Iraqis. And you can see in those photos . . . how once it starts, it becomes this Dante-esque hell, this kind of play palace of the darkest recesses of human consciousness.

"That's why it's necessary to maintain an absolute prohibition on torture. There is no such thing as a little bit of torture. The whole myth of scientific surgical torture—that torture advocates, academic advocates in this country came up with—that's impossible. That cannot operate. It will inevitably spread."

The Bush administration has gone to great lengths to give the appearance of legal cover to its torture policies. When top Justice Department lawyers warned that new interrogation rules violated international law, the White House found midlevel attorneys at the department, such as John Yoo and Jay Bybee, to draft memos (some of which the administration has been forced to rescind) arguing that torture was legal.

Then there was the Detainee Treatment Act of 2005, the so-called McCain amendment. What began as an attempt to stop the United States from torturing detainees has ended up giving torturers legal immunity. As Professor McCoy explained, the McCain amendment put into law several key principles that torture advocates coveted:

"In his signing statement [of the Detainee Treatment Act of 2005] on December 30, President Bush said . . . 'I reserve the right, as commander in chief and as head of the unitary executive, to do what I need to do to defend America.' Okay, that was the first thing. The next thing that happened is that McCain, as a compromise, inserted into the legislation a provision that if a CIA operative engages in inhumane treatment or torture but believes that he or she was following a lawful order, then that's a defense. So they got the second principle—defense for CIA torturers. The third principle is that the White House had Senator Lindsey Graham of South Carolina amend McCain's amendment by inserting language into it saying that for the purposes of this act, the U.S. Navy base at Guantánamo Bay is not on U.S. territory."

McCoy concluded, "They have, in fact, used [the Detainee Treatment Act of 2005] to quash legal oversight of their actions."

When the eulogy for American democracy is written, this will stand out as a signal achievement: how an American president and vice president championed torture, how Congress acquiesced, how the courts provided legal cover for the sadists, all while sage media pundits politely debated the merits of our descent into barbarism.

10. Exporting Abuse

Of course, there is an alternative to terrorism. It's called justice.

—Arundhati Roy, author and activist

The American military personnel who earned worldwide notoriety for torturing prisoners at Abu Ghraib prison did not become monsters upon arriving in Iraq. They honed their skills in the prisons of America. The murder and torture that they inflicted on Iraqis was merely the latest and most public chapter in the sagas of these serial abusers. But rather than punish American jailers who had long rap sheets as human rights abusers, the Bush administration rewarded them: They were sent to run Iraq's prisons.

Harold C. Wilson had personal experience with the climate of abuse that prevailed at Abu Ghraib—while he survived on Pennsylvania's death row.

It was 1989, and Wilson, then 31, stood in a Philadelphia courtroom to hear the jury's verdict in a triple homicide. Despite Wilson's protests that he did not kill anyone, that he had been framed by the Philadelphia Police Department and that evidence was planted in his home, authorities insisted he was the perpetrator of the grisly killings.

A gasp arose in the room when the verdict was announced: Wilson was guilty of three counts of first-degree murder. He was sentenced to death—three times.

"It was like something had invaded my body, my spirit, when he announced the sentence of death," Wilson said in a soft-spoken voice on *Democracy Now!* in December 2005. It was just a month after he had been released after over sixteen years of being wrongfully imprisoned, and the first time he was speaking publicly about his ordeal. "He's giving out three verdicts. Three punishments of death. And I'm standing up there in shock, thinking, like, 'How can he do that? How is it possible to die three times by electrocution?'"

Wilson was eventually sent to State Correctional Institution Greene, a supermax prison that houses most of Pennsylvania's death row prisoners. Enduring abuse became part of his normal routine. One method of breaking down prisoners was to blow freezing air into their cells. Wilson told us that he was repeatedly sent to solitary confinement for "covering my vent, protecting myself from the freezing cold temperatures. . . . Cold was used as a punishment to silence most of the condemned, to put you in a sickly state where you had to totally depend on its medical department." As Wilson has since learned, this "was a practice not only in SCI Greene, but at Abu Ghraib."

The cold, said Wilson, "affected my bones. You know, at some points it was so cold in my cell that I could scrape the inside window with an ink pen. I could scrape ice off. And a lot of times I had to sleep in my clothes. I couldn't wash up at the sink because the temperatures were unbearable."[1]

The abuses at SCI Greene were well known. Amnesty International Secretary General Pierre Sané declared after visiting the supermax prison in 1997, "Death row in Pennsylvania looks and feels like a morgue. . . . From the moment that condemned prisoners arrive, the state tries to kill them slowly, mechanically and deliberately— first spiritually, and then physically."[2] The Amnesty delegation was told by prisoners, most of them black, of being beaten by guards and subjected to racist taunts and false disciplinary charges.

In 1998, a major prison abuse scandal erupted at SCI Greene. Pennsylvania Corrections Secretary Martin Horn revealed that there were three dozen reported incidents of using excessive force during the previous twelve months at the prison. Among these were numerous complaints about inmates being choked, kicked, punched, and beaten with nightsticks, some of them while hand-cuffed, and being subjected to racial taunts.[3] Four guards were fired, twenty-one others demoted, and the prison superintendent and one of his deputies were transferred.[4]

"What they're running there is a concentration camp. It's like an Alcatraz mentality. It's horrible," said Grisel Ybarra, an attorney who represented an inmate at SCI Greene. She charged that she had been ordered to remove her bra to walk through a metal de-tector, and had been subjected to racist and sexist treatment. "In my 22 years as an attorney, I have never, ever, ever seen a place such as Greene. I have never seen such bigots in my life."[5]

Prisons are a flourishing industry in Pennsylvania, as they are all around the United States. The Pennsylvania Department of Cor-rections houses over 42,000 inmates in twenty-five prisons; the state corrections budget was more than $1.3 billion in 2005. SCI Greene is the most secure of Pennsylvania's prisons, and is home to most of the state's 223 death row prisoners.[6]

Death row epitomizes the racism in America's criminal justice system. The United States has always been far more eager to exe-cute blacks than whites. In Pennsylvania, 60 percent of the death row prisoners are black.[7] In Philadelphia, blacks are four times more likely to be sentenced to death than whites.[8] Nationwide, blacks comprise 12 percent of the national population, but they ac-count for 42 percent of the country's 3,314 death row inmates (as of 2004),[9] and one in three of those executed since 1977.[10]

Methods of execution in the United States have evolved only slightly since medieval times. Thirty-six states and the federal gov-ernment have the death penalty. Three states—Idaho, Oklahoma, and Utah—allow death by firing squad; Delaware, New Hampshire, and Washington opt for hanging; while Arizona, California, Mis-souri, and Wyoming allow the gas chamber.[11] The remaining death penalty states kill people either by electrocution or lethal injection.

Pennsylvania once held itself up as a model of how civilized so-cieties treat prisoners. Two hundred years ago, the Pennsylvania

Quakers established modern prisons that abolished whipping, flogging, the pillory, and cruel and inhumane punishments. Eastern State Penitentiary was established in Philadelphia in 1829. Built at a cost of $780,000, it was the most expensive building of its time in the United States. It was a place where lawbreakers were given a Bible in order to reflect and do penance—the root of the word *penitentiary*.[12]

But when British novelist Charles Dickens visited Eastern State Penitentiary in 1842, he recoiled at what he saw. "I believe that very few men are capable of estimating the immense amount of torture and agony which this dreadful punishment, prolonged for years, inflicts upon the sufferers," Dickens wrote. "I hold this slow and daily tamperings with the mysteries of the brain to be immeasurably worse than any torture of the body."[13]

With mandatory sentences and three-strikes-and-you're-out laws, the prison population in America exploded in the 1990s. American prisons are home to over 2 million inmates—an increase of 600,000 prisoners since 1995. One in 136 Americans is now in jail, and the prison population grows by about 1,100 prisoners per week.[14] African-Americans are disproportionately thrown behind bars: According to the Justice Department, almost 17 percent of black men in 2001 had prison experience, compared with 8 percent of Hispanic men and 3 percent of white men. Black males born in 2001 have a one in three chance of doing time, compared with one in six for Hispanic males and one in seventeen for white males. If 2001 incarceration rates remain the same, about 7 percent of people born that year can expect to serve a prison sentence during their lifetimes; that compares with 2 percent of people born in 1974.[15]

These days, rehabilitation is out, and punishment is the rage. In the 1970s, there were only a few supermax prisons (a supermax is designed to hold prisoners in single cells for twenty-three hours per day, offering minimal contact with staff or other prisoners). Today, more than two-thirds of states have supermax facilities, housing some 20,000 prisoners.[16]

"We're working under the burden of laws and practices that have developed over thirty years that have focused on punishment and prison as our primary response to crime," said Malcolm Young, executive director of the Sentencing Project, which promotes alternatives to prison.[17]

When it comes to punishment, money is no object: The cost of keeping an inmate in a maximum security prison is now about $57,000 per year—double the cost of regular prison and far more than the cost of most colleges.[18] As Randy Gauger of the Pennsylvania Prison Society told the *Pittsburgh Post-Gazette,* "The current direction in corrections—building expensive prisons, focusing on punishment rather than treatment—is simply a dead end. It's being dumb on crime."[19]

It was within this culture of rampant abuse that Harold Wilson single-mindedly pursued justice to save his life. He was incarcerated at SCI Greene alongside Mumia Abu-Jamal, the noted death row inmate, author, and activist, who advised Wilson in researching and mounting legal challenges (we chronicled Abu-Jamal's story in our book *The Exception to the Rulers*). In 1999, Wilson's lawyers successfully argued that his trial attorney, Willis Berry, provided ineffective counsel. Wilson charged that Berry refused to respond to him and failed to properly investigate his case. As a result of this legal victory, Wilson's death sentence was commuted to life in prison. Berry later became a Pennsylvania judge.

In 2003, Harold Wilson successfully proved that prosecutors had used racial bias to eliminate black jurors in his original trial, earning him the right to a new trial. This followed the discovery of a training tape made by Philadelphia assistant district attorney Jack McMahon, who prosecuted Wilson. In the video, McMahon explained to other prosecutors how to pick a jury that would convict:

> You are there to win . . . and the only way you're going to do your best is to get jurors that are as unfair and more likely to convict than anybody else in that room. Let's face it again.

There's the blacks from the low-income areas who are less likely to convict. It's just—I don't understand it. It's an understandable proposition. There's a resentment for law enforcement, there's a resentment for authority. And as a result, you don't want those people on your jury. And it may appear as if you're being racist or whatnot, but again, you are just being realistic, you're just trying to win the case. . . .

You don't want smart people, because smart people will analyze the hell out of your case. They have a higher standard. They hold you up to a higher standard. They hold the courts up to a higher standard, because they are intelligent people. They take those words "reasonable doubt," and they actually try to think about them. And you don't want those people. Bad luck with teachers, bad luck with social workers, bad luck with—intelligent doctors are bad. I always feel doctors are bad, too.[20]

Wilson and his new attorneys fought on. In May 2005, they finally got a new trial on the murder charges, only to have it end in a mistrial after just one day, following prejudicial remarks that were made to the jury by the prosecutor. For his next trial, Wilson took a new tack: For the first time, he submitted to DNA testing.

In November 2005, Wilson, now forty-eight and sporting a gray beard that made him look older than he is, returned to court. His large frame towered over others in the courtroom. This time, his defense lawyers presented stunning new evidence: A bloody jacket found at the murder scene—prosecutors had long insisted it belonged to Wilson, despite his vehement denials—was subjected to DNA testing. It was stained with the blood of the three victims, and a fourth person—not Harold Wilson.

After three days of deliberation, the jury rendered its verdict. On November 18, 2005, Wilson stood between his two public defenders, Marc Bookman and Karl Schwartz. His round face was etched with the strain of all he had endured: In the course of sixteen years of incarceration, most of it on death row, Wilson had had two death warrants signed and delivered to him. The jury foreman rose to announce the decision: "On the count of murder in the first degree, we find the defendant *not guilty.*"

Wilson crumpled into his chair in shock. His attorney hurriedly asked the judge's permission for his client to be seated. His mother flung her arms into the air and declared, "Hallelujah!" His sister bent over in prayer.

After the verdict, he was returned to county jail to be processed for release. At 9:00 P.M., the judicial system of Pennsylvania—which fought for decades to execute an innocent man—conceded a colossal miscarriage of justice. In compensation for robbing him of one-third of his life, his former jailers handed Harold C. Wilson a subway token, 65 cents, and a change of clothes. Wilson wandered out of jail onto the state highway, into a chilly autumn night.

Homegrown Torturers

When the infamous Abu Ghraib photos were made public in 2004, one man appeared in many of them: a grinning, toothy, bespectacled soldier in a T-shirt and camo pants standing over naked Iraqi detainees, giving the thumbs-up. His name was Charles Graner, and he had a well-known track record as an abuser long before arriving at Abu Ghraib.

Charles A. Graner Jr. took a job in 1996 as a correctional officer at SCI Greene, which had opened two years earlier. Graner came directly from the Marine Corps, where he had served for eight years. He fit right in to the racist prison culture of Greene, where 93 percent of the guards were white, and 77 percent of the inmates were black.[21]

Within a year of Graner's arrival at SCI Greene, the 1998 abuse scandal exploded at the jail. Forty-one guards were investigated for routinely beating handcuffed inmates, using crude racial slurs, and falsifying reports of inmate misconduct.

Graner was not disciplined at that time, but in 1999, he was sued in federal court by an inmate, Horatio Nimley, who was serving a five-year sentence at Greene for burglary. Nimley charged that in June 1998, Graner and three other guards slipped a razor blade into his potatoes, then assaulted him when he asked to see a nurse. Nimley wrote that Graner and three other guards "picked me up and slammed me to the floor head first and then started hitting me in [my] face and head with their closed fists, giving me black eyes, bloody nose and worsening the razor injury I was already suffering in my mouth."[22]

A federal magistrate in Pittsburgh determined that the complaint "has a reasonable opportunity to prevail on the merits," but Nimley disappeared after being released from SCI Greene in 2000, so the lawsuit was dismissed.

Harold Wilson says he was "familiar with Officer Graner's demeanor, his method of torture, his method of abuse of others," although Graner did not personally abuse Wilson. He suspects that Graner avoided him because he frequently filed grievances against guards.

Nick Yarris was another death row prisoner at SCI Greene. He served twenty-two years for a crime he did not commit; he was exonerated by DNA evidence in 2003. After seeing the photos of his jailer at Abu Ghraib, Yarris commented on CNN, "Charles Graner smiling in that photograph over a dead human being is the same Charles Graner that smiled over a [food] tray that he had spit in."[23]

Yarris added, "Charles was just filled with the glee of opportunity to go over there, because he said, as we were walking down the corridor, 'I can't wait to go kill some sand niggers.' That smile he showed, he showed best when he was getting some prisoner to lose it, to snap, to lose his mind and scream at Charles. He loved it."

Graner also had a history of violence at home. His wife filed three protection orders against him, charging that he stalked and threatened her. Graner was forced to admit in court that he "did pull [his wife] around by her hair and banged her head on the floor."[24]

Graner was fired from SCI Greene in 2000, after receiving numerous reprimands and suspensions for job infractions. Unemployed and with a reputation for violence, Graner joined the Army Reserve in early 2002. By the fall of 2003, he had landed a new assignment: guarding inmates at Iraq's Abu Ghraib prison.

It wasn't long before Army Specialist Charles Graner was back to his old ways. He was accused by other soldiers of torturing and abusing prisoners in his new post at Abu Ghraib. In one incident, he punched and kicked a naked detainee so hard in the temple that the prisoner passed out.

Were it not for the infamous photos that Graner and his fellow soldiers took of one another torturing Iraqi prisoners, Graner's sadistic treatment of the inmates, honed at SCI Greene, would have gone unnoticed. Indeed, he received a commendation from the Army in November 2003 for his work as an MP in Iraq. Far from being a rogue officer, Graner was just the kind of tough-on-crime guy the Bush administration was looking for in Iraq.

The photos that splashed across the world's front pages in April 2004 of a smiling Graner standing over a stack of hooded, naked Iraqi men were a public relations disaster for Bush, who claimed to be bringing democracy to Iraq. The Army needed a fall guy, and the grinning grunt from rural Pennsylvania was an easy one. Graner was depicted as an out-of-control low-ranking soldier who acted alone. In January 2005, Graner was sentenced to ten years in federal prison for charges including assault, indecency, and obstruction of justice. That, the Bush administration hoped, would close the book on Abu Ghraib.

Instead, the Abu Ghraib photos threw light into an invisible underworld that extends from America's prisons, to Abu Ghraib, Afghanistan, Guantánamo Bay, and to a network of secret CIA prisons located around the world. The torture of prisoners did not happen by accident, but by design: Charles Graner was one of numerous abusive American prison professionals who were put in charge of Iraq's jails.

The Prison Pros

Lane McCotter oversaw a prison system in Utah where a mentally ill patient died after being stripped and strapped naked to a restraining chair. Gary DeLand was accused of overseeing jails in Utah where a prisoner was forced to lie naked on a concrete floor for weeks. Prison guards under the supervision of John Armstrong savagely beat a mentally ill man to death in Connecticut.

For committing human rights abuses like these, one might expect McCotter, DeLand, and Armstrong to be sent to prison. And they were—but not as inmates. These were the American officials the Bush administration sent to Iraq to advise and run prisons. One prison in particular: Abu Ghraib.

Many of the men sent by the Bush administration to consult on rebuilding Iraq's prisons were forced out of their jobs running U.S. prisons by lawsuits or political controversy. There was, for example, Lane McCotter. A former director of the prison systems in New Mexico, Texas, and Utah, McCotter was sent by the U.S. Department of Justice in May 2003 to be part of a four-man team of advisors helping to reconstruct Iraq's notorious prisons. If the Justice Department had been seeking an expert in prisoner abuse, it couldn't have done much better than McCotter. Salt Lake City Mayor Rocky Anderson recounted on *Democracy Now!* in 2004 that when McCotter ran Utah's prisons, he "had very, very serious human rights abuses taking place, and without any real effort to resolve them."

One such case involved Michael Valent, a 29-year-old schizophrenic inmate. In 1997, when the mentally ill patient refused to take a pillowcase off his head, he was stripped and strapped naked to a restraining chair by Utah prison guards. After his release sixteen hours later, Valent collapsed and died from a blood clot that blocked an artery to his heart.

Before being elected mayor, Rocky Anderson was an attorney who represented Valent's family in a lawsuit filed after Michael's death in jail. Anderson said, "This turns out not to have been a rare instance at all. We obtained affidavits of a number of inmates, many of them suffering from mental illness, who were subjected to restraint in the chair, some of them for a number of days, and also other inmates who were strapped down on a metal board. . . . They had their wrists and ankles tied down. Some of them were tied for a number of days also. In some of the instances, it was reported to us that the inmates were held completely naked and left either sitting or lying in their own feces and urine."

It turned out that Michael Valent's assault by guards was videotaped. McCotter, who defended the action, resigned following the lawsuit brought by Valent's family, although he denied that his resignation was related to the lawsuit.

Gary DeLand, McCotter's predecessor as head of Utah's prisons, joined McCotter in 2003 on the mission to Iraq. Mayor Anderson said the United States Court of Appeals for the Tenth Circuit "describes what I think could be characterized as absolutely medieval treatment of a mentally ill inmate at the Salt Lake County Jail while Gary DeLand was commander of the jail." In one incident, Anderson says an inmate at DeLand's jail was "held naked without any bedding, without even a blanket, left lying naked on the concrete floor in his cell for fifty-six days without ever a hearing, and without any medical treatment."[25]

Anderson charged that both McCotter and DeLand have "a record of real disdain toward inmates and their rights."

After leaving his job running Utah's prisons, McCotter went to work for Utah-based Management and Training Corporation (MTC), a firm that runs private prisons. The company's Web site proclaims that "MTC creates nurturing environments."[26]

In August 2001, McCotter, then MTC's director of corrections business development, visited Santa Fe to close a three-year deal for MTC to run the Santa Fe County Detention Center. Santa Fe was about to get a taste of McCotter's version of justice.

As Dan Frosch reported in *The Nation,* less than a year after Mc-Cotter arrived, "a team of Justice Department correctional experts was inside the Santa Fe jail investigating civil rights violations. In March 2003, their report concluded that certain conditions violated inmates' constitutional rights, and that inmates suffered 'harm or the risk of serious harm' from, among other things, woeful deficiencies in healthcare and basic living conditions. The report documented numerous and horrifying examples, and threatened a lawsuit if things didn't get better. Amid the fallout, the Justice Department pulled its approximately 100 federal prisoners out of Santa Fe and MTC fired its warden and pressured its medical subcontractor, Physicians Network Association, to ax one of its medical administrators."

Frosch reported that on May 20, 2003, "in a case of unfathomable irony, Attorney General John Ashcroft announced that McCotter, along with three other corrections experts, had gone to Iraq. The very same day, Justice Department lawyers began their first negotiations with Santa Fe County officials over the extensive changes needed at the jail to avoid legal action."[27]

McCotter's reign in Santa Fe was a chilling precursor of tactics to come in Iraq. Mark Donatelli, a Santa Fe attorney who specializes in criminal justice issues and was a court-appointed member of the Prison Oversight Board, told *Democracy Now!,* "As soon as McCotter came in, he took the position that despite the horrendous history we had in New Mexico [prisons] of physical abuse and murders, it was nobody's business to come into his prison system and monitor conditions. The federal court was without jurisdiction."[28]

Joining McCotter and DeLand as consultants in Iraq was Terry Stewart. Stewart had been head of the Arizona Department of Corrections. In 1997, the Justice Department Civil Rights Division sued the Arizona Department of Corrections "for allegedly failing to prevent sexual misconduct by correctional officers and staff toward female inmates."[29] The allegations included charges that guards were involved in sexual misconduct, abuse, and rape in an Arizona women's prison. The investigation began while Stewart worked for the department, but just before he became director.

Another American prison official sent by the Justice Department to consult in Iraq was John Armstrong, commissioner of the Connecticut Department of Corrections from 1995 to 2003. Armstrong left his job following a sexual harassment scandal involving female guards in Connecticut's prisons. During Armstrong's tenure, two mentally ill patients were killed by prison guards—including one who was savagely beaten to death on videotape. Armstrong punished the guards by demoting one and suspending several others for a short time. Antonio Ponvert, a Connecticut attorney who has represented inmates, criticizes Armstrong for "his failure to train his staff when it became crystal clear that they had no conception of how to properly discipline and how to deal with mentally ill inmates."[30] Armstrong was part of a team that arrived in September 2003 and advised prison staff at Abu Ghraib, shortly before the abuses became an international scandal.

In February 2005, following a demand by Senator Charles Schumer, the Justice Department completed an investigation into the hiring of the abuse-tainted prison officials. The Justice Department report revealed that many of the prison consultants did not undergo thorough background checks. But it added that the numerous lawsuits filed against the men—alleging everything from torture, to rape and murder that occurred in their facilities—"were standard complaints filed by inmates against correctional officials." The director of the Justice Department program that hired the men said that even in light of what he had learned about McCotter, DeLand, Armstrong, and Stewart, "none of the information would have caused [the Department] to forego retaining the men."[31]

The Justice Department investigation also said all of the men "denied witnessing any acts of abuse at Abu Ghraib and said they were unaware of the abuse until it became public. They also said that had they witnessed any such abuse, they immediately would have reported it."

Just like they reported abuse in the United States.

Salt Lake City mayor Rocky Anderson reflected, "It's hard for me to understand, when people have the record of such disdain toward basic human civil rights of inmates, how it is that they're out making a living—and I understand they fared well financially consulting in the prison. Unfortunately, it's taken the abuse of the Iraqi prisoners for much of our nation's media to focus on the abuse of American inmates, and especially the mentally ill."

The Torture Two-Step

The Bush administration insists that the torture of Iraqi prisoners had an immaculate conception. "There were some people on a night shift who engaged in mistreatment of detainees," insisted a dismissive Defense Secretary Donald Rumsfeld, adding, "This, of course, was an event where the policy of the president and the policy of the government was for humane treatment and was against torture."[32]

This "rogue soldiers" cover story has been unraveling from the moment it was floated.

The first to expose the complicity of top officials in the prison abuse scandal was veteran investigative reporter Seymour Hersh. He revealed in *The New Yorker* in May 2004 that the torture at Abu Ghraib was part of a Pentagon-approved black ops program authorized by Rumsfeld. "The roots of the Abu Ghraib prison scandal lie not in the criminal inclinations of a few Army reservists but in a decision, approved [in 2003] by Secretary of Defense Donald Rumsfeld, to expand a highly secret operation, which had been focused on the hunt for al Qaeda, to the interrogation of prisoners in Iraq," Hersh reported. "Rumsfeld's decision embittered the American intelligence community, damaged the effectiveness of elite combat units, and hurt America's prospects in the war on terror."[33]

And so we learned about America's Torture Two-Step: The Bush administration provided the strategy and legal cover, and low-level grunts provided the muscle. And who better than rough-and-ready American jailers to show the Iraqis how it's done?

The epicenter of the U.S. detainee abuse scandal was Abu Ghraib. It was there that the most notorious photos of detainee abuse were taken: A hooded Iraqi man forced to stand on a box with electrical wires connected to various parts of his body. Naked Iraqis stacked on top of each other. U.S. military personnel posing with Iraqi corpses. And Iraqi detainees held on leashes. In April 2004, a secret Pentagon report concluded that U.S. soldiers had committed "egregious acts and grave breaches of international law" at Abu Ghraib. Like a festering wound, more—and increasingly grisly—photos of prisoner abuse periodically continue to surface.

When jails become torture chambers, prisoners die. According to the ACLU, at least twenty-one detainees have been murdered at U.S. facilities in Iraq and Afghanistan. The ACLU came to the conclusion after a lawsuit yielded reams of Pentagon documents. The documents show that detainees were hooded, gagged, strangled, beaten with blunt objects, and subjected to sleep deprivation and to hot and cold environmental conditions.

ACLU Executive Director Anthony Romero said, "There is no question that U.S. interrogations have resulted in deaths. High-ranking officials who knew about the torture and sat on their hands and those who created and endorsed these policies must be held accountable."[34]

The Torture Two-Step has worked to protect its masters: Only the grunts have taken a fall. Since the torture photos first appeared, no senior Bush administration officials have been reprimanded for what happened at Abu Ghraib. By mid-2006, ten low-ranking soldiers had been convicted for their roles in the detainee abuse. In 2005, Lynndie England—Graner's girlfriend, who was photographed holding an Iraqi prisoner on a leash—was sentenced to three years in prison, and Graner is currently serving his ten-year sentence. The highest ranking military officer reprimanded was Brig. Gen. Janis Karpinski, who was commanding officer at the prison. She was demoted to colonel in May 2005. She oversaw all military police in Iraq and was the first female ever to command soldiers in a combat zone.

Contending that she has been scapegoated, Karpinski has decided to talk about what she witnessed at Abu Ghraib. While human rights advocates insist that she is more involved than she admits, her revelations nevertheless shed further light on how top-level Bush administration officials were complicit in torture. She explained on *Democracy Now!* what happened when Maj. Gen. Geoffrey Miller arrived in late 2003. Karpinski recounted that Rumsfeld and Undersecretary of Defense for Intelligence Stephen Cambone sent Miller "to assist the military intelligence interrogators with enhancing their techniques."

Karpinski recounted her first conversations with Miller: "He used the term, he was going to 'Gitmo-ize' the operation and use the MPs to assist the interrogators to enhance interrogations and to obtain more actionable intelligence. I explained to him that the MPs were not trained in any kind of interrogation operations."

General Miller dismissed Karpinski's objections. He told the military police that "they were being too nice to [Iraqi prisoners]. They were not being aggressive enough. . . . He said, 'You have to treat them like dogs.' "[35]

Karpinski insisted that she did not know of the abuses going on at her prison because much of the prison was being run by military intelligence people and private contractors from American companies who were not under her command.

The abuse at Abu Ghraib started soon after Miller's visit, and as a result of orders that came directly from Secretary of Defense

Donald Rumsfeld. Karpinski said she learned of these orders from a memorandum that was signed by Rumsfeld and posted on a cell-block wall. "It discussed interrogation techniques that were authorized," she said. "It was one page. It talked about stress positions, noise and light discipline, the use of music, disrupting sleep patterns, those kind of techniques. . . . And there was a handwritten note out to the side of where the list of interrogation tactics were. It said, 'Make sure this happens.'"

Who were these dangerous people who were to be treated like dogs? The International Committee of the Red Cross estimated that 90 percent of the prisoners classified as "security detainees" at Abu Ghraib—the ones being interrogated—were being held without charges, and "there was no effective release process in place for them," said General Karpinski. Of the remaining prisoners, she said that "probably 75 or 80 percent of those individuals didn't have a piece of evidence in their file that would hold them or convict them in a U.S. court."

Then there were the "ghost detainees"—the prisoners being hidden from the Red Cross, in violation of the Geneva Conventions. Karpinski described how she was instructed to hide one prisoner, a so-called high-value detainee dubbed "Triple X" by the Pentagon. "When he was turned over to my control," said Karpinski, "we were told specifically by memorandum, by order from Secretary Rumsfeld, not to enter his name on any database."

Karpinski recounted, "When I returned to Baghdad and saw these instructions, I went right to Colonel Warren, who was the legal advisor, and I said, 'This is a violation.' And he said, 'Well, we'll try to get clarification, but this is from Rumsfeld's office.' And I said, 'It's a violation. You have to put people on the database. And how much longer are we going to be held responsible for him? *You* take control of him. If you want to violate a Geneva Convention, that's up to you, but I don't want to keep him in one of our camps this way.'"

Karpinski reflected on who bears ultimate responsibility for torturing Iraqi prisoners: "We have to start at the very top. The original memorandum directing harsher interrogation techniques and the departure from the Geneva Conventions starts at—[former White House counsel] Alberto Gonzales was one of the people who made the recommendations to the president. I don't know if he talked about each detail of that departure or what that may imply, but I do know that the secretary of defense signed a very lengthy memorandum authorizing harsher techniques to be used in Afghanistan and specifically at Guantánamo Bay. This was the global war on terrorism. This was a prisoner of a different kind. You needed to get down at the same level as they were to be effective."

Karpinski feels that she and low-level soldiers "have been unfairly and unjustly held accountable for all of this, as if they designed these techniques, as if Lynndie England deployed with a dog collar and a dog leash. And that's unfair, and that's a tragedy in all of this. Should they be punished for doing what they did, for agreeing to do what they did? Absolutely. But singled out? No."

Quest for Justice

Human rights activists have demanded an independent investigation into the policies that led to the Abu Ghraib scandal, but none has been undertaken. So in November 2004, the Center for Constitutional Rights filed suit in Germany against top U.S. officials, including Rumsfeld, former CIA director George Tenet, Undersecretary of Defense Stephen Cambone, and Janis Karpinski. The suit invoked the doctrine of "universal jurisdiction," in which suspected war criminals may be prosecuted irrespective of where they are located. The lawsuit called for a criminal investigation into the culpability of U.S. officials in the Abu Ghraib torture. CCR president Michael Ratner, who traveled to Berlin to file the complaint, stated, "From Donald Rumsfeld on down, the political and military leaders in charge of Iraq policy must be investigated and held accountable. It is shameful that the United States of America, a nation that purports to set moral and legal standards for the world, refuses to seriously investigate the role of those at the top of the chain of command in these horrible crimes.

"Indeed," Ratner added, "the existence of 'torture memos' drafted by administration officials and the authorization of techniques that violated humanitarian law by Secretary Rumsfeld, Lt. Gen. Sanchez and others make clear that responsibility for Abu Ghraib and other violations of law reaches all the way to the top."[36]

In late 2005, German prosecutors declined to take the case, incorrectly claiming that the United States would and should investigate the matter. However, the suit almost grounded Rumsfeld: He nearly canceled a trip to Germany in early 2005 due to the threat that he might be arrested as an international war criminal. Such travel restrictions may be the fate of top Bush administration officials who are being accused of war crimes.

Human rights supporters have continued their quest for justice. In March 2005, the ACLU and Human Rights First filed suit against Rumsfeld on behalf of eight men who were tortured by U.S. forces in Iraq and Afghanistan (the list of plaintiffs has since grown to nine). "Secretary Rumsfeld bears direct and ultimate responsibility for this descent into horror by personally authorizing unlawful interrogation techniques and by abdicating his legal duty to stop torture," said Lucas Guttentag, lead counsel in the lawsuit and director of the ACLU's Immigrants' Rights Project. "He gives lip service to being responsible but has not been held accountable for his actions. This lawsuit puts the blame where it belongs, on the Secretary of Defense."[37] Similar ACLU complaints have been filed against Col. Thomas Pappas, Brig. Gen. Janis Karpinski, and Lt. Gen. Ricardo Sanchez on behalf of the torture victims who were detained in Iraq.

One month after being released from over sixteen years on Pennsylvania's death row, Harold Wilson sat in a restaurant in New York City, still visibly shaken as he recounted to us what happened to him. With his release, he became the 122nd inmate freed from America's death row.[38]

Wilson moves and speaks slowly and deliberately, as if unaccustomed to describing or unable to share the lengthy story of the injustices that he endured. Why, we asked, did the system go so wrong in his case? He spoke of how "the death penalty is politically motivated," and how convicting him helped the careers of his prosecutors. Then he stopped and pondered.

"America," he concluded softly, "has a rage to punish."

Wilson's freedom has been bittersweet. Being "an exonerated former death row prisoner leaves me to fend for myself, to survive at a level higher than a homeless person. Because at this time, I don't know where my next meal is coming from other than the support of family. I don't have any financial income. I don't have any work. . . . After eighteen years of dealing with the injustice system, all the abuse—the physical, mental abuse—I'm placed back in society with nothing, just the shelter of family. You know, no means of livelihood, no means of support, no financial bank account, no credit card. No compensation whatsoever."

When Harold Wilson went to prison, he left behind a two-year-old son and a year-old daughter. He emerged from prison to deal with the lives they had created in his absence. His son joined the Marines and was on the front lines in Iraq, where he saw his best friend blown up. And his daughter—"I don't like to tell people this," he says softly—is now a prison guard in Arizona.

Wilson, who converted to Islam, says of his son's military service, "Knowing the Bush administration and knowing how unjust the war is, being inflicted on the minds and spirits of American citizens and the families and parents, my son's service in the United States military was worse than three death penalties. . . .

"You know, nothing meant more to me than my son's safety. At times it was unbearable. . . . He was trained and he was brainwashed to believe that he was fighting for the safety and the protection of the United States people and citizens, and his life is being sacrificed. . . . And it was just painful," he said, "knowing that his death penalty was going to be greater than mine."

For Harold Wilson, like others around the world who have suffered at the hands of America's prison officials, the future is uncertain. He reflects about his new freedom, "Now you do what you have to do to get your life back together."

Anger is energy, it's a force. . . . It's injustice that motivates us to do something, to take
risks, knowing that if we don't, things will remain the same.
— **Digna Ochoa (1964–2001), slain Mexican human rights lawyer**[1]

In 2004, the United States launched two major assaults on Fallujah,
the Sunni city west of Baghdad that had come to symbolize Iraqi
resistance to the U.S. occupation. The first offensive was in April
2004, and it came a few days after four American military contractors from the private security firm Blackwater USA were brutally
killed in the city. The second assault took place in November 2004.
In that attack, a U.S. military spokesman later confirmed to *Democracy Now!* that U.S. troops used white phosphorus—a chemical
that can be used for illumination and obscuring troop movements,
or as an incendiary weapon like napalm that melts the skin. This
offensive use may violate international law.

The attacks on Fallujah were an extraordinary action by the
U.S. military. As Marti Hiken, co-chair of the National Lawyers
Guild Military Law Task Force, declared while filing a lawsuit
against the military to obtain information about the assaults, "Not
since the destruction of Guernica (1937), the Warsaw Ghetto (1942),
Nagasaki, Hiroshima, or Dresden (1945) has there been such a total
devastation of a city the size of Cincinnati or Oakland, housing
350,000 people or more. Having no apparent purpose other than a
'show of power' and a demand for revenge for four civilian American security contractors killed in March 2004, the Bush government
unmercifully leveled one of the largest cities in Iraq."

The U.S. military made clear that revenge was its motive in

attacking Fallujah in April 2004. "We will pacify that city," said Brig. Gen. Mark Kimmitt, the U.S. military spokesman in Baghdad, the day after the killings. "We will be back in Fallujah. It will be at the time and place of our choosing."[2]

The siege that followed was one of the bloodiest assaults of the U.S. occupation. In two weeks that April, thirty Marines were killed as local guerillas resisted U.S. attempts to capture the city. Some 600 Iraqis died and over 1,000 were wounded.

The American military insisted that there were almost no civilian casualties among the Iraqis reported killed, despite the fact that fierce fighting raged in the heart of a densely populated city. "What I think you will find is 95 percent of those were military-age males that were killed in the fighting," said Marine Lt. Col. Brennan Byrne. "The Marines are trained to be precise in their firepower. . . . The fact that there are 600 [dead] goes back to the fact that the Marines are very good at what they do."[3]

Embedded American reporters described the firefights from the vantage point of the Marines. As Jeffrey Gettleman reported in the *New York Times:*

> The Marines were pros. Nobody panicked. They crawled behind a berm, got on their knees and judiciously fired back, bullet after bullet. We escaped that firefight with no casualties. But soon we were in another. And then another. The countryside was so lush and pretty. But it was swarming with insurgents.
>
> "Man, I think some of those guys were kids," a lance corporal told me afterward. "Or they were midgets."[4]

American press coverage also included the usual worshipping of weapons, and assurances that high technology would minimize civilian casualties. The *New York Times* reported on April 30, 2004:

> By day, AH-1W Super Cobra helicopters have hovered over the city, launching Hellfire missiles at guerrillas who fire on

the Marines. By night, lumbering AC-130 gunships have pounded trucks and cars ferrying fighters with the distinctive thump-thump of 105-millimeter howitzers. . . .

Commanders say they go to great lengths to avoid civilian casualties, but they acknowledge they do not know how many civilians have died in recent attacks. Pilots concede that in at least one case, an American warplane mistakenly bombed the wrong building in Fallujah. . . .

The stepped-up air assault has sought to minimize the risks to both civilians and the military, senior officers said. Bombs guided by lasers or satellites permit American forces to attack weapons caches or clusters of fighters more precisely and with less risk to civilians than with ground fire, they say.

Al Jazeera had some of the only unembedded journalists inside the besieged city, and its exclusive footage was being broadcast by every network from CNN to the BBC. Al Jazeera's reporting enraged the U.S. government. To the Bush administration, determined to control the flow of information, Al Jazeera had to be taken out. No one could imagine just how far this would go: In a White House meeting with British prime minister Tony Blair on April 16, 2004, George W. Bush actually proposed bombing Al Jazeera's international headquarters in Qatar. This revelation came from top secret minutes of the Bush-Blair summit leaked to Britain's *Daily Mirror* in November 2005. The British government swiftly invoked the Official Secrets Act and banned the *Daily Mirror* and any British media outlet from publishing further details of the leaked documents.[5] Two civil servants were arrested for leaking the memo.

Blair was apparently able to persuade Bush to abandon the idea of incinerating the Al Jazeera headquarters, but the United States maintained its offensive against the Arab news network. On April 9, 2004, the Bush administration demanded that Al Jazeera leave

Fallujah as a precondition for a cease-fire. Al Jazeera initially refused.

Al Jazeera, with a worldwide viewership of some 50 million people, has been under constant attack by the Bush administration. As the *Guardian* (UK) reported:

> Last November [2003], George Bush declared that successful societies "limit the power of the state and the military . . . and allow room for independent newspapers and broadcast media." But three days earlier, an Al Jazeera camera man, Salah Hassan, had been arrested in Iraq, held incommunicado in a chicken-coop-sized cell and forced to stand hooded, bound and naked for up to 11 hours at a time. He was beaten by U.S. soldiers who would address him only as "Al Jazeera" or "bitch." Finally, after a month, he was dumped on a street just outside Baghdad, in the same vomit-stained red jumpsuit that he had been detained in. Twenty other Al Jazeera journalists have been arrested and jailed by U.S. forces in Iraq and one, Tariq Ayoub, was killed last April when a U.S. tank fired a shell at the Al Jazeera offices in Baghdad's Palestine Hotel. It was an accident, the Pentagon said, even though Al Jazeera had given the Pentagon the coordinates of its Baghdad offices before the war began.[6]

In addition, the Al Jazeera offices in Afghanistan and Basra were bombed by American planes, and two of its correspondents have been imprisoned on unspecified terrorism charges—one in Spain and one at Guantánamo Bay.

Al Jazeera's journalists are not the only ones under siege. The Iraq War has been among the deadliest conflicts ever for journalists. The Committee to Protect Journalists (CPJ) reported that by mid-2006, over 100 journalists and media assistants had been killed in Iraq while doing their jobs. By comparison, 66 journalists lost their lives over the course of the 20-year-long Vietnam conflict.[7] More than half of those killed in Iraq were Iraqi and other Arab journalists. Fifteen journalists have been killed by U.S. fire. Reporters Without Borders has declared, "Repeated statements by the U.S. military command in Iraq saying troops had acted in accordance with 'the rules of engagement' or in 'legitimate self-defense' are not enough."[8]

Journalists also risk arrest while reporting on the war in Iraq: In 2005 alone, U.S. forces arrested seven Iraqi journalists "for prolonged periods without charge or the disclosure of any supporting evidence," according to CPJ. All were eventually released, and no charges were ever filed. CPJ concluded that the Pentagon has "displayed a pattern of disregard when confronted with issues involving the security of Iraqi journalists and citizens."[9]

In February 2006, the Al Jazeera journalists who reported from Fallujah in April 2004 spoke about their experience for the first time on *Democracy Now!* Ahmed Mansour and his cameraman Laith Mushtaq were reporting from inside Fallujah for much of the siege. Mansour, a senior Al Jazeera journalist, has been a special focus of American wrath. The *Observer* (UK) reported in 2005, "According to Sami Muhyideen al-Hajj, an Al-Jazeera cameraman arrested in Afghanistan in 2001 and detained in Guantánamo Bay, U.S. interrogators are obsessed with the idea of al Qaeda infiltration of the channel and asked about Mansour more than 100 times."[10]

It was Mansour's shocking dispatches from Fallujah that infuriated the Bush administration and the military. Mansour recounted, "The ninth of April 2004 was really like the day of judgment in Fallujah. We were under siege for two days from the U.S. forces and the snipers."

Mansour and his crew decided to leave their offices and observe the battles in the heart of the city, at great risk to themselves. What they saw around Fallujah shocked them. "We found children, women, elderly, all lifting white flags and walking, or in their cars leaving the city," he said. "When we reached the heart of the city at the hospital, I almost lost my mind from the terror that I saw, people going in each and every direction. . . . I felt like we need a thousand cameras to grab those disastrous pictures: fear, terror, planes bombing, ambulances taking the dead people.

"At the end, I felt that I have to control myself. . . . There were no reporters in the city. We were the only team that was able to enter the city. . . . We felt that we are responsible for all these civilians being bombed from the planes and who are threatened with death, so we have to transfer this picture of suffering to the whole world. It was extremely difficult."

The U.S. military responded by ordering Al Jazeera out of Fallujah, so that the killing could continue without witnesses. Gen. Mark Kimmitt declared, "The stations that are showing Americans intentionally killing women and children are not legitimate news sources. That is propaganda, and that is lies." Four days later, on April 15, Donald Rumsfeld said that Al Jazeera's reporting was "vicious, inaccurate and inexcusable. It's disgraceful what that station is doing."[11]

"They did not stop those accusations leveled against us," Mansour asserted. "If there's anyone who lies, then it is the person who belies those pictures that we presented to the world."

Cameraman Laith Mushtaq described the images that he captured: "There were a lot of children in the hospital that were wounded. Some children were brought, and their families were dead already."

The cameraman described a wrenching scene that he encountered with a man named Hamiz, who lived in a neighborhood attacked by U.S. troops. "There were about four families in one place, children and women. Usually men leave to give some privacy for the children and the ladies. The planes bombed this house, as they did the whole neighborhood, and they brought the corpses and bodies to the hospital. I went to the hospital. I could not see anything but a sea of corpses of children and women—

mostly children, because peasants and farmers usually have a lot of children. I was taking photographs and forcing myself to photograph. At the same time I was crying, because I used to move the camera from one picture of a child to the father Hamiz, who was the only one left alive from that family. He was speaking with his dead children. They had an infant named Ahmed. His nickname was Hamudi. In the child's hand was a toy the shape of a car. Half the boy's head was gone. Hamiz said to him: 'Come back, my beloved. Come to my lap. I am your father.'"

Laith Mushtaq reflected, "Every time I look at a wounded girl or one who lost her family or is killed, I always remember my own little daughter. And I remember that I have to be here to protect those children."

When Mushtaq returned to the Baghdad bureau, he said Al Jazeera "took an initiative to cover both sides." So the network sent him and a journalist back to Fallujah, this time embedded with U.S. forces. His first task was to cover a press conference in Fallujah in which the spokesman for the Marines announced that they had made advances into the city and killed terrorists. When the Al Jazeera reporter asked about civilian casualties, Mushtaq recalled the Marine spokesman replying, "Oh, there are no civilians. The people whom you see their corpses on Al Jazeera TV and on the media, it is fighters wearing civilian clothing."

"What about the child?" Mushtaq challenged him. "Is he a fighter disguised in civilian clothes?"

"This Is Our Duty Toward Humanity"

Few journalists have faced the dual burden that has confronted Ahmed Mansour and his Al Jazeera colleagues: Not only must they survive reporting from a war zone, but they must maintain their professionalism and reputation in the face of relentless criticism by U.S. and British leaders.

Brig. Gen. Mark Kimmitt issued a veiled threat in April 2004 in response to Mansour's Fallujah coverage: "If somebody sees it a different way than we do, that's OK. If somebody's got a different editorial view, that's OK. But when they start telling intentional lies, that goes beyond the pale," said the U.S. military spokesman in Baghdad.

Kimmitt continued, "Much of what we are doing over here depends on the consent and trust of the Iraqi people. When an organization intentionally tries to break that trust and confidence, that puts us in a more precarious position"—such as when Iraqis avenge killings "that we did not do."[12]

"What I can say is that we did our duty as journalists," Mansour told *Democracy Now!* He remains deeply committed to his work. "If this battle took place on the land of the U.S. and I was the one covering it and American civilians were vulnerable to killing, I would not have done any different than what I have done at Fallujah. This is our duty toward humanity in general, as journalists, to report the truth from any place that we are in.

"Our role was to present the truth about what is happening to the civilians. We did that with documents and pictures, and no one could deny this. The whole world reported and transferred this truth and these facts."

But as Mansour quickly learned, the Bush administration tolerates only its own version of the truth. By embedding journalists with U.S. troops, the Pentagon maintained near total control of what the reporters could see and say. It was a brilliant propaganda coup for Bush, and a devastating compromise of journalistic integrity by the Western press.

"Why did the Americans refuse the entering of any journalists or media or TV stations to Fallujah in the second battle [in November 2004] and they only limited to those who are embedded with them?" asked Mansour. From his vantage point among the civilians, Mansour saw the Western media abdicating their commitment to cover all sides of the story. "Is it professionalism that the journalists wear U.S. clothing and they go with them in the planes and tanks to cover this and report this? The battles have to be reported from both sides. We were among the civilians, and we reported. They had embedded journalists with those who launched this attack from the U.S. forces who occupied Iraq, and they reported what they wanted. We were trying to create an equilibrium or a balance, so that the truth was not lost."

The penalty for presenting unofficial truths soon became apparent: U.S. bullets and bombs were ultimately trained on Al Jazeera. Mansour was left to draw his own conclusions. "We were going live and from this roof. We had three telephones, and we were doing satellite signals, so they could have monitored that," he recounted. "We photographed the battles in the al-Julan neighborhood, because this was the highest building in the area and it's well known. Everybody knows that in this area is Al Jazeera's team. So we photographed the battles of Fallujah, of airplanes bombing and cars taking bodies to the hospitals. And we were live with Al Jazeera, and the whole world was seeing that. And General Kimmitt came at night and said, 'Ahmed Mansour spreads lies.' After that we were fired upon. I think they know exactly where their tanks were firing upon."

Laith Mushtaq added, "I do feel that we were targeted. . . . I was afraid as a journalist. I was extremely frightened. . . . I shouldn't be afraid to do my duty with professionalism. We were standing on the roof and taking pictures. They fired upon us."

The Al Jazeera team continued to broadcast from Fallujah at great risk to their lives. Mansour insisted, "I wanted the whole world to know what's happening to those besieged people. I wasn't thinking about leaving the city at all. I decided to stay and let my destiny be as those of the people. If they die, I'll be with them. If they escape, I'll be with them. I decided not to think about what the U.S. forces will do with me if they catch me, and not to think about my family or anything. I only think about those people. . . . Despite that, they accused us of lying, only because they don't want the world to see the truth and the reality."

In an extraordinary attack on the press, the U.S. military declared in April 2004 that there could be no peace for Fallujah unless Al Jazeera abandoned the city. For Mansour to remain would mean even more Iraqis would die. "The extreme stresses and pressures leveled against Al Jazeera because of my reporting of what happened in Fallujah made Al Jazeera unable to help me to go back one more time," he said. "I left Fallujah when I had to leave Fallujah. I was leaving as one who was carrying a funeral within himself. I did not want to leave those people, simple people, alone and abandon them."

In August 2004, the U.S.-backed Iraqi government ordered Al Jazeera's Baghdad bureau closed. It was an important milestone in Bush's war against independent media.

Ahmed Mansour remains ready to return. "Anytime and any day, and for any oppressed people subject to death, I am willing to go to report the truth and express those people anywhere in the world—even if it's in the United States of America."

The first week of August 2005 was supposed to be uneventful. President Bush was on vacation in Crawford, Texas—again. But when peace activist Cindy Sheehan arrived in Crawford on August 6, 2005, to begin her month-long protest, the administration's business-as-usual was suddenly under a spotlight. What was the administration doing that week that George W. Bush couldn't walk outside his door to speak with the grieving mothers of dead American soldiers? The answers revealed much about the Bush administration's priorities.

On the day that Sheehan arrived, Vice President Dick Cheney and former president George H. W. Bush were in Riyadh, Saudi Arabia, with King Abdullah, whose father, King Fahd, had just died. For the Bushes, this was a death in the family. The Bush connection to the Saudi royal family dates back decades. Even through the 9/11 attacks, in which fifteen of the nineteen hijackers were Saudi, the OILYgarchies of both countries remained fiercely loyal to one another. When all air traffic was grounded after the 9/11 attacks, Bush ensured that members of the Bin Laden family and other Saudi tycoons would be flown out of the country without being seriously questioned by the FBI. Saudi ambassador Prince Bandar—nicknamed "Bandar Bush" for his chummy relationship with the First Family—was sitting with George W. Bush on the White House balcony two days after the attacks. Meanwhile, George H. W. Bush enjoyed profitable business dealings with the Saudis while he sat on the board of the Carlyle Group, a multibillion-dollar investment firm that has extensive holdings in defense and oil businesses.

George W. Bush was too busy to meet with Sheehan, but he did have time that week to travel to New Mexico to sign the Energy Act of 2005—an epic giveaway to the energy corporations. You would think that while American troops are fighting and dying to maintain the flow of oil from countries that hate America, the U.S. government would seek ways to reduce its dependence on foreign oil; after all, 60 percent of the 21 million barrels that the United States consumes daily comes from foreign sources.[1]

Bush's approach to the energy crisis mirrors his approach to war: Give the illusion of caring about it, while privately enabling the plundering and profiteering to continue. So when President Bush declared in his 2006 State of the Union speech, "America is addicted to oil," he hoped we wouldn't remember that the energy bill that the president signed five months earlier, which was brokered by Dick Cheney, encouraged Americans to use even more oil. The Bush administration's morning-after retractions and "clarifications" are by now a well-rehearsed disinformation two-step: In a conference call with reporters the day after Bush's State of the Union, Energy Secretary Samuel Bodman told reporters the president was giving "purely an example" when he spoke about making dependency on Middle Eastern oil "a thing of the past."

Bush is so quickly ensnared in his own web of deceit that it would be funny—if the issues weren't so serious. Take, for example, Bush's new embrace of renewable energy. In his 2006 State of the Union speech, the president called for new research and investment "to develop cleaner, cheaper, and more reliable alternative energy sources." It didn't take long for his rhetoric to collide with reality: The day after his speech, the Department of Energy's primary renewable energy laboratory announced that as a result of a $28 million budget cut, it was forced to lay off thirty-two researchers in ethanol and wind technology—both areas that Bush cited in his address as having great potential. Making matters worse, Bush was visiting the lab three weeks later. So the day before he arrived, the Energy Department announced that it had found $5 million to rehire the thirty-two laid-off employees, and hurriedly called them on President's Day so Bush's photo op wouldn't be riddled with empty spaces where real researchers once stood. None of the employees returned in time for his photo, and the lab announced that it was still facing a $23 million budget shortfall.[2]

"My message to those who work here is, we want you to know how important your work is," President Bush told what remained of the renewable energy staff when he visited the lab. "We appreciate what you're doing. And we expect you to keep doing it. And we want to help you keep doing it."

Let the Good Times Roll

Instead of actually doing something about America's oil addiction, Bush put the drug pushers in charge of finding a cure. Cheney's Energy Task Force, formed in January 2001, was charged with developing a national energy policy, which it released four months later. This policy formed the basis of the 2005 energy bill. The national energy policy read like an industry wish list. It recommended:

- Opening up the Arctic National Wildlife Refuge for oil and natural gas drilling
- Giving tax breaks and subsidies to encourage the construction of more coal and nuclear power plants
- Not requiring new technology on cars that would increase fuel economy
- Dumbing down the fuel economy rules for light trucks and SUVs, the most inefficient vehicles
- Deregulating the electricity market and gutting rules that protect consumers from price gouging.

It was as if the energy barons had written the policy themselves—which they did. "If you were King, or Il Duce [the nickname of Benito Mussolini, the fascist dictator of Italy], what would you include in a national energy policy, especially with respect to natural gas issues?" e-mailed Joseph Kelliher, a policy advisor in Bush's Department of Energy, to energy industry lobbyist Dana Contratto in March 2001.[3] The lobbyist obliged with a three-page wish list and—*voilà!*—many of his ideas appeared in the national energy policy. Kelliher solicited a "dream list" from an Enron lobbyist as well, parts of which also became national energy policy, and succeeded in delivering several presidential executive orders at the request of the American Petroleum Institute.[4]

The Cheney Energy Task Force met almost exclusively with industry executives and lobbyists. But you're not supposed to know that: Cheney has gone to extremes to protect the identities of the bill's architects—who also happen to be its beneficiaries. In one of the most protracted secrecy battles of the Bush administration (and that's saying a lot), Cheney has refused to disclose whom he met with to shape national energy policy. The meetings of the task force were held in secret, and the Bush administration refused to say who participated. Despite an unprecedented lawsuit by the General Accounting Office, and another lawsuit filed by the conservative group Judicial Watch and the Sierra Club that went to the Supreme Court, Cheney has successfully protected the identity of his corporate patrons.

But a little light has now shone into the White House back rooms where the energy giveaways were doled out. In November 2005, in the wake of record gas prices and oil company earnings, the heads of the major oil companies were called to testify in the Senate to publicly explain their orgy of profits. But Senate Commerce Committee chair Ted Stevens (R-Alaska), who had received $370,390 in contributions from gas and oil companies since 1989,[5] refused demands from Democrats that the executives be sworn in so that their testimony would be given under oath. The senators were eager to avoid a replay of the Big Tobacco CEOs who, after raising their hands to swear to tell the truth, famously proceeded to lie about whether they knew that smoking caused cancer.

Sen. Frank Lautenberg (D-N.J.) used the opportunity to find out what Cheney wanted to hide. He asked the executives whether they had met with the Cheney Energy Task Force in 2001. The chief executives of ExxonMobil, Chevron, and ConocoPhillips said they had not, while the president of Shell Oil said his company did not participate "to my knowledge," and the head of BP America said he did not know.[6]

The *Washington Post* checked Secret Service logs and learned that, in fact, executives from each of these oil companies did meet at the White House with Cheney Energy Task Force staff members in 2001. Meanwhile, the Commerce Department released documents as a result of a lawsuit that revealed that in early 2001, the Cheney Task Force was examining maps of Iraqi oil fields, pipelines, and foreign corporations that were vying for Iraqi oil contracts.[7] It appears that long before the 9/11 attacks, U.S. energy companies had designs on Iraq's oil. The Saudi-linked terror attacks provided a convenient pretext to take control of Iraq's oil spigots.

How to Make $144,573 a Day

Writing the 2005 Energy Bill was the opportunity to turn the Cheney Task Force recommendations into law—and lots of cold cash. The energy companies left nothing to chance. Since 2001, energy corporations have plied federal politicians with $115 million in campaign contributions. It was a bipartisan orgy, but lucky Republicans received three-quarters of these corporate bribes.[8] You were especially well compensated if you were on the House-Senate Energy Bill conference committee, whose sixty-five members have received some $9.7 million in contributions since 2001.[9]

As the payoffs were handed out, Texans were at the front of the line. As the *Boston Globe* observed, the bill is "a $14.5 billion extravaganza . . . that highlighted the clout of [Texas], home to the president, the House majority leader, and the chairman of the committee overseeing the energy legislation. . . . Energy companies based in Texas will be eligible for billions in tax benefits."[10] This point was driven home by the fact that President Bush had two Texas congressmen join him when he signed the bill: Rep. Joe Barton, the chair of the Energy and Commerce Committee, and the Democrat-turned-Republican Rep. Ralph Hall, a member of the same committee.[11] Barton has received $2 million in contributions from PACs and individuals in the energy industry since entering Congress in 1989, half of it from the oil and gas industry. Hall received $908,000 in contributions from the energy industry during that same period.[12]

A leading skeptic on global warming, Barton was accused in 2005 of conducting a "witch hunt" against three of the country's leading climate change scientists. Barton demanded that the scientists, who had established links between man-made carbon emissions and global warming, hand over details of their funding, methods, and everything they had ever published.[13]

In July 2005, Representative Barton was determined to give away everything he could to his patrons in the energy industry in the bill about to be signed by President Bush. So, in a vote held after midnight, his committee passed a provision in the energy bill that allowed the oil and gas industry to avoid paying royalties on oil and gas drilled in publicly owned waters in the Gulf of Mexico. "There is no cost" to taxpayers, he assured his fellow congressional representatives.[14] In early 2006, the real cost was revealed: The Bush administration had waived $7 billion in royalties over the next five years, an amount that may rise to $28 billion if a lawsuit filed by the oil company Kerr-McGee is successful. Rep. Edward Markey, a Massachusetts Democrat on the committee, fumed, "Taxpayers are being asked to provide huge subsidies to oil companies to produce oil—it's like subsidizing a fish to swim."[15]

Another highlight of the energy bill is the hundreds of millions of dollars in tax breaks, loan guarantees, and insurance for operators and builders of nuclear power plants.[16] No new nuclear plants have been built in the United States since the 1970s, reflecting intense public skepticism about the safety and costs of nuclear power. According to Public Citizen, the energy bill also gave the oil and gas industry $6 billion in subsidies, while coal subsidies totaled $9 billion.[17]

A coalition of environmental groups including the National Audubon Society, the Wilderness Society, and the Sierra Club declared, "When it comes to solving America's pressing energy problems, this bill can only be classified as a miserable failure. Instead of moving toward a new energy future, the energy bill provides tens of billions of dollars to the oil, gas, coal, and nuclear industries, significantly weakens environmental protections such as the Clean Water Act and Safe Drinking Water Act, and undermines numerous consumer protections."[18]

All of this has translated into a mind-boggling windfall for oil companies. In 2005, ExxonMobil, whose fortunes had already been soaring, hit the jackpot: Its $36 billion annual profit was the largest in history for any corporation in the world. Unfortunately, the only thing most Americans would experience from this windfall would be price gouging and emptier pockets: While ExxonMobil's profit shot up 45 percent over the company's 2004 result, its tax bill rose only 14 percent. Just to make sure ExxonMobil didn't feel any pain, President Bush rejected an attempt in early 2006 to levy a onetime windfall profits tax on the oil industry.

Congress certainly wouldn't want to put the squeeze on struggling Exxon employees—such as former Exxon chairman Lee Raymond, who was paid $686 million from 1993 to 2005. That works out to $144,573 per day while he ran the company.[19] But when it came time to explain to Congress why gas prices were so high, Raymond insisted in 2005 it was all because of global supply and demand, and he was feeling the pain like any average Joe. "We're all in this together, everywhere in the world," he said.[20]

To put ExxonMobil's bonanza into perspective, the company's 2005 revenue of $371 billion surpassed the $281 billion gross domestic product of Saudi Arabia that year, and also exceeded the $245 billion GDP of Indonesia, the world's fourth most populous country and an OPEC member.[21]

This orgy of corporate profits prompted Ralph Nader to write a letter to new ExxonMobil chairman Rex Tillerson: "Over $36 billion last year, after modest taxes, yet you blithely ignored urgent pleas by members of Congress, especially that of the powerful Chairman, Senator Chuck Grassley (R-Iowa) to contribute some significant deductible money to charities which help impoverished American families pay the exorbitant prices for heating oil this past winter. Rarely has there been such a demonstration of corporate greed and insensitivity by a company that has received huge government welfare subsidies, de-regulation and tax expenditures over the years at the expense of the smaller taxpayers of America."[22]

The good times just keep on rolling for the energy industry. No wonder Boone Pickens, head of BP Capital Management, a billion-dollar hedge fund that trades energy futures, said of the high times: "I've never had so much fun in my life."[23]

Fighting Back

Somebody's gotta stop those lying bastards.
  —**Cindy Sheehan, addressing the Veterans for Peace Convention, Irving, Texas,**
  August 5, 2005, the day before she went to Crawford

Beware of mothers who have nothing left to lose.

On the eve of President Bush's January 2005 inauguration, Cindy Sheehan and Celeste Zappala set out on a mission. For weeks they had been trying to arrange a personal meeting with Defense Secretary Donald Rumsfeld. They e-mailed, wrote letters, called. Rumsfeld never responded.

So on January 19, 2005, the pair headed to the Pentagon holding photos of their sons who were killed in Iraq. "The real reason I wanted to meet with Rumsfeld was so he could see the face of my son, Specialist Casey Sheehan, who was killed in Sadr City," Sheehan said. "I wanted him to look me in the face and see my red swollen eyes and to see all the lines that grief has etched. I wanted him to see the unbearable pain his ignorance and arrogance has caused me and my family. I wanted him to know that his actions have terrible consequences."[1] Joining Sheehan and Zappala was a group of military families and former soldiers who opposed the Bush administration's war policies, including ex–Army ranger Stan Goff.

Goff recalled what happened next. As the group left the Pentagon parking lot, they suddenly saw through the driving snow "a phalanx of black clad, armed and body-armored police waiting for us, the blue lights whipping around on top of their cruisers."[2]

Sheehan—who was not yet a household name—never made it inside the Pentagon that day.

Just weeks before, Specialist Thomas Jerry Wilson had a chance to do what Sheehan and Zappala never got to do: question Donald Rumsfeld about the administration's war policies. An active-duty member of the 278th Regimental Combat Team, the 31-year-old Tennessean had the temerity to question his boss during a televised event from Kuwait.

"Why do we soldiers have to dig through local landfills for pieces of scrap metal and compromised ballistic glass to up-armor our vehicles?" Wilson asked. "We do not have proper armored vehicles to carry us north."[3]

Rumsfeld famously replied, "You go to war with the army you have."

While Rumsfeld, standing in the glare of TV lights, was forced to answer that question, he never had to answer to the mothers who were turned away at gunpoint from the Pentagon, leaving only a stack of photos of the sons they no longer have. The heavily armed police who greeted the grieving mothers probably had better armor than Casey Sheehan did in Iraq.

On April 4, 2004, five days after arriving in Baghdad, Casey was on patrol in the Sadr City section of Baghdad. Shiite militiamen loyal to the cleric Muqtada al Sadr ambushed his vehicle, repeatedly firing rocket-propelled grenades. Casey stood little chance of surviving the attack.

"They didn't even have their armor from Kuwait yet. They didn't have their tanks. They didn't have their Bradleys," Sheehan told *Democracy Now!* "And they sent our children to be sacrificial lambs, to be slaughtered in the city. And it just really proves that our babies, our precious, precious children are nothing but cannon fodder to these people."[4]

U.S. Army specialist Tomas Young was also in Sadr City that day. He recalled driving in a similarly unprotected vehicle. "The truck had no canvas top to it, so it was just open. Nor did it have any armor on the sides," Young said.[5] The soldiers were sitting ducks. Young was shot, but he survived—barely. He was paralyzed from the chest down after being struck by a round from an AK-47 while sitting in the open truck bed. He had been in Iraq for just four days.

Though Young never met Casey, he, like so many others, would meet Casey's mother in Crawford, Texas. While the media largely ignored her previous efforts to question the men who sent her son to war, nobody could ignore the determination of Cindy Sheehan in the first week of August 2005.

On August 2, President Bush left Washington for Crawford to start the longest presidential vacation in history. By the end of his retreat that summer, he would have spent a year—more than a fifth of his presidency—in Crawford.

The following day, August 3, fourteen Marines from a unit based in the Cleveland suburb of Brook Park, Ohio, died when their lightly armored amphibious assault vehicle was hit. It was the deadliest roadside bombing of the war to that point. Six other Marines from the same unit died earlier in the week. Later that day, President Bush said, "I hear all the time, well, when are you bringing the troops home? And my answer to you is, as soon as possible, but not before the mission is complete."

On August 4, President Bush held a joint press conference in Crawford with Colombian president Alvaro Uribe where they conflated the so-called wars on terror and drugs. Bush used the opportunity to send a message to the families of the dead Marines: "Take comfort in the understanding that the sacrifice was made in a noble cause."

On August 5, Cindy Sheehan had had enough. There were only so many times she could relive her son's death. She addressed the Veterans for Peace convention in Irving and announced that she would head to Crawford the next day. She didn't even know where the place was, but she vowed to stay until President Bush would meet her and answer one question: For what noble cause did my son die?

On August 6, Sheehan arrived in Crawford and set up what became known as Camp Casey. Her month-long vigil outside Bush's estate had begun.

The fiercely tenacious tall woman with short blond hair is an unlikely activist. A stay-at-home mother of four from California, she was a youth minister at her local Catholic church, where her son Casey was an altar boy. He joined the Army in 2000 and reenlisted in 2003. She tried to dissuade him from going into the military, but he felt it would help give him some direction.

"Casey was such a gentle, kind, loving person. He never even got in one fistfight his whole life," Sheehan told *Democracy Now!* in Texas at her protest. "Nobody even hated him enough to punch him, let alone kill him. And that's what George Bush did. He put our kids in another person's country, and Casey was killed by insurgents. He wasn't killed by terrorists. He was killed by Shiite militia who wanted him out of the country. When Casey was told that he was going to be welcomed with chocolates and flowers as a liberator, well, the people of Iraq saw it differently. They saw him as an occupier."[6]

Sheehan's presence on the side of the road in Crawford offered a stark contrast with Bush, who was enjoying his vacation while 160,000 American troops were under fire in Iraq. Cindy Sheehan said she can never fully enjoy another vacation again. "This is really hard. Not only am I trying to stop the war, but I am grieving my son every day," she said. "Every day I wake up, it's like April 4 all over again. I have to realize that I have to go for another day without my son and it's really, really hard. And then I do this," she said, pointing to the protesters who had gathered around her in Texas, "on top of that."

The picture of this grieving mother demanding answers from a war president was too much for Bill O'Reilly of Fox News. He and Rush Limbaugh launched a relentless right-wing smear campaign against her. O'Reilly called her actions "treasonous." Limbaugh dismissed Sheehan's protests as "the latest effort made by the coordinated left."

The Gold Star Mother was unbowed. "I believe that it is my right and responsibility as an American to question our government when our government is wrong. I'm not one of the immature patriots who say, 'My country, right or wrong.' Because my country is wrong now. And the policies of my country are responsible for killing tens of thousands of innocent people, and I won't stand by and let that happen anymore. I believe that anybody who tries to tell me that I don't have the right to say what I'm saying, they're unpatriotic. They're un-American. And their attacks are not going to stop me."[7]

Beware of reporters in the dead of a Texas summer trying to cover a president on the longest presidential vacation in history, who prides himself on divulging nothing to the media, while just down the road sits a determined mother with a single request: to ask the president a question. On August 13, the media finally repeated her question to President Bush. He responded, "I think it's important for me to be thoughtful and sensitive to those who have got something to say. But I think it's also important for me to go on with my life, to keep a balanced life." As the *Atlanta Journal-Constitution* reported, Bush spent that day going on a two-hour mountain bike ride with journalists and aides, attending a Little League baseball game, having lunch with Secretary of State Condoleezza Rice, taking a nap, going fishing, and reading. Yes, reading.[8]

A few days later, Cindy had to leave Crawford suddenly to care for her mother, who had just suffered a stroke. At the airport, she said she was determined to come back, but said that the peace camp would continue because the movement was much larger than her.

Cindy Sheehan lit a flame that blazed across the country. By the time *Democracy Now!* arrived in Crawford, hundreds of people were there. Veterans came. Active-duty soldiers showed up. Ordinary citizens gathered. And more mothers—mothers from every walk of life—arrived.

Democracy Now! broadcast next to the ditch on the road where
the families had taken up residence in the hundred-degree sun—
Cindy said it was nothing compared to what the soldiers face in
Iraq right now. Some of the remarkable women of what became
known as Camp Casey shared their stories.

Nadia McCaffrey's son, Patrick, joined the Army National
Guard the day after the 9/11 attacks. She said he was living the
perfect life: He had two little kids, a wife, and was very happy. But
immediately after 9/11, he felt he had to give something back. He
thought that if he joined the Army National Guard and there were
disasters at home, he would be there to help. He never dreamed he
would be deployed to Iraq. When he was called up to go to Iraq,
she sat with him. Patrick said again and again that it was his duty
to protect those in his unit. Then he left.

Patrick McCaffrey was killed a few months after Casey Sheehan.
Nadia McCaffrey immediately decided she would challenge President Bush's executive order banning photographs of the flag-
draped caskets of returning soldiers. The casualties of Bush's war
are invisible. Even injured soldiers are out of sight when they return. They are brought back under the cover of night to be treated
in underfunded Department of Veterans Affairs (VA) hospitals.

The Bush administration knows the power of images—and so
does Nadia McCaffrey. Defying President Bush, she invited the press
to Sacramento International Airport and allowed them to take pictures of her son's coffin as it came off the plane. She said it was a gesture for her grandchildren. It was also a gesture for the world.

Nadia talked about the e-mails that Patrick sent home. He
wrote, "I don't understand why we're here. They hate us. They
just hate us." But Patrick never stopped trying to reach out to the
Iraqis he met. Among his last e-mails were requests for candy for
the children, and for deflated soccer balls. The last picture of him
was taken a few hours before he died. He was holding white flowers that the children had given him.

And then there was Becky Lourey. She is a Minnesota state

senator who introduced an antiwar resolution in her state legislature just before the invasion of Iraq. Her son Matt was in the military.

In December 2003, Becky Lourey attended a meeting of the National Council of State Legislatures. Donald Rumsfeld was addressing state lawmakers from around the country. A number of legislators in attendance used the opportunity to tell him that their communities were in financial crisis while billions were being spent on the wars in Iraq and Afghanistan. Lourey decided to express her concerns to Rumsfeld about war profiteering by Halliburton, which by that time had already landed $5 billion in contracts for the war on Iraq: "I thought that I would suggest an area where perhaps you could find some savings in the military. And I want you to know that my second son is flying helicopters in Baghdad, so every time a report comes out, I hold my breath until I find out whether or not it is his plane that has gone down."

She added, "I wrote a resolution in the Minnesota Senate against going to war unilaterally." The crowd broke into applause.

"That's why we went in with thirty-two other countries," Rumsfeld shot back.

Lourey continued, "I'm very upset about the services to our servicemen that Halliburton is providing. . . . It is a great concern when our servicemen and -women are over there, and an entity, non-bid, such as Halliburton, is not doing the job that our own Army had always done much better."

Rumsfeld replied, "There has not, to my knowledge, been any overpayment, and I wouldn't want your comment to leave these good folks with a misimpression."[9]

Seventeen months after she confronted the defense secretary, Becky Lourey's son lay dead in the sands of Iraq. His helicopter was shot down by small-arms fire. Three months later, Becky came to Crawford to stand with Cindy Sheehan. And to speak up for her son.

Becky said of her encounter with Rumsfeld, "I remember thinking, he's like a massive tree, and I'm just shoving my fist into the tree and getting nothing but scratches from the bark. I remember thinking, How are we going to move away from this, you know, the whole way that he talks about morality? . . . How do we counter all of these things? . . . Because it's not just all of the service people who are dying now. It is why they are dying, and what's going to be happening. Who are going to be our leaders?"

Becky, Cindy, and Nadia are answering those questions. They are the leaders, these mothers who have lost their sons, and who are speaking out.

Coleen Rowley accompanied Becky Lourey on her trip to Crawford. Rowley was Person of the Year in *Time* magazine in 2002. She is the FBI whistle-blower who said the U.S. government had been warned before the 9/11 attacks, and charged that her investigation into Zacarias Moussaoui, the so-called twentieth hijacker, who was arrested before 9/11, had been blocked by her FBI superiors. At Camp Casey, she pointed out that she had also spoken out a few weeks before the invasion of Iraq was launched. She warned that launching an attack on Iraq would undermine counterterrorism efforts. She said before the invasion, "A continuing question that needs to be asked and answered from the people who are waging the war in Iraq is, 'How is this making us safer?'" She said the media were not terribly interested in her comments then.

Coleen Rowley was not the only one within the government saying that the evidence linking Iraq to terrorism and weapons of mass destruction just didn't add up. Throughout the military and intelligence services, people were saying the same thing. Like Rowley, former UN weapons inspector Scott Ritter had been a media darling, especially when he quit the UN weapons inspection program in 1998 and declared that the Clinton administration was not being aggressive enough in confronting Saddam Hussein. But when Ritter, a former intelligence officer in the Marines, insisted in 2003 that Iraq did not have WMDs and spoke out forcefully against a military invasion, he became a media pariah. Joe Scarborough, host of the MSNBC show *Scarborough Country*, said on April 9, 2003, that Ritter "played chief stooge for Saddam Hussein." He ridiculed Ritter for predicting that "the United States is going to leave Baghdad with its tail between its legs, defeated."[10]

Instead of seriously considering the views of war skeptics, the networks provided a megaphone for a small circle of pundits, who know so little about so much, who cheerlead for war. Consider a sample of what American pundits had to say in 2003, as collected by the media watch group FAIR:[11]

- "It is amazing how thorough the victory in Iraq really was in the broadest context. . . . And the silence, I think, is that it's clear that nobody can do anything about it. There isn't anybody who can stop [Bush]. The Democrats cannot oppose him politically."— *Washington Post* reporter Jeff Birnbaum, speaking on Fox News Channel, May 2, 2003

- "Well, the hot story of the week is victory. . . . The Tommy Franks–Don Rumsfeld battle plan, war plan, worked brilliantly, a three-week war with mercifully few American deaths or Iraqi civilian deaths. . . . There is a lot of work yet to do, but all the naysayers have been humiliated so far. . . . The final word on this is, hooray."—Fox News Channel's Morton Kondracke, April 12, 2003

- "He looked like an alternatively commander in chief, rock star, movie star, and one of the guys."—CNN's Lou Dobbs, on Bush's "Mission Accomplished" speech, May 1, 2003

- "Oh, it was breathtaking. . . . It was reminiscent, I think, of the fall of the Berlin Wall. And just sort of that pure emotional expression, not choreographed, not stage-managed, the way so many things these days seem to be. Really breathtaking."— *Washington Post* reporter Ceci Connolly, appearing on Fox News Channel on April 9, 2003, discussing the pulling down of a Saddam Hussein statue in Baghdad; the event was later revealed to have been a carefully stage-managed psy-ops mission by the U.S. military—*Los Angeles Times*, July 3, 2004

This is what passes for a "mainstream" media today: jingoistic cheerleaders who beat the drums for war. The real mainstream are those opposed to war. They are not a fringe minority or a silent majority. They are a *silenced* majority—silenced by the corporate media.

Celeste Zappala has experienced this phenomenon firsthand. Her son, Sergeant Sherwood Baker, was killed in Iraq on April 26, 2004, in an explosion in Baghdad. Baker was the first member of the Pennsylvania Army National Guard to die in combat since World War II. His mother was the cofounder of Gold Star Families for Peace, with Cindy Sheehan. On *Democracy Now!*, she responded to an MSNBC commentator who referred to the mothers in Crawford as "extremists":

"I proudly wear the badge of being a person for peace. People can criticize. It's okay. They need to do that. They get paid to do that. . . . But I would say to any of those folks, especially the rabid commentators: talk to me after you have a loved one serving. Then we can have a different conversation."

She continued, "What does that mean, 'antiwar extremist'? I'm a peace extremist, you know? I want people to start taking responsibility for the behavior of their nation. I want my representatives to get a spine and stand up and start leading. I want accountability for all the terrible mistakes that have occurred that have put us in this dreadful situation."

We also found Patricia Roberts in the ditch in Crawford. Her son, Jamaal Addison, was the first soldier from Georgia killed in Iraq. As an African-American woman, she felt it was particularly important for her to be there. "I believe that this is a poor man's war. They have solicited the minorities to go in, and if you look at all of the statistics, you have more minorities die in this war than [anyone] else. . . . You have wiped out generations of minorities. So I think that because it's us that's dying, we need to be the ones speaking out and standing up more than anyone else."

Mimi Evans was also staying in that ditch outside President

Bush's vacation home. Her son had just been deployed. She kissed him good-bye on Monday, and on Tuesday, she came to join Cindy at Crawford. She'd just learned that her son and his wife were expecting their first child.

"My son is going to Iraq based on lies. It's very clear. I wanted to believe and my son wanted to believe, too. But nothing has come forward—nothing—to show any of us mothers that our sons are going there to fight for a noble cause. My son is going there not for weapons of mass destruction. Not because we've declared war. Not because a mushroom cloud is imminent. And not to fight terrorism—because no Iraqis were involved in 9/11 or in London or in Spain. And I really want to know why he's going. I think that's a fair question."

In late August 2005, this contingent of military families piled into vans to deliver a letter to President Bush to demand that he meet with the grieving mothers. They made their way to the Secret Service checkpoint and they all got out of the vans that had PEACE emblazoned on the side. They walked beneath the searing midday sun bearing the letter and some roses. The Secret Service refused to take the letter and ordered them to step back across the road. And then two of the mothers stepped forward.

Mimi Evans and Beatrice Saldivar, whose nephew Daniel Torres had recently died in Iraq, put their arms around each other. They clutched the letter and the rose and they walked across the street. As the Secret Service agents ordered them to "get back, get back," they put the letter down on the road. The agents told them not to dare leave it there. But the women did it anyway.

The Secret Service agents looked confused and disturbed. They did not know what to do, especially with reporters looking on. Beatrice asked them to pick up the letter just as so many soldiers have had to pick up the pieces of their fallen comrades on the roads in Iraq. "It's the least you can do to pick up the letter and give it to the president," said Beatrice. But the Secret Service agents refused and ordered them to leave.

These are the women of Cindy's Crawford, who are refusing to grieve politely and in silence.

Then there are the men who have returned from Iraq. Army Specialist Tomas Young decided to spend his honeymoon in Crawford. Sitting in his wheelchair, he talked about his experience in Sadr City: "All of the higher-ups were trying to tell us that the Iraqis were just mindless terrorists who wanted to come over and destroy the American way of life and that we were going to defend freedom. That was definitely the rah-rah, gung ho kind of attitude they were trying to instill in us so that we could feel more comfortable with going in and, I guess, killing them."

Cindy Sheehan said of Young, "Tomas has more courage and integrity in his pinky than George Bush has in his entire body." She proposed building a veterans' rehabilitation center near Bush's vacation home "so for the rest of his life, George Bush will have to look and see what his policies did."

Charlie Anderson was another soldier recently returned from Iraq who stayed at Camp Casey. "We're seeing a Veterans Administration that is being horribly underfunded. It's been ignored for years. Right now, the Veterans Administration needs $1 billion just to provide services for the veterans that are going to be entering the system next year. We need $4 billion in the Veterans Administration to be able to provide care for all veterans for a reasonable amount of time, for the veterans that are going to enter from this conflict, as well as those that are seeking treatment from previous conflicts," Anderson said. "The VA is in crisis now. We don't need yellow ribbons. We need help. We need jobs. We need health care. We need education. We need the promises fulfilled that were made to us when we signed our enlistment contracts."

Cindy Sheehan's mission since her son's death in Iraq is to make sure there is a face—of a mother, a soldier, a movement—on every casualty in Iraq. Sheehan and the other military families ensure that everywhere Bush goes, he is confronted with those faces. So when Bush returned to Crawford for Thanksgiving in November 2005, Cindy was there. When he delivered his State of the Union address in Congress in January 2006, Cindy was there. She was wearing a black T-shirt that said in bold white letters, "2,245 dead. How many more?" Capitol Police arrested her for wearing the shirt, only to drop charges and apologize the next day. In March 2006, Sheehan was arrested at the U.S. mission to the United Nations while trying to deliver a petition with more than 60,000 signatures calling for the withdrawal of all troops from Iraq. Police manhandled Sheehan, tearing ligaments in her shoulder.

The venues change, but Sheehan's focus does not. As she said at Camp Casey in August 2005, "I know we speak for thousands of [military families] when we want to know 'What is the noble cause our children died for, what is the noble cause they are still fighting for and dying for every day?' And that is what we want—answers to these questions. And there's millions of Americans here with us—thousands here actually in Crawford—who want the same answers. They don't have what I like to call 'skin in the game,' but we are all affected. Our entire humanity is affected when one country wages an illegal and immoral war on another country. And that's why America is behind us, saying we want the answers to those questions, too."

In March 2006, near the second anniversary of her son's death, Cindy Sheehan wrote an open letter explaining why she continues her struggle: "I started working for peace shortly after Casey was killed to be sure that Casey would not be forgotten by America, that he would not just be a number. I started this so Casey's sacrifice would count for love and peace; not hatred, killing, and lies. I started on my journey for peace to make sure it didn't happen to other Caseys and their families. Casey and the millions of others who have been tragically killed by our leaders in worship of greed for money and power will never die as long as there are people working for peace and justice. This is their gift to us. Let's never forget them. Their deaths can't be in vain."[12]

General, a man is quite expendable.
He can fly and he can kill.
But he has one defect:
He can think.

 —Bertolt Brecht (1898–1956),
   playwright and poet[1]

Mike Hoffman would not be the guy his buddies would expect to see leading a protest movement. The son of a steelworker and a high school janitor from Allentown, Pennsylvania, he enlisted in the Marine Corps in 1999 as an artilleryman to "blow things up." His transformation into an activist came the hard way—on the streets of Baghdad.

When Hoffman arrived in Kuwait in February 2003, his unit's highest-ranking enlisted man laid out the mission in stark terms. "You're not going to make Iraq safe for democracy," the sergeant said. "You are going for one reason alone: oil. But you're still going to go, because you signed a contract. And you're going to go to bring your friends home." Hoffman, who had his own doubts about the war, was relieved—he'd never expected to hear such a candid assessment from a superior. But it was only when he had been in Iraq for several months that the full meaning of the sergeant's words began to sink in.

"The reasons for war were wrong," he said. "They were lies. There were no WMDs. Al Qaeda was not there. And it was evident we couldn't force democracy on people by force of arms."

When he returned home and got his honorable discharge in August 2003, Hoffman said, he knew what he had to do next. "After being in Iraq and seeing what this war is, I realized that the only way to support our troops is to demand the withdrawal of all occupying forces in Iraq." He cofounded a group called Iraq Veterans Against the War (IVAW) and soon found himself emerging as one of the most visible members of a growing movement of soldiers who openly oppose the war in Iraq.

Dissent about Iraq within the military is not new. Senior officers were questioning the optimistic projections of the Pentagon's civilian leaders from early on, and some retired generals strongly criticized the war. Retired Gen. Anthony Zinni, the head of Central Command before Gen. Tommy Franks and once President George W. Bush's special Middle East envoy, told *60 Minutes* in May 2004: "To think that we are going to 'stay the course'—the course is headed over Niagara Falls. . . . It's been a failure."

In what has become a familiar ritual, neoconservatives questioned Zinni's patriotism, and the conservative *National Review* slammed him as an "anti-Semite" for criticizing the war. He fired back at the critics, insisting that speaking out as a soldier "is part of your duty." He scoffed at "the idea that when the troops are in combat, everybody has to shut up. Imagine if we put troops in combat with a faulty rifle, and that rifle was malfunctioning, and troops were dying as a result. I [don't] think anyone would allow that to happen, that would not speak up."

Soldiers and their families are now speaking out in growing numbers. Hoffman founded Iraq Veterans Against the War in July 2004 with eight members; within two years, its membership had grown to over 300. Another organization, Military Families Speak Out, began with two families in 2002; four years later, its membership included over 2,400 military families. And soldier-advocacy groups are reporting a rising number of calls from military personnel who are considering refusing to fight. Rather than go to Iraq, numerous soldiers have fled to Canada.

Most troops now question the official rationale for occupying

Iraq. In a first-ever survey of American troops in Iraq conducted in February 2006 by Zogby and LeMoyne College, an overwhelming 72 percent of them thought the United States should leave the country within the next year; one in four advocated an immediate withdrawal.[2] In a 2005 poll by *Military Times,* a bare majority (54 percent) of soldiers approved of President Bush's Iraq policy.[3] In a poll in Pennsylvania in 2003, 54 percent of households with a member in the military said the war was the "wrong thing to do." Doubts about the war have contributed to the decline of troop morale—nearly three-fourths of soldiers described morale as "bad" in 2004[4]—and may, some experts say, be a factor in why Army suicide rates in Iraq have risen up to 40 percent since the start of the war.

"That's the most basic tool a soldier needs on the battlefield—a reason to be there," said Paul Rieckhoff, a platoon leader in the New York National Guard and former JPMorgan banker who served in Iraq. Rieckhoff has founded a group called Iraq and Afghanistan Veterans of America, which provides a freewheeling forum for soldiers' views on the war.[5] "When you can't articulate that in one sentence, it starts to affect morale. You had an initial rationale for war that was a moving target. [But] it was a shell game from the beginning, and you can only bullshit people for so long."

With his baggy pants, red goatee, and moussed hair, Mike Hoffman looks more like a guy taking some time off after college than a 25-year-old combat veteran. But the urgency in his voice belies his relaxed appearance; he speaks rapidly, consumed with the desire to get his point across. Talking in a coffee shop in Vermont after one of his many speaking engagements, he conceded, "A lot of what I'm doing is basically survivor's guilt. It's hard: I'm home. I'm fine. I came back in one piece. But there are a lot of people who haven't."

More than a year after his return from Iraq, Hoffman was still battling depression, panic attacks, and nightmares. "I don't know what I did," he said, noting that errors and faulty targeting were common in the artillery. "I came home and read that six children were killed in an artillery strike near where I was. I don't really know if that was my unit or a British unit. But I feel responsible for everything that happened when I was there."

When he first came home, Hoffman says, he tried to talk to friends and family about his experience. It was not a story most wanted to hear. "One of the hardest things when I came back was people who were slapping me on the back saying 'Great job,'" he recalled. "Everyone wants this to be a good war so they can sleep at night. But guys like me know it's not a good war. There's no such thing as a good war."

Hoffman finally found some kindred spirits in fall 2003 when he discovered Veterans for Peace, the antiwar group founded in 1985. Older veterans encouraged him to speak at rallies, and steadily, he began to connect with other disillusioned Iraq vets. In July 2004, at the Veterans for Peace annual meeting in Boston, Hoffman announced the creation of Iraq Veterans Against the War. The audience of silver-haired vets from wars in Vietnam, Korea, and World War II burst into applause. Hoffman smiled wryly. "They tell us we're the rock stars of the antiwar movement."

A number of Hoffman's Marine Corps buddies have now joined Iraq Veterans Against the War, and the stream of phone calls and e-mails from other soldiers is constant. Not long ago, he said, a soldier home on leave from Iraq told him, "Just keep doing what you're doing, because you've got more support than you can imagine over there."

Members of IVAW led the protest march that greeted the 2004 Republican convention in New York, and their ranks swelled that week. But the protest's most poignant moment came after the march, as veterans from wars past and present retreated to Summit Rock in Central Park. Joe Bangert, a founding member of Vietnam Veterans of America, addressed the group. "One of the most painful things when we returned from Vietnam was that the veterans from past wars weren't there for us," he said. "They didn't support us in our questioning and our opposition to war. And I just want to say," he added, peering intently at the younger veterans, "we are here for you. We have your back."

Soldiers of Conscience

There was no Iraq veterans' group for Brandon Hughey to turn to in December 2003. Alone and terrified, sitting in his barracks at Fort Hood, Texas, the 18-year-old private considered his options. He could remain with his Army unit, which was about to ship out to Iraq to fight a war that Hughey was convinced was pointless and immoral. Or he could end his dilemma—by taking his own life.

Desperate, Hughey trolled the Internet. He e-mailed a peace activist and Vietnam veteran in Indianapolis, Carl Rising-Moore, who made him an offer: If he was serious about his opposition to the war, Rising-Moore said, he would help him flee to Canada.

The next day, an officer knocked on Hughey's door: His deployment date had been moved up, and his unit was leaving within twenty-four hours. Hughey packed his belongings in a military duffel, jumped in his car, and drove north. He met up with Rising-Moore in Indianapolis, and the two headed north together. As they approached the Rainbow Bridge border post at Niagara Falls, Hughey was nervous and somber. "I had the sense that once I crossed that border, I might never be able to go back," he recalled. "It made me sad."

Months after fleeing Fort Hood, the baby-faced 19-year-old still sported a military-style buzz cut. Sitting at the kitchen table of the Quaker family that was sheltering him in St. Catharines, Ontario, Hughey talked about growing up in San Angelo, Texas, where he was raised by his father. In high school he played trumpet and loved to soup up cars. But when his father lost his job as a computer programmer, he was forced to use up his son's college fund.

So at 17, Hughey enlisted in the Army, with a $5,000 signing bonus to sweeten the deal.

Quiet and unassuming, Hughey grew intense when the conversation turned to Iraq. "I would fight in an act of defense, if my home and family were in danger," he said. "But Iraq had no weapons of mass destruction. They barely had an army left, and Kofi Annan actually said [attacking Iraq was] a violation of the UN charter. It's nothing more than an act of aggression." As for his duty to his fellow soldiers, he insisted, "You can't go along with a criminal activity just because others are doing it." By early 2006, an estimated 200 U.S. soldiers had fled to Canada rather than fight in Iraq and Afghanistan, and about 25 of them had applied for refugee status.[6]

There are growing signs of resistance in the military to fighting Bush's wars. The Pentagon estimates that as of late 2005, more than 8,000 members of the U.S. military had deserted since the start of the Iraq War[7] (military personnel are classified as having deserted after not reporting for duty for more than a month), and many observers believe the actual number may be even higher. The Army has acknowledged that it is not aggressively hunting down soldiers who don't show up—although in a bizarre twist, the military has lately been hunting down and arresting Vietnam-era deserters to send a message to current soldiers that desertion is a lifelong stigma. In 2004, the overstretched Army called up 4,000 former soldiers and ordered them back to duty; half of them have resisted the orders.[8] The GI Rights Hotline, a counseling operation run by a national network of antiwar groups, reports that it now receives between 3,000 and 4,000 calls per month from soldiers seeking a way out of the military; before the war, it received about 1,000 calls per year. Some of the callers simply never thought they would see combat, said J. E. McNeil, director of the Center on Conscience and War. But others are turning against the war because of what they saw while serving in Iraq, and they don't want to be sent back there. "It's people learning what war really is," she said. "A lot of people are naïve—and for a while, the military was portraying itself as being a peace mission."

Unlike Vietnam, when young men facing the draft could convincingly claim that they opposed all war, enlistees in a volunteer military have a tough time qualifying as conscientious objectors. In 2004, about 110 applied for conscientious objector (CO) status, four times the number who applied in 2000.[9] Roughly half of the applications were denied. "The Army does understand people can have a change of heart," noted spokeswoman Martha Rudd. "But you can't ask for a conscientious objector discharge based on moral or religious opposition to a particular war."

With the military turning down so many CO applications, war resisters are now landing in jail. The first Iraq War soldier sent to prison for refusing to fight was 28-year-old Sgt. Camilo Mejia, a Nicaraguan-born member of the Florida National Guard who fought in Iraq for six months. Upon returning to the United States in October 2003 for a two-week leave, he refused to go back to Iraq. He went into hiding for five months before turning himself in and applying to be a conscientious objector. Mejia claims to have witnessed and participated in prisoner abuse and the killing of civilians. Former attorney general Ramsey Clark, who was part of Mejia's defense team, spoke of the "incredible irony that we're prosecuting soldiers in Iraq for violations of international law and we're prosecuting a soldier here because he refused to do the same things."

On May 21, 2004, Camilo Mejia was convicted of deserting his unit. In June 2004, Amnesty International declared Mejia a prisoner of conscience and called for his immediate and unconditional release. He served a year-long sentence in the brig at Fort Sill, Oklahoma, and was released in February 2005.

Mejia spoke on *Democracy Now!* shortly after his release. As he sat absorbed in thought in the studio waiting for the interview to begin, he suddenly broke into a smile. A familiar song was playing during the break, "Quincho Barrilete," the anthem of the Sandinista revolution that overthrew the U.S.-backed Somoza dictatorship in 1979. The singer was his father, Carlos Mejia Godoy, a noted Nicaraguan musician and later an ambassador in the Sandinista government.

Mejia, a hint of his jarhead haircut still evident beneath a flock of brown curls, explained what drove the son of a rebel leader to join the U.S. military. "I guess the pressure to be like your parents and to be like your father, who is such a public figure, and who has contributed so much to the Sandinista revolution—I guess I just turned my back on it, because I wanted to find my own way."

The Iraq War veteran talked about why he went to Iraq in the first place: "Politically, I was very much in disagreement with the war, but I didn't really want to make a stand, because I was terrified, because I didn't want to go through a court-martial, because I didn't want to go to jail, because I was a squad leader in an infantry unit, and I didn't want my friends to think I was a coward or a traitor."

His feelings changed when he was stationed at a former Iraqi air force base. Mejia described how unidentified "spooks" would decide which of the Iraqi prisoners were "enemy combatants." "No one knows who [the spooks] are or where they come from. They wear no unit patch or anything." Prisoners deemed "enemy combatants" were hooded and singled out for abuse. Mejia was told to deprive these prisoners of sleep for days. Soldiers from another unit explained how to keep someone awake: "Yell at them, tell them to get up and get down," he recounted. "Let them sleep for five seconds, so they will get disoriented. Bang a sledgehammer on a wall to make it sound like an explosion. Scare them. And if all of that fails, then, you know, cock a nine-millimeter gun next to their ear, so as to make them believe that they're going to be executed. And then they will do anything that you want them to do. In that manner, keep them up for periods of 48 to 72 hours in order to soften them up for interrogation."

He also described what he did when he went on house-to-house raids: "You go in there at two or three in the morning, put every-body from the household in one room and then take the owner of the house, who is usually a man, all through the house into every room. Open every closet and everything and look for weapons and look for literature against the coalition. And then get your de-tainees and move out." Mejia and his mates could not, of course, understand the Arabic literature they were sent to find. And the in-telligence his unit had was often vague or meaningless. "Some-times they would tell us, you are looking for a man who's 5'7", dark skin, has a beard—which is like about 90 percent of men in Iraq."

For many immigrants, joining the military is a fast track to gain-ing American citizenship. Some 41,000 "permanent resident aliens" are in the United States armed forces. By mid-2005, sixty-three immigrants had been killed fighting in Iraq.[10]

Seeing the Iraq War close-up, including prisoner abuse, awoke something in Camilo Mejia that has "just been dormant for a long time. I guess that family background has finally kicked in and given me a new conscience."

Following his release from jail, Mejia wrote this advice to other soldiers: "Peace does not come easily, so I tell all members of the military that whenever faced with an order, and everything in their mind and soul, and each and every cell in their bodies screams at them to refuse and resist, then by God do so. Jail will mean noth-ing when breaking the law became their duty to humanity."[11]

Antiwar Refugees

Jeffry House is reliving his past. An American draft evader who fled to Canada in 1970 (he was number 16 in that year's draft lot-tery), he is now fighting to persuade the Canadian government to grant refugee status to American deserters.

"In some ways, this is coming full circle for me," said the slightly disheveled, 57-year-old Toronto lawyer. "The themes that I thought about when I was 21 years old now are reborn, particularly your obligation to the state when the state has participated in a fraud, when they've deceived you." A dormant network has been revived, with Vietnam-era draft dodgers and deserters—an estimated 50,000 of them came to Canada to avoid fighting in Vietnam—quietly contributing money to support the legal defense of the newest American fugitives.

House's strategy is bold: He is challenging the very legality of the Iraq War, based on the Nuremberg principles. Those principles, adopted by a UN commission after World War II in response to the Nazis' crimes, hold that military personnel have a responsibility to resist unlawful orders. They also declare wars of aggression a violation of international law. House hopes that in Canada, which did not support the war in Iraq, courts might sympathize with the deserters' claims and grant them legal refugee status.

Private Jeremy Hinzman was the first American soldier to flee to Canada and publicly protest fighting in Iraq. He settled in Toronto with his wife and their 2-year-old son, Liam. The clean, preppy-looking 25-year-old veteran of the Army's storied 82nd Airborne Division had been spending much of his time reading history and politics, and following the news from Iraq.

For Hinzman, the way the Abu Ghraib prison torture scandal was handled captures the immorality of the Iraq conflict—and the hypocrisy of how justice is meted out in wartime. "[CENTCOM Commander Ricardo] Sanchez and Rumsfeld—the higher policymakers knew what was going on. Were the brass punished? No, they scapegoated the trailer trash. They are being punished for carrying out command decisions, instead of punishing those who formulated these command decisions."

Hinzman applied for CO status while in Afghanistan. When it was denied by the Army, he felt he had no option but to flee. "The whole enterprise in Iraq was illegal and essentially criminal. By participating in it, I would have been participating in a criminal enterprise."

In March 2005, the Canadian Immigration and Refugee Board turned down Hinzman's application for refugee status. The board sidestepped his argument about the illegality of the Iraq War and ruled that he would not face serious persecution if he returned to the United States. Brandon Hughey's application was turned down six months later. Hinzman and Hughey are appealing the rulings. Hinzman, who periodically runs marathons, is now in his longest and toughest race.

When Jeremy Hinzman traveled the lonely mile across the Rainbow Bridge into Canada rather than fight in an immoral and illegal war, he unwittingly catalyzed a movement. The War Resisters Support Campaign of Canada has formed to provide financial and legal assistance and offer housing to the growing number of American soldiers arriving in Canada. The Canadians and the American soldiers hope to rekindle the spirit of former Canadian prime minister Pierre Trudeau, who declared in 1969: "Those who make a conscientious judgment that they must not participate in this war . . . have my complete sympathy. . . . Canada should be a refuge from militarism."[12]

A Dissenting Voice

The San Diego Naval Station was abuzz with activity. It was December 6, 2004, and thousands of Marines from Camp Pendleton were boarding the USS *Bonhomme Richard*, an amphibious assault ship, to be transported to the Middle East for combat duty. As the Marines boarded, one sailor stood apart: Petty Officer 3rd Class Pablo Paredes sat on the pier and refused to move. There was a standoff, as Paredes informed senior officers that he was refusing to go in protest against the Iraq War. The 23-year-old weapons control technician told reporters, "I don't want to be a part of a ship that's taking 3,000

Marines over there, knowing a hundred or more of them won't come back. I can't sleep at night knowing that's what I do for a living."[13]

Paredes, a Hispanic-American, expected to be arrested for his actions. For nearly two hours, the sailor sat on the pier and spoke to reporters, explaining why he was refusing to board. Paredes told the journalists he was young and naïve when he joined the Navy and "never imagined in a million years we would go to war with somebody who had done nothing to us."

"I really wanted to use my position to show the world a dissenting voice that is not afraid to suffer some consequences for principles," he told *Democracy Now!*[14] But the Navy declined to arrest him with the media present. It was only after he left the pier that day that he was classified as a "deserter and fugitive."

Paredes had spent the previous two years in the Navy in Japan. It was there, he said, "I saw a different perspective. I got to see news from a different point of view, and it got me very interested. First as a Latino, I got very interested in the politics of Latin America and all of the interventions, the CIA operations, the coups. I got very interested in everything that's happened in history, which up until then, I was clueless to." Paredes says he felt he was "part of the system that allowed those things to happen, so I started to have a very serious conflict about what I was doing."

Paredes was jarred by being surrounded by a massive military operation that was deploying in Afghanistan and Iraq, while talking to family back home who seemed oblivious. "I was seeing the disconnect that happens in the U.S. Then I wondered what makes people so apathetic. I see that the monster of the mainstream media is a big reason."

Paredes's application to be a conscientious objector was denied. He was court-martialed for taking an unauthorized absence from the Navy. A friend and supporter of his, an active-duty member of the elite Navy SEALS, drove him to the trial. Sitting in the courtroom to support him were a number of others who have spoken out against the war: Sgt. Camilo Mejia, Cindy Sheehan, Fernando Suarez del Solar—whose son, Marine Lance Cpl. Jesus Suarez, was one of the first to die in Iraq—and Aidan Delgado, who served as a military policeman at Abu Ghraib and subsequently succeeded in getting CO status.

Paredes stated at his court-martial: "If there's anything I could be guilty of, it is my beliefs. I am guilty of believing this war is illegal. I'm guilty of believing war in all forms is immoral and useless, and I am guilty of believing that as a service member I have a duty to refuse to participate in this war because it is illegal."[15] To the surprise of Paredes and his attorneys, Lt. Cmdr. Bob Klant, presiding judge at the court-martial, conceded at one point, "I think the government has successfully proved that any seaman recruit has reasonable cause to believe that the wars in Yugoslavia, Afghanistan and Iraq were illegal."[16]

Navy prosecutors asked for Paredes to be sentenced to nine months in prison and that he be given a bad conduct discharge. "He is trying to infect the military with his own philosophy of disobedience. Sailors all over the world will want to know whether this will be tolerated," declared prosecutor Lt. Brandon Hale.

Instead, the judge sentenced the seaman to three months of hard labor on his Navy base for refusing deployment, and demoted him from petty officer third class to seaman recruit, the lowest rank in the Navy. He was discharged "under honorable conditions." Defense lawyer Jeremy Warren described the sentence, which pointedly did not include jail time, as "a stunning blow to the prosecution. This is an affirmation of every sailor's and military person's right to speak out and follow their conscience."[17]

Since Paredes was released in October 2005, he has been on a mission to speak out against war. He has been to Venezuela for the World Social Forum, and to Colombia, where he went to advocate for legal recognition of CO status. The goateed young man with deep brown eyes was quick to laugh, but intensely focused when it came to discussing what he cares about.

"Counter recruitment," said the young man who grew up in the South Bronx, "is my passion." Paredes described how he "attended high school part-time, and worked full-time" in a family that struggled after his father was seriously injured in a workplace accident. An easy paycheck for a cash-strapped Latino kid was always waiting for him, if only he would talk to the guys in uniform who were ubiquitous around his high school.

"Here I was an average Joe, and somewhere along the line my new best friend became a guy in working whites." He decries the militarization of schools, especially in minority communities. "It's not just this great, witty, charming guy who comes into school. It's a process of romanticizing everything to do with the military and uniforms and arms. Now you have grammar schools where Hummers and tanks come. In the malls, [recruiters] show up with virtual reality machines. So in the inner city, you are targeted and indoctrinated with a love of all things military."

The Army has a $200 million advertising budget, and recruiters now travel the country with flight simulators, Hummers with state-of-the-art audio-visual systems, and a fleet of thirteen trailers, each costing $1 million, that show off the latest in high-tech military equipment and Xbox military video games. The toys are intended to dazzle and seduce young recruits. "It's more like an Army version of 'Pimp My Ride,'" said Lt. Col. Mark V. Lathem, commander of the battalion that runs the fleet.[18]

"It's disgusting," said Paredes. "On the one hand, you have high schools where the education budgets are being cut and the coaches are being cut. Then you have the recruitment manual that instructs recruiters, 'High schools are getting their budgets cut, so if you volunteer as a coach, you will be the hero of all the students. That heroic posture will make it easier to recruit.' You invade their school and try to become their hero. They've got Ronald McDonald beat."

Paredes said that "learning all these things makes you feel like you have to work towards change to balance this. Students have no one on their side. . . . They have recruiters working for years at a time to get them into the military. So this is a passion for me. Someone has to advocate for the students."

Filling the Ranks

The U.S. military is broken. One in four soldiers returning from Iraq and Afghanistan suffers from post-traumatic stress disorder (PTSD). In 2004, 215,871 veterans received PTSD benefit payments at a cost of $4.3 billion, a 150 percent jump since 1999.[19]

As soldiers return from Iraq and Afghanistan and talk candidly about the horrors of war and the realities of occupying countries that do not want them, the military is struggling to fill its ranks. In the fiscal year ending September 30, 2005, the Army fell 8 percent short of its annual goal of 80,000 enlistees—the Army's biggest shortfall since 1979. In that same time, the Army Reserve only managed to muster 84 percent of its quota, while the Army National Guard signed up just 80 percent, 12,783 recruits shy of its goal of 63,002.[20]

"The Army's recruiting shortfalls have put the future of the all-volunteer armed forces in jeopardy," wrote retired Lt. Col. Charles A. Krohn, the Army's former deputy chief of public affairs. "We have basically committed most of the Army's active forces (including much of the National Guard), rotating them to the point of exhaustion."[21]

The military is digging deep to attract new soldiers. Recruiters have been added; the Army has doubled the maximum enlistment bonus from $20,000 to $40,000 (to stock our "all-volunteer" military); the maximum enlistment age for reservists has been raised from 34 to 39; restrictions have been relaxed on enlisting high school dropouts; and more people with substandard scores on the Army aptitude test are now signed up.[22] The *Washington Post* reported, "To fill its ranks nationwide, the Army in fiscal 2005 accepted its least qualified pool in a decade—falling below quota in high school graduates (87 percent) and taking in more youths scoring in the lowest category of aptitude test (3.9 percent)."[23]

When even these efforts fail, the Bush administration just fakes the numbers. For example, despite sagging sign-ups, the Army announced it had exceeded its recruiting quotas for October 2005. An impressive feat—until you learn that the Army simply lowered its October quota by one-third, from about 7,000 recruits in October 2004 to 4,700 recruits a year later.[24]

Recruiters are becoming increasingly desperate to make quota. Charges of recruiting improprieties almost doubled from 2000 to 2004, with some 957 incidents reported in 2004.[25] David McSwane, a 17-year-old high school journalist in Arvada, Colorado, decided "to see how far the Army would go during a war to get one more soldier." CBS News picked up the story from there:

McSwane contacted his local Army recruiting office, in Golden, with a scenario he created.

For one thing, he told his recruiter, he was a dropout and didn't have a high school diploma.

No problem, McSwane says the recruiter explained. He suggested that McSwane create a fake diploma from a nonexistent school.

McSwane recorded the recruiter saying on the phone: "It can be like Faith Hill Baptist School. Whatever you choose."

So, as instructed, McSwane went to a Web site and, for $200, arranged to have a phony diploma created. It certified McSwane as a graduate of Faith Hill Baptist High School, the very name the recruiter had suggested, and came complete with a fake grade transcript.

What was McSwane's reaction to them encouraging him to get a phony diploma? "I was shocked. I'm sitting there looking at a poster that says, 'Integrity, honor, respect,' and he is telling me to lie."[26]

McSwane continued the ruse, telling the recruiter: "I have a problem with drugs. I can't kick the habit. Just marijuana." The Army does not accept people with drug problems—or so it says. The recruiter told him, "Not a problem. Just take this detox." The recruiter even offered to pay half the cost of the treatment, and drove McSwane to a store where he could buy it.

Economic hard times have been a boon to the military. In 2004, nearly half of recruits came from lower-middle-class or poor households, and 44 percent came from rural areas. In these depressed areas, the risk of going to war is outweighed by the threat of going jobless or hungry.

As support for the Iraq War has dropped dramatically among African-Americans, the military has made recruiting Latinos a top priority. Between 2001 and 2005, the number of African-American recruits dropped from 22 percent to 15 percent, while Latino enlistment shot up 26 percent. Latinos now make up 11 percent of the military; they account for 14 percent of the population. But critics point out that Latinos are being used as cannon fodder: They comprise less than 5 percent of the officer corps.[27] The Army is spending millions on advertising in Spanish-language media. President Bush has added another sweetener: Instead of being hunted down at the border, he has promised that Latino recruits will be fast-tracked for citizenship.

Pablo Paredes shakes his head in disgust about the Latino recruitment effort, and vows to counter it. "It's bad enough that the poor of the U.S. are targeted to fight wars of the U.S. But when the poor of another country are targeted to fight the wars of the U.S., that's criminal."

Lately, the military has been outsourcing its recruitment efforts. Where high school students could once easily identify recruiters by their crisp military uniforms, today the person making a pitch to join may simply be a well-dressed civilian. That's because the military has been steadily privatizing its recruiting operation. In 2002, the Pentagon awarded a $100 million contract to Military

Professional Resources, Inc. (MPRI)—which boasts of "having more generals per square foot than the Pentagon"[28]—to take over recruiting in five areas (Tacoma, Washington; Jackson, Mississippi; Oklahoma City; Dayton, Ohio; and the Delaware, Maryland, and Virginia region). Another firm, Resource Consultant, Inc. (now Serco), won a $72 million contract to cover recruiting in Harrisburg, Pennsylvania; Wilmington, North Carolina; Granite City, Illinois; Homewood, Illinois; and Salt Lake City.[29] In November 2005, Serco won another contract worth up to $30 million to provide 102 recruiters to the Army in the southern United States.[30]

"We simply provide a product, like Coca-Cola," said MPRI Vice President Ed Soyster, a retired army general and the former director of the Defense Intelligence Agency.[31] It's a Coke that can kill.

Students in the Crosshairs

As recruiters go bottom feeding to meet quota, the Pentagon is busy creating a high-tech database to reach out and snare unsuspecting students. First there was the obscure provision of the No Child Left Behind Act that forces high schools to turn over the names and contact details of all juniors and seniors, effectively transforming President George Bush's signature education bill into the most aggressive military recruitment tool since the draft.

Then, in June 2005, privacy advocates were shocked to learn that for two years, the Pentagon had been amassing a database of information on some 30 million students. The information dossiers on millions of young Americans were to help identify college and high school students as young as sixteen to target them for military recruiting.

The massive database includes an array of personal information including birth dates, Social Security numbers, e-mail addresses, grade point averages, ethnicities, and what subjects the students are studying. The Pentagon has hired the Massachusetts-based company BeNow to run the database. By turning to private firms to do this work, the government is circumventing laws that restrict its right to collect or hold citizen information.

The Pentagon's Joint Advertising, Market Research and Studies Group (JAMRS) oversees this massive data mining project. The Pentagon, which is spending $243 million on JAMRS, is collecting data from commercial data brokers, state driver's license records, and other sources.[32] The JAMRS Web site describes the consolidated database located at BeNow as "arguably the largest repository of 16–25-year-old youth data in the country, containing roughly 30 million records."[33] If you're concerned that the information might be used by other agencies, well, you should be: The Pentagon has stated that it can share the data with law enforcement, state tax authorities, other agencies making employment inquiries, and foreign authorities, among others. Students will not know if their information has been collected, and they cannot prevent it from happening.

The main obstacle to getting kids into the military—concerned parents—has at long last been circumvented. Private companies can now harvest data on children and provide private recruiters with the information they need to contact kids directly. If skeptical parents find out that the "Mr. Jones" calling for Johnny is offering their child a free ticket to Iraq, the military is spending millions to learn how best to persuade or bypass these negative "influencers." One JAMRS study is focused exclusively on how to change mothers' attitudes. In March 2004, 271 mothers from Atlanta, Chicago, Los Angeles, Denver, Dallas, and New York City were interviewed in order to enable recruiters to "better understand ways to motivate mothers currently on the fence to be accepting of military service, [and] exert some influence on mothers who are currently against military service."[34]

Now rebellious teens have a new ally in challenging their overprotective mothers—the Pentagon. And in case the prospective recruit has dropped out of school, has a criminal record, or is a single

parent—each normally a bar to acceptance into the military—
JAMRS is also studying "moral character waiver policies" to help
recruiters sign them up anyway.

Data mining—which the Pentagon claimed it had stopped in 2003
after an earlier program, the Total Information Awareness Project,
was exposed—is fraught with risk. As Mark Rotenberg, director of
the Electronic Privacy Information Center (EPIC), told *Democracy
Now!*, "There is a real problem with the security of information data-
bases in this country right now. The most recent breach was about 40
million records maintained by a credit card processing company, and
this is also having a direct impact on the crime of identity theft, which
according to the Federal Trade Commission cost American consumers and businesses over $50 billion in 2004."[35]

In late 2005, over one hundred groups wrote to Secretary of Defense Donald Rumsfeld demanding that "because of the potential
for abuse and the threat to the personal privacy rights of a generation of American youth, we request that the JAMRS project be immediately ended."[36] But the program continues.

As the military secretly gathers personal information about students and passes it around, abuse has followed close behind. In In-
diana, six female high school recruits were sexually assaulted by a
recruiter in 2002 and 2003. According to the *Indianapolis Star*, Indi-
ana National Guard Sgt. Eric P. Vetesy "picked out teens and
young women with backgrounds that made them vulnerable to
authority. As a military recruiter, he had access to personal information, making the quest easier."[37] The local prosecutor noted
that of the victims, young women between the ages of 17 and 21,
"most were in single-parent families with no father figure. Because
Vetesy assembled background information on each recruit . . . he
was able to target those he most likely could coerce."

The *Star* continued, "Nationwide, military recruiters reportedly
have been linked to at least a half-dozen sexual assaults during the
past few years, since the creation of the federal No Child Left Behind Act. This broad education law requires, among other things,

that high schools give military recruiters greater access to students."

Groups are mobilizing against the Pentagon's massive student recruitment and data mining campaigns. Leave My Child Alone (www.leavemychildalone.org) offers online opt-out forms that students and parents can download and submit to schools to keep their names off recruiter contact lists. The group estimates that as of 2006, 37,000 students have opted out of the No Child Left Behind requirement. Students can also file another form to send to the Pentagon to have their names removed from the JAMRS database.

It's little wonder that the Pentagon must invent new ways to find bodies for the front lines. Support for America's foreign wars has dropped to new lows among young Americans: One study showed that just 25 percent of teens support the Iraq War.[38] As more returning soldiers speak out against the war, today's soldiers may just follow the lead of their commander in chief: Go AWOL.

Vietnam figures prominently in soldiers' conversations about Iraq. Numerous Iraq veterans have relatives who served in the military, and they tell a similar story: When they grew cynical about the Iraq War, the Vietnam veterans in their family immediately recognized what was happening—another generation of soldiers was grappling with the realization that they were being sent to carry out a policy determined by people who cared little for the grunts on the ground.

Resistance in the military "is growing, but it's going to take a little while," said Mike Hoffman, whose cousins, uncle, and grandfather all did their time in uniform.

Hoffman recalled the GI Revolt, the groundswell of resistance within the military in Vietnam and the breakdown of morale that hastened the end of that war. "There was a progression of thought that happened among soldiers in Vietnam. It started with a mission: Contain communism. That mission fell apart, just like it fell apart now—there are no weapons of mass destruction. Then you are left with just a survival instinct. That, unfortunately, turned to racism. That's happening now, too. Guys are writing me saying, 'I don't know why I'm here, but I hate the Iraqis.'

"Now you realize that the people to blame for this aren't the ones you are fighting," Hoffman continued. "It's the people who put you in this situation in the first place. You realize you wouldn't be in this situation if you hadn't been lied to. Soldiers are slowly coming to that conclusion. Once that becomes widespread, the resentment of the war is going to grow even more."

If you see something, say something.
—**Terror warning posted in the New York City subways, 2006**

In a time when supposedly civilized world leaders weigh the merits of different torture techniques, Craig Murray is that rarest of public servants: He is a defender of human rights. For that, the former British ambassador to Uzbekistan was sacked, his writing was suppressed, and he has been threatened with punishment and even jail by the administration of British prime minister Tony Blair. Murray's experience both during and after his time in Uzbekistan offers a stunning inside view of how human rights has been sacrificed to advance the narrow interests of the United States in its war on terror.

Uzbekistan is a California-size republic in Central Asia. From 1924 to 1991, it was part of the Soviet Union. It gained its independence in 1992 as a supposedly secular and democratic republic. Islam Karimov, the Communist Party chief in Uzbekistan, became president in 1990, and was reelected after independence. Karimov's regime has been marked by brutality and authoritarianism. All genuine opposition parties were banned in the early 1990s, and the crackdown on Muslims has been especially brutal. In its 2006 *World Report*, Human Rights Watch described Uzbekistan as having a "disastrous human rights record."[1]

Craig Murray arrived in Tashkent as British ambassador in August 2002. He quickly began castigating the Uzbek regime for its human rights abuses. Three months after his arrival, Ambassador Murray gave a speech to an Uzbek human rights group in which he spoke with undiplomatic bluntness:

Uzbekistan is not a functioning democracy, nor does it appear to be moving in the direction of democracy. The major political parties are banned; parliament is not subject to democratic election and checks and balances on the authority of the executive are lacking.

There is worse: we believe there to be between 7,000 and 10,000 people in detention whom we would consider as political and/or religious prisoners. In many cases they have been falsely convicted of crimes with which there appears to be no credible evidence they had any connection. . . .

No government has the right to use the war against terrorism as an excuse for the persecution of those with a deep personal commitment to the Islamic religion, and who pursue their views by peaceful means. Sadly the large majority of those wrongly imprisoned in Uzbekistan fall into this category.[2]

The London *Daily Telegraph* reported that Murray's speech "stunned those present, including John Herbst, the American ambassador. . . . The speech was a gift to human rights organizations and a disaster for the Tashkent government and its new best friend, the White House."[3]

In confidential memos to the British Foreign Office, Murray was harshly critical of the United States. A month after assuming his post in Tashkent, Murray sent a secret memo to his superiors with the subject heading "U.S./UZBEKISTAN: PROMOTING TERRORISM." He denounced the "sham reform" that was certified by the U.S. State Department, which claimed that Uzbekistan was improving in both human rights and democracy, a prerequisite for disbursing $140 million in U.S. aid to Uzbekistan in 2002.

Murray described President Karimov as a "dictator" whose goal was "not the development of his country but the diversion of economic rent to his oligarchic supporters through government controls." The U.S. claim of reform, insisted Ambassador Murray, "is either cynicism or self-delusion."

Murray charged that a U.S. motivation for backing Karimov was to establish strategic air bases in the country. Nevertheless, the U.S. alliance with the dictator "is misconceived. In the short term it may help fight terrorism but in the medium term it will promote it. . . . And it can never be right to lower our standards on human rights. . . . Above all," Murray concluded, "we need to care about the 22 million Uzbek people, suffering from poverty and lack of freedom. They are not just pawns in the new Great Game."[4]

In response to Murray's insistent human rights appeals and pointed criticism, the British government attempted to muzzle him, then smear him, and finally sack him. In late December 2005—after the British government moved to suppress publication of his explosive book, *Murder in Samarkand*—Murray defied Britain's draconian Official Secrets Act by posting a series of classified memos on his Web site (www.craigmurray.co.uk) that he wrote while an ambassador. Fearing that the British government would shut down the site, Murray encouraged other Web site owners to republish the material. Hundreds took up the call.

In one classified memo from July 2004, Murray wrote, "We receive intelligence obtained under torture from the Uzbek intelligence services via the U.S. We should stop. . . . This is morally, legally and practically wrong."

Perhaps the most damning memo is one that was written by a British legal advisor asserting that using information extracted through torture is not technically a violation of the United Nations Convention Against Torture.

In January 2006, shortly after Murray posted the confidential memos, Human Rights Watch released its annual report. It included an unprecedented criticism of U.S. global human rights policy. In presenting the annual report, Human Rights Watch director Kenneth Roth declared, "The global defense of human rights was profoundly compromised over the last year by the Bush administration's policy-level decisions to flout some of the most basic human rights norms, out of a misguided sense that that's the best way to fight against terrorism."

Roth charged that the U.S. violation of human rights had spawned "a copycat phenomenon," offering as an example his conversation with the prime minister of Egypt the previous year. Roth was protesting the "torture of scores, if not hundreds, of suspects" in the aftermath of the bombing of the Hilton Hotel in the Egyptian resort town of Taba. The Egyptian prime minister told Roth, "Well, what do you want? That's what the United States does."

White House Press Secretary Scott McClellan responded to the scathing criticism from Human Rights Watch, saying, "The United States of America does more than any other country in the world to advance freedom and promote human rights. Our focus should be on those who are denying people human dignity and who are violating human rights."

"A Country Which Lives in Fear"

On January 19, 2006, Craig Murray came to the *Democracy Now!* firehouse studio to give his first interview in the United States since he publicly released the confidential memos. He described what he encountered when he became ambassador to Uzbekistan in 2002. "I found a country which lives in fear. . . . It's a totalitarian state. Effectively they haven't reformed much from the old Soviet system, and then they have added a new level of brutality and violence and an extra level of corruption to that. It's a state where everyone is scared of their neighbor, where there are 40,000 secret police in the city of Tashkent alone. And the astonishing thing was it was a state where people were being disappeared and tortured on an industrial basis and which was being financed and organized by the United States of America."

Murray couldn't keep silent about the horrors of the situation. "One of the things you have to do as a new ambassador is call on your fellow ambassadors, pay courtesy calls. And I kept saying to them, you know, to the French, the German, the Italian: 'This is awful. It's terrible what's happening here. There are thousands of people being rounded up in prisons, tortured, killed, disappeared, and it all seems to have the backing of the USA.'

"And they said to me absolutely straight, they said, 'Yes, but we don't mention that. You know, President Karimov is an important ally of George Bush in the war on terror, so there's an unspoken agreement that we keep quiet about the abuses.' " Murray decided that this conspiracy of silence would end with him.

One of the first human rights cases that came to Ambassador Murray's attention occurred shortly after he arrived in the summer of 2002. "Two Muslim prisoners in Jaslyk gulag—which is an old Soviet gulag in the middle of the Garagum Desert, a sort of forced-labor camp, a terrible place where people are sent to die, effectively—were boiled to death," he explained. "The mother of one of the prisoners received her son's body back in a sealed casket. She was ordered not to open the casket, and just to bury it the next morning. Despite being in her sixties, she managed to get the casket open in the middle of the night, even though police were guarding the house outside."

The victim's mother took a series of detailed photos, which she then passed to the British Embassy. Murray sent the photos to be examined by the pathology department at the University of Glasgow. The pathologists issued an autopsy report which stated that the prisoner's fingernails had been extracted, he had been severely beaten, and he died from being immersed in boiling liquid. This "gives you some idea of the level of brutality of this regime," said Murray. The victim's mother was later sentenced to hard labor for exposing what happened to her son.

The Uzbek government was unhappy with Murray's scolding, so they sent him a message. In March 2003, the ambassador went to have dinner with Jamal Mirsaidov, a professor of Tajik literature at the University of Samarkand, who was a dissident in Soviet times. "While we were having dinner, his grandson, who lived in his house, was abducted off the streets, severely tortured, and murdered. His elbows and knees were smashed. His right hand was dipped in boiling liquid until the flesh peeled away. And, ultimately, he was killed with a blow to the back of the head," Murray said. The boy's body was dumped on the professor's doorstep several hours after Murray left.

"This was intended as a warning, both to the professor and to me, a warning not to meet dissidents and for dissidents not to meet me." Murray said that the boy's death "had a profound effect on me. It has troubled my own conscience greatly. Because if I hadn't met his grandfather, he probably wouldn't have died that terrible death."

Uzbekistan's sordid human rights record did not deter the United States, which had a large military air base in the country. Uzbekistan is located immediately north of Afghanistan, and the air base was used for U.S. military operations there. Halliburton was building facilities on the Uzbek base, and the airfield was being turned into a permanent military base. Murray explained, "The United States was pumping huge amounts of American taxpayers' money into the Uzbek regime. According to a U.S. Embassy press release of December 2002, in 2002 alone, the United States government gave Uzbekistan over $500 million, of which $120 million was in military support and $80 million was in support of the Uzbek security services who were working alongside their CIA colleagues."

While Murray was raising human rights issues publicly, he was also pressing the British government internally about the intelligence that they were receiving from the Uzbek secret service. "I was seeing CIA reports, which were passed on to MI6 [the British equivalent of the CIA], which had been extracted from the Uzbek torture chambers," he said.

"I had been there for two or three months, which was long enough to know that any Uzbek political or religious detainee is going to be tortured. There's no question of . . . 'Is that or is that not torture?' We're talking about people having their fingernails pulled, having their teeth smashed with hammers, having their limbs broken, and being raped with objects including broken bottles—both male and female rape—extremely common in Uzbek prisons. And from the security service, which was operating right alongside the CIA, we were getting this intelligence.

"The intelligence itself was nonsense," Murray insisted. "The purpose of the intelligence was to say that all the Uzbek opposition were related to al Qaeda, that the democratic Uzbek opposition were all Islamic terrorists, that they'd traveled to Afghanistan and held meetings with Osama bin Laden. It was designed to promote the myth that Uzbekistan was, in total, part of the war on terror, and that by aligning himself with Karimov, Bush and the Bush administration were backing or improving United States security, which wasn't true at all. I mean, the intelligence was false. If you torture people, they will say anything. I couldn't believe that the CIA was working so closely with these dreadful security services and then were accepting intelligence which was obviously untrue."

"Fabric of Deceit"

For Tony Blair's government, which had hitched its star tightly to the Bush administration, there was little patience for this outspoken ambassador's persistent criticism of U.S. and British complicity in the Uzbek abuses. In March 2003, just before the invasion of Iraq, Murray was summoned back to London for a meeting. It was there that Sir Michael Wood, chief legal advisor to the British Foreign Office, made an astonishing pronouncement: He said that it wasn't illegal for the UK to use intelligence that was obtained under torture. He confirmed this view in a memo, which Murray later published on his Web site. "He said that as long as we didn't specifically ask for an individual to be tortured—if he was tortured and we were passed the material—then that was not breaking the

UN Convention Against Torture, and therefore the CIA and MI6 were acting perfectly legally in getting this information from torture," recounted Murray. He was told that this was also the view of British Foreign Secretary Jack Straw and the head of MI6. "They had decided that we should continue to receive this intelligence material, which was all CIA-sourced, even though it was obtained through torture."

Murray went so far as to confirm his allegations about torture with the CIA. "I asked my deputy to call up the American Embassy just to make sure I wasn't missing something here and to ask the CIA station there whether they, too, believed that this Uzbek intelligence was probably coming from torture. And so, my deputy went off to the American Embassy. . . . and the American Embassy had said, 'Yes, it probably did come from torture.' But they didn't see that as a problem."

The Western intelligence agencies, he explained, are careful to maintain "a fabric of deniability over the whole thing. They don't actually go into the torture chamber. They receive the intelligence that comes out of the torture chamber, but they don't enter it. The CIA will then process the material, so that when it actually arrives on the desk of Colin Powell, as it was then, or Condoleezza Rice or Donald Rumsfeld, or on the desk of a British minister, it just says this intelligence was got from an Uzbek prisoner related to al Qaeda. It doesn't say who he was. It doesn't say his name. It doesn't say when he was interrogated. So you can't trace it back, in order to say it was that individual and he was tortured in this way. . . . So [Condoleezza Rice] can say, 'I, to my knowledge, have never seen information obtained under torture.' And that's a fabric of deceit set up to enable her to say that."

For Ambassador Murray, the reasons given to justify the invasion of Iraq pushed him to the edge. "I saw George Bush on CNN making a speech the day the real fighting started, where he said we are going in basically to dismantle the torture chambers and the rape rooms. And yet, the United States was subsidizing the torture chambers and the rape rooms in Uzbekistan." Murray said "the sheer hypocrisy of that" led him to cable the British Foreign Office:

> As seen from Tashkent, US policy is not much focused on democracy or freedom. It is about oil, gas and hegemony. In Uzbekistan the US pursues those ends through supporting a ruthless dictatorship. We must not close our eyes to uncomfortable truth.
>
> I watched George Bush talk today of Iraq and "dismantling the apparatus of terror . . . removing the torture chambers and the rape rooms." Yet when it comes to the Karimov regime, systematic torture and rape appear to be treated as peccadilloes, not to affect the relationship and to be downplayed in international fora. Double standards? Yes.[5]

The Blair government was furious at its outspoken ambassador. In August 2003, Murray was called back early from vacation in Canada and told to resign as ambassador to Uzbekistan. He was offered the job of ambassador to "somewhere peaceful, like Copenhagen." Murray declined, saying he was arguing his case internally, as required. He was then handed a list of eighteen "disciplinary allegations" that the British government was going to investigate—including that he was stealing money, drinking, issuing visas in exchange for sex, and a charge that he drove a Land Rover down a flight of stairs to a picnic area (Murray does not drive).[6] He was told he had a week to consider whether or not to resign. Murray refused, insisting the allegations were false. The smears were then leaked to the media. The message was clear: Complaining about British and American complicity in human rights abuses would be punished by character assassination, for starters.

The smear campaign backfired. There were protests at the British Embassy in Tashkent. Fifteen British businessmen in Uzbekistan signed a letter of support for Murray. A formal government investigation ultimately cleared Murray of all charges. But the incident took a personal toll on the human rights crusader: While awaiting the outcome of the investigation, Murray suffered a nervous breakdown and spent ten days recuperating in a London hospital.

Ambassador Murray returned to Uzbekistan for another year. In October 2004, one of his confidential memos was leaked to the *Financial Times*. In it he said that "Uzbekistan is morally beyond the pale, that we shouldn't be treating it as an ally, and we certainly shouldn't be cooperating with the Uzbek security services," he recounted. He was promptly removed as ambassador; he resigned from the Foreign Office four months later. Murray denies leaking the document, and suspects it was done by officials in the British government in order to provide a pretext for sacking him.

James McGrory, a British businessmen in Uzbekistan who co-signed a letter of support for Murray, said there was a "common belief that Mr. Murray is being sacrificed to the Americans."[7]

Bush and the Barbarians

George W. Bush's association with Uzbekistan dates back to his days as governor of Texas, when Enron CEO Kenneth Lay asked him to meet with the Uzbek ambassador. It was 1997, and Enron was arranging a $2 billion deal with Uzbekistan to exploit its natural gas reserves. Bush lent a helping hand, prompting Lay to write that he was "delighted" that Bush would meet the Uzbek officials.

Murray explained that Uzbekistan's energy reserves and its authoritarian government made it irresistible to foreign oil companies. "Central Asia has the largest untapped reserves of oil and gas in the world. Uzbekistan doesn't have much oil; it has a terrific amount of natural gas. And Uzbekistan dominates Central Asia. It has half the population of the whole region. It has, by far, the biggest army and the most muscle. So Uzbekistan was key to the energy policy, and that's why Enron and Halliburton and all of the companies you very much associate with the Bush administration were in there plugging this policy of staying close to Karimov. And that's why he was such a welcome guest in the White House.

"The war on terror was a cover for these activities," asserted the former ambassador. "That's why they needed this false intelligence saying that the Uzbek opposition was all Islamic terrorists . . . the wellspring of the whole policy of the United States was the ruthless pursuit of sectional oil and gas interests, and that originated with Enron. Obviously, once Enron collapsed, those interests passed on to other major U.S. oil companies."

The Bush administration was so tightly allied with the Karimov regime that it provided them with political cover for a notorious massacre in the eastern Uzbek town of Andijan. On May 10, 2005, protests began over the jailing of twenty-three businessmen who the Uzbek government claimed were Islamic extremists. The protesters broke the men out of jail, and in the process freed thousands of other prisoners. By May 12, the protests had intensified, and demonstrators tried to take over government buildings in Andijan. The Uzbek government responded by sealing off the city and then killing over seven hundred people.

Initially, the United States downplayed the killings. On May 13, State Department spokesman Richard Boucher was asked whether the United States blamed the violence on the government of Uzbekistan. Boucher responded: "I would note that while we have been very consistently critical of the human rights situation in Uzbekistan, we're very concerned about the outbreak of violence in Andijan, in particular the escape of prisoners, including possibly members of the Islamic Movement of Uzbekistan, an organization we consider a terrorist organization. I think at this point we're looking to all the parties involved to exercise restraint to avoid any unnecessary loss of life."

Murray, who was no longer ambassador by that time, described the incident as "a dreadful massacre. I mean, what was happening in Andijan was effectively no different from the pro-democracy demonstrations that you saw in Ukraine or in Georgia, that brought down a dictatorial regime." Which is just what the White House was afraid of.

Murray says he "was completely flabbergasted by the White House's approach. On one hand, you've got unarmed pro-democracy demonstrators, and on the other side you've got the government troops with tanks and heavy weapons shooting them down, and the White House called for restraint on both sides. What do they want the people to do, die more peacefully? It really was a sickening response from the United States, but, you know, of a piece with their relationship with the Karimov regime, which they were trying desperately to maintain."

Ultimately, Bush's policy toward Uzbekistan failed in all of its goals. Despite the United States investing about $1 billion in the Karimov regime and even supporting them during the Andijan massacre, the Uzbeks eventually made their lucrative gas deal with Gazprom of Russia in August 2005. Then, on August 1, 2005, the Uzbek government ordered the United States out of the Khanabad military base within six months. Thus was lost a key staging area for the U.S. war in Afghanistan.

Murray mused, "The Bush administration is trying now to put the best possible gloss on it and say, 'We left because of the human rights situation.' Absolutely untrue. The human rights situation seemed not to bother them at all. They left because they were kicked out. . . . They kicked out the Peace Corps, kicked out most American NGOs [non-governmental organizations] and USAID operations.

"We had the very pathetic sight of America having really kow-towed to this terrible dictator, then being humiliated by him and chucked out of the country. So all that loss of moral authority, all that waste of money and resources has come to nothing."

Craig Murray did something remarkable. Confronting an on-slaught of political and media pressure to look the other way in the face of horrendous abuse, he said no. He declined to pull the "fabric of deceit" over the suffering the Uzbek people. And he refused to treat human rights as just another bargaining chip for governments or oil companies to trade with tyrants.

"I think it's just what any decent person would do," Murray told *Democracy Now!* "I mean, when you come across people being boiled and their fingernails pulled out or having their children raped in front of them, you just can't go along with it and sleep at night."

"The emperor's new suit is incomparable!" . . . Nobody wished to let others know he saw nothing, for then he would have been unfit for his office or too stupid.

"But he has nothing on at all," said a little child at last. . . . One whispered to the other what the child had said. "But he has nothing on at all," cried at last the whole people.

—**Hans Christian Andersen (1805–1875),** *The Emperor's New Clothes*

Karen Bauer, Leslie Weise, and Alex Young were eager to hear their president. They had obtained tickets to what was billed as a "conversation on saving Social Security" in Denver in March 2005, at which President Bush was to speak. The three friends obtained tickets from the office of Rep. Bob Beauprez (R-Colo.). But when the trio showed up at a museum for the taxpayer-funded event, they quickly learned that this was to be a one-sided conversation: Bush was only interested in talking with people who agreed with him.

The Denver stop was part of a lavish "60 Stops in 60 Days" road show that the Bush administration undertook in March and April 2005 to sell its controversial plan to privatize Social Security. The tour was one of the most expensive in memory, costing millions of taxpayer dollars. It included 31 administration officials visiting 127 cities, including numerous appearances by President Bush and Vice President Cheney.[1]

Congressmember Henry Waxman, the ranking Democrat on the House Government Reform Committee, requested that the Government Accountability Office determine the exact cost of the Social Security tour. In his letter, Waxman questioned "whether the Bush administration had crossed the line from education to propaganda. . . . There is a vital line between legitimately informing the public, as the President did in his State of the Union address, and commandeering the vast resources of the federal government to fund a political campaign for Social Security privatization."[2]

Privatizing Social Security is part of a longstanding conservative crusade to dismantle or gut most of the major social welfare programs enacted since the Great Depression. President Bush's Social Security tour was intended to scare Americans into thinking that their national retirement plan was about to go broke, despite numerous studies that showed this was untrue. The Bush administration employed its usual propaganda tactics on the tour—limiting the media's access to the president, manufacturing news stories, and mounting elaborate theatrical sets behind the president ("Keeping Our Promise to Seniors" was the slogan that adorned the stage in Denver).

But the Bush administration has taken image control to another level: It has tried to banish anyone who doesn't cheerlead for its policies from getting anywhere near the president.

Throughout the country, wherever President Bush or Vice President Cheney appear, similar stories are told: Anyone who is even suspected of being insufficiently enthusiastic about the president finds him- or herself on lists of banned persons, or is arrested, barred, or harassed. This is occurring at taxpayer-funded events.

Bauer, Weise, and Young were conservatively dressed for the Denver event. But there was one way to glean their political leanings: The car they arrived in sported a "No More Blood for Oil" bumper sticker.

As they approached the auditorium, two of them were stopped by a man wearing a smiley-face tie. But he wasn't smiling. He ordered them to wait "for the Secret Service to arrive."

Minutes later another man appeared. He started threatening them, telling them that they "would be sent to prison and arrested if they pulled anything" while they were inside, Alex Young told *Democracy Now!*

The unidentified man allowed them to enter—but only briefly. About twenty minutes later, the unidentified man "came and grabbed us from the audience and started pushing and shoving us out of the hall," said Young. "We kept asking: 'Why are you doing this? Who are you? Where are we going?' He wouldn't answer any of those questions. This man was wearing a wire. He had one of those earpiece microphones on, and he had a lapel pin similar to a Secret Service agent, wearing a navy blue suit."

But the Secret Service denied that one of their agents was involved in ejecting them. They claimed that it was a member of the Republican host committee that forced them out.

As they were shoved outside, President Bush began his presentation. "We're going to have a serious dialogue on Social Security," he said, sitting beside Sen. John McCain. "It's an issue that requires a lot of dialogue and a lot of discussion."[3]

Alex Young told *Democracy Now!*, "I think that if he's having conversations in America, then we need to have all voices at the table. We need to have dissenting opinions on these programs."[4]

The Denver Three, as they soon dubbed themselves, decided they, too, were interested in dialogue: They demanded to know the name of the self-appointed thought policeman who evicted them while impersonating a Secret Service agent. They were hearing about other people being blocked and ousted from Bush events around the country. Was this part of a pattern?

They brought their case to Washington, where a number of Colorado lawmakers took it up. "Who kicked three of my constituents out of a taxpayer-funded event?" demanded Rep. Diana DeGette (D-Colo.).[5] Inquiries were launched and lawsuits threatened. The Secret Service announced that they knew who the person was, but they weren't telling.

When White House press secretary Scott McClellan was asked about the incident, he said, "If they want to disrupt the event, then I think that obviously they're going to be asked to leave the event."[6]

But the trio have consistently denied that they planned to disrupt anything. The reason they were thrown out of the event was a bumper sticker that Republican operatives didn't like. The Denver Three had political views that were disruptive.

In reality, there was little support for Bush's plan to gut Social Security. A *Washington Post*/ABC News poll in June 2005 found just 34 percent of the country approved of his plan.[7] But reality has always been pliable for Bush. He has learned that if you control the images, you can control the people. The administration that brought us preemptive war was asserting that it could preempt free speech.

In November 2005, Leslie Weise and Alex Young filed a lawsuit against Michael Casper, Jay Bob Klinkerman, and five unnamed individuals who worked with the White House advance team. They charged that these operatives violated their civil rights. Weise and Young believe Casper, a local volunteer for the White House who runs a government office building, was the man posing as a Secret Service agent. Klinkerman, the head of the Colorado Federation of Young Republicans, is accused of being the person who first stopped them.

But these were just the foot soldiers; the orders came from the top. In March 2006, the *Denver Post,* citing a Secret Service report obtained under a Freedom of Information Act request, revealed that the person responsible for ordering the Denver Three ejected was a White House staff member. The staffer had identified the trio as "potential protesters."[8]

"The government should not be in the business of silencing Americans who are perceived to be critical of certain policy decisions," said Chris Hansen, the ACLU senior staff attorney representing Weise and Young. "The president should be willing to be in the same room with people who might disagree with him, especially at a public, taxpayer-funded town hall."[9]

Smart Ass

The Denver Three were just another casualty in the Bush administration's war on dissent—or even the potential for dissent. Hunting down and ferreting out those who disagree with President Bush has become a familiar routine.

The week before the Denver Three became taxpayers non grata at a Bush event, University of Arizona student Steven Gerner was surprised to find that he was deemed too dangerous to be allowed into a town hall meeting with the president. Gerner showed up at the Tucson Convention Center on March 21, 2004, to attend a Social Security forum. He had obtained tickets to the event from Congressman Raúl Grijalva (D-Ariz.). The ticket had his name printed on it.

Gerner, a political science and pre-pharmacy sophomore, happened to be wearing a University of Arizona Young Democrats T-shirt that read, "Don't be a smart [image of a donkey, the Democratic Party symbol]. UA Young Democrats."

"I really wanted a chance to hear the Bush side of the Social Security debate," Gerner told the *Arizona Daily Wildcat*.[10]

After waiting in line for forty minutes, he was approached by an event staffer, who asked to read his T-shirt. Then the man, who refused to provide his name, asked for Gerner's ticket and crumpled it. Twenty minutes later, the man returned and said that Gerner's name had been added to a list of people banned from entering the event. Gerner, who offered to put on a different T-shirt, was told he was a "potential risk."[11]

Blacklisted

"The following are names of area people included on a list of those not to be admitted into the Bison Sports Arena for today's visit by President Bush, according to two unnamed officials close to the visit."

So began a newspaper story in the *Fargo Forum* about President Bush's visit to Fargo, North Dakota, for a town hall meeting about Social Security in February 2005. What followed were the names of forty-two local citizens who had been blacklisted. Among the banned: letter writers to the newspaper who criticized Bush policies; university professors; the producer of a liberal radio talk show; the 2004 Democratic candidate for governor in North Dakota; a high school student who had helped in a campaign supporting civil unions for gay men and lesbians; and a glass artist.[12] Some thirty-three of the forty-two banned people were or had been members of the Fargo-Moorhead Democracy for America meet-up group, liberal Democrats who originally came together around the unsuccessful presidential bid of Howard Dean.

Clearly, these people posed a serious threat to the president. They might . . . disagree with him.

The blacklistings and bannings were supposed to be a stealth operation, made to look as if turning the people away was routine. Everyone entering the event was supposed to write down his or her name and address. Those that matched the blacklist would be denied entry to hear the president. Following the embarrassing revelation of the list in the newspaper, White House spokesperson Jim Morrell promptly announced, "It was the result of an overzealous volunteer. We weren't aware of it here at the White House."[13]

But a spokesperson for North Dakota's Republican governor said he received the list from a White House advance team. And Fargo City Commissioner Linda Coates, whose name was on the list, was told by people at the venue that the list was the work of an "overzealous staffer," not a volunteer. Once again, the identity of the zealot remains a mystery. But the intended effect was obvious.

City Commissioner Coates insisted that people on the list were singled out because of "our history of outspoken opposition to many of the administration's policies."

"Last time I checked that was called democracy," she said. "You know, that noble governance that our country's current leaders are so hot to spread—by force if necessary—around the world."[14]

Bush ended the event in Fargo by saying, "Getting out of Washington is healthy, and getting out amongst the people is invigorating, and I want to thank you for coming out to say hello."

And if you try to say anything else, you'll be arrested.

"I Really Like This Crowd"

During the 2004 election campaign, the Bush administration was obsessed with stage-managing public events to make it appear as if adoring crowds followed Bush and Cheney everywhere they went. One way they accomplished this was by borrowing a technique from the McCarthy era: administering loyalty oaths.

When Vice President Dick Cheney campaigned in Rio Rancho, New Mexico, on July 31, 2004, people interested in attending were told they had to sign a form. John Wade, a 72-year-old retiree from Albuquerque, was astonished by what the form said: "I . . . herby (sic) endorse George W. Bush for reelection of the United States (sic)." The form also noted, "In signing the above endorsement you are consenting to use and release of your name by Bush-Cheney as an endorser of President Bush."[15]

"Whose vice president is he?" asked Wade. "I just wanted to hear what my vice president had to say, and they make me sign a loyalty oath."[16] Wade eventually decided against swearing allegiance to Bush, and demanded his signed form back, which he received after returning the tickets to the event.

Peering out over the throng of people who had sworn allegiance to him, Cheney declared at Rio Rancho Mid-High School, "I really like this crowd."[17]

Obscene

When President Bush traveled to Oregon in 2004 for a campaign rally, he faced what his handlers described as "potential risks." Was it al Qaeda? A deranged assassin?

Not quite. It was three teachers from Medford, Oregon, wearing T-shirts that read, "Protect Our Civil Liberties."

The teachers had heard about the crackdown on dissent at other Bush rallies. "We chose this phrase specifically because we didn't think it would be offensive or degrading," said Tania Tong, 34, a special education teacher.[18]

The women cleared several security checkpoints until they were intercepted by campaign officials, who allegedly told them their T-shirts were "obscene." The three teachers were threatened with arrest and thrown out of the rally.

A month earlier, Vice President Cheney visited Eugene, Oregon. Perry Patterson, 54, was hauled out and cited for criminal trespassing for shouting in the middle of a speech by the vice president.

Patterson, who has sons ages 16 and 22, hadn't planned her outburst. She had intended to ask about the reinstatement of the draft, which she worries about for her sons. She is a registered Democrat and had never demonstrated at a political event. But she was struck by something in the crowd: There were no protesters, no signs, nothing that would suggest anything but support for America's leaders. "It felt eerily un-American," she told the *Eugene Weekly*.[19]

After Cheney declared that Bush had "made the world a safer place," Patterson suddenly blurted out, "No! No! No!" "It emotionally felt like if your child ran into the street. It was not conscious, but it had to be done," she recounted. A judge dismissed the trespassing charge the following month, but in early 2006, Patterson filed a lawsuit against the "men in black"—the Secret Service suggested that they were members of Cheney's staff—who physically ejected her from the event.

The Bush campaign was also being vigilant in Iowa. The *Boston Globe* told the story of Nick Lucy, a 64-year-old veteran. He was barred from a Bush rally in Dubuque on May 7, 2004, even though a local Republican leader had given him a ticket. Lucy has gone to see every president since Ronald Reagan. So much for his patriotic winning streak: Although he is a past commander of the American Legion in Dubuque who plays taps at veterans' funerals, he is not a registered Republican.

"They asked the police to escort me out of there," Lucy told the *Globe*. "I wasn't going to disrupt anything, but I probably wasn't going to clap a lot, either. Every rally the president goes to everyone is cheering for him because they're handpicked. No wonder he thinks everything's just fine."[20]

Four More Years!

When President Bush is in trouble, he often dispatches his wife to put a kinder, family-friendly face on his policies. But when Laura Bush came to campaign for her husband in New Jersey in September 2004, she didn't bargain for confronting another mother—one who was suffering the consequences of Bush's policies.

Sue Niederer of Hopewell, New Jersey, decided to confront the First Lady at a campaign rally at a local firehouse. Niederer's son, Army 1st Lt. Seth Dvorin, 24, was killed in Iraq in February 2004 while trying to disarm a bomb. Niederer showed up at the firehouse rally wearing a T-shirt that read, "President Bush You Killed My Son," over a picture of Dvorin.

Niederer, a short, bespectacled suburban mom, interrupted the First Lady and demanded to know why her son died. As if on cue, the audience broke into a chant: "Four more years!" The grieving mom was undeterred. When the chanting died down, she persisted. When Bush mentioned the troops in Iraq, Niederer interrupted again. "When are yours going to serve?" she challenged, referring to Bush's 22-year-old twin daughters, who are not in the military. At this point, she was handcuffed, placed in a police van, and charged with trespassing, despite the fact that she held a ticket for the event.

Laura Bush continued her speech, following her husband's script of connecting the 9/11 attacks with the war in Iraq, despite the fact that no such link has ever been found. "Too many people here had a loved one that went to work in New York that day," Bush said. "It's for our country, it's for our children, our grandchildren that we do the hard work of confronting terror."[21]

Meanwhile, Niederer held a makeshift news conference in the police station lobby. "I was denied my freedom of speech," she declared.

It turns out that the "spontaneous" crowd response to the grieving mom was carefully planned. As CBS News reported, 20-year-old volunteer Karolina Zabawa was deployed in the crowd with instructions for what to do in case of an outburst of free speech.

"If anybody acts up, I just start chanting, 'Four more years!'" said the college student.[22]

Bursting Bush's Bubble

President Bush travels inside a hermetically sealed safety zone. Inside this zone, there are no protesters, no unanticipated questions, just his acolytes. His safety zone has steadily shrunk in tandem with his job approval ratings; he now rarely addresses audiences outside of people in uniform, government employees, deep-pocketed fund-raisers, or Republican supporters.

Take the days following Bush's State of the Union Address on January 31, 2006. On February 2, he attended the National Prayer Breakfast at the Washington Hilton Hotel. Then it was off that evening to speak on "American competitiveness" at the Minnesota headquarters of the 3M Corporation (total spent on 2004 election: $256,860; 85 percent to Republicans).[23] The next day, he was off to New Mexico to speak at Intel Corporation (total spent on 2004 election: $286,864; 77 percent to Republicans). On February 6, it was over to the Federal Reserve for the swearing in of new Federal Reserve chairman Ben Bernanke, a Bush appointee.

But on February 7, in a rare moment, President Bush was forced to step outside his bubble. The occasion was the funeral for Coretta Scott King, wife of slain civil rights leader Martin Luther King Jr. There at New Birth Missionary Church in Lithonia, Georgia, the president was exposed, ever so briefly, to the public. It was an event Bush couldn't miss—Presidents Clinton and Carter and his father, George H. W. Bush, attended, as did three governors, at least fourteen senators, and dozens of Congress members. As speakers rose to honor the life and work of Mrs. King, Bush—who was sitting onstage in the camera view, just behind the podium— had no choice but to listen to people who thought differently than he did. It was that rare event that Bush couldn't script or control, and it provided an opportunity for Bush's critics—the two-thirds of the country who didn't approve of his presidency at that moment— to let him know what was on their minds.

The Reverend Joseph Lowery, cofounder of the Southern Christian Leadership Conference, praised Mrs. King by criticizing the priorities of the current administration: "She extended Martin's message against poverty, racism, and war. She deplored the terror inflicted by our smart bombs on missions. We know now that there were no weapons of mass destruction over there. But Coretta knew, and we know, that there are weapons of misdirection right down here. Millions without health insurance. Poverty abounds. For war billions more, but no more for the poor."[24] Lowery's remarks were followed by a standing ovation by much of the audience of fifteen thousand.

Former President Jimmy Carter spoke at King's funeral and made a pointed reference to Bush's warrantless wiretapping of

Americans: "The efforts of Martin and Coretta have changed America. They were not appreciated even at the highest level of government. It was difficult for them personally—with the civil liberties of both husband and wife violated as they became the target of secret government wiretapping, other surveillance, and as you know, harassment from the FBI."

Carter continued, "The struggle for equal rights is not over. We only have to recall the color of the faces of those in Louisiana, Alabama, and Mississippi, those who are most devastated by Katrina, to know that there are not yet equal opportunities for all Americans. It is our responsibility to continue their crusade."

Poet Maya Angelou also eulogized her friend, and announced that she was standing on the stage for, among others, the famous entertainer and activist Harry Belafonte, a close friend of the King family. It wasn't until a month later that Belafonte revealed on *Democracy Now!* that he had been disinvited from delivering a eulogy for his friend Coretta Scott King. Weeks before the funeral, Belafonte made international headlines when he denounced President Bush as "the greatest terrorist in the world" while appearing alongside President Hugo Chavez in Venezuela. King's children had asked Belafonte to deliver a eulogy. But the day before the funeral—and two days after President Bush announced he would be attending—Belafonte was informed by family representatives that plans had changed: He could attend the service, but he could not speak. Belafonte chose not to attend. (In late April 2006, the King family issued a statement denying that Belafonte had been disinvited or that the White House had pressured them, but said that they "sincerely regret any hurt feelings over this misunderstanding.")

Belafonte was saddened by what he saw of his friend's funeral on TV. It appeared to be an extension of Bush's bubble—with a few notable exceptions. "I saw all of the power of the oppressor represented on the stage, and all those who fought for the victories that this nation was experiencing and enjoying sat in the outhouse, sat out in the field, sat removed. And if it had not been for Lowery, for President Carter, and for Maya Angelou, we would have had no voice and no representation at all."

Following the funeral, President Bush swiftly retreated back to his bubble: The next day he addressed the Business and Industry Association in Manchester, New Hampshire, and two days later, he was speaking about the war on terror before the National Guard Association of the United States.

While Bush moved on, the media was abuzz about the funeral—slamming what Bush's critics said.

Speaking on Fox's *Special Report with Brit Hume,* *Weekly Standard* editor Fred Barnes said, "This happens to be Jimmy Carter's style right now. He is a cheap partisan, very petty man, picking at George Bush."[25]

On that same show, Fox re-aired part of the Reverend Lowery's remarks, editing out the twenty-three seconds of applause and standing ovation that followed his statement on Iraq. After seeing the doctored clip, *Roll Call*'s Morton Kondracke concluded that the audience "wasn't exactly uproarious in its response to Lowery."[26]

"It's all hate, and it's all anger," said Republican strategist Mary Matalin on Fox's *Hannity & Colmes.* "These civil rights leaders are nothing more than racists. And they're keeping their constituency, they're keeping their neighborhoods and their African-American brothers enslaved, if you will, by continuing to let them think that they're—or forced to think that they're victims."[27]

It made us think: What would Martin Luther King have done in this situation? For an answer, we turned to King's famous "Letter from Birmingham Jail," written in April 1963 to fellow Southern clergymen. King was responding to "A Call for Unity" issued by eight Alabama clergymen, who pointedly criticized civil rights demonstrations being undertaken by King and others in Birmingham. "We recognize the natural impatience of people who feel that their hopes are slow in being realized," declared the clergymen, "but we are convinced that these demonstrations are unwise and untimely." The Alabama clergymen praised the restraint of local police and counseled blacks to be patient. "When rights are consistently denied, a cause should be pressed in the courts and in negotiations among local leaders, and not in the streets," they stated.

King responded four days later from the Birmingham city jail, where he was placed after being arrested during a peaceful demonstration against segregation. Scribbling in the margins of newspapers and on scraps of paper that a sympathetic black guard provided to him, King insisted that civil rights would never be attained without direct action. "Freedom is never voluntarily given by the oppressor; it must be demanded by the oppressed," he wrote.

King scoffed at the idea that African-Americans should confine their protest to polite private conversations or the courts. He chastised his critics for being more concerned about protests than they were about the racism that inspired the marches. As for the accusation that he was pushing too far, too fast, King countered, "The world [is] in dire need of creative extremists."

King could just as well be writing about America under George W. Bush. But if he was—especially if he were at an event with this president—he'd probably end up back in the Birmingham jail.

17. We Interrupt This Program . . .

L'etat, c'est moi. —Louis XIV (1638–1715), King of France

I am the decider. —George W. Bush (2006), U.S. President

Just after midnight on December 3, 1984, residents of Bhopal, India, awoke to the sound of screams. People were staggering into the street, their eyes, noses, and mouths burning. Residents described a thick white cloud entering their homes, followed by a burning and suffocating sensation. All hell broke loose in the densely populated city. People ran in panic. Soon they began coughing and vomiting up blood. A survivor, Champa Devi Shukla, remembers, "Those who fell were not picked up by anybody. They just kept falling, and were trampled on by other people. People climbed and scrambled over each other to save their lives—even cows were running and trying to save their lives and crushing people as they ran."[1]

The toxic cloud came from the Union Carbide plant located in Bhopal. In all, some 27 tons of the deadly gas methyl isocyanate leaked out after the six safety systems designed to contain the leak failed. A half million people were exposed to the gas. About 7,000 people died immediately, and roughly 20,000 more people have died as a result of being poisoned.[2] The shuttered Union Carbide plant has never been completely cleaned up, and toxic waste continues to poison residents of Bhopal. In 2001, Dow Chemical purchased Union Carbide, acquiring the company's liabilities. Dow has continued where Carbide left off: It has refused to clean up the site or provide safe drinking water, or fairly compensate victims.

Some 150,000 people continue to suffer chronic illnesses that stem from the 1984 accident.[3]

Union Carbide has long denied responsibility for the world's worst industrial accident. It claimed that its Indian subsidiary, in which it owned a 51 percent stake, was to blame. But documents obtained in 2004 by the London daily *The Independent* reveal "the intimate and extensive involvement of UCC [Union Carbide] in procuring equipment, designing and providing technical services to the plant in Bhopal." The American company was involved in procuring "safety equipment" and "control instrumentation"—both of which failed on that December night in 1984. Another company memo revealed that Union Carbide slashed 335 jobs from its Bhopal plant the year before the accident, saving $1.25 million. "Future savings will not be easy," the confidential Union Carbide memo concluded, hinting that the cuts might jeopardize the plant's operations. Warren Anderson, then chairman of Union Carbide, has refused to answer a summons in India to face charges of culpable homicide.[4] He was recently discovered living comfortably in retirement in the Hamptons.

This tale of corporate negligence and the continuing tragedy of Bhopal has received scant mention in the world's press, save for the obligatory anniversary stories. So Jacques Servin was surprised to receive an e-mail from the BBC at his Paris apartment in late November 2004. The BBC was airing a story to mark the twentieth anniversary of the disaster. The e-mail, which was addressed to the website www.dowethics.com, requested an interview with a Dow spokesman to discuss the company's position on the Bhopal disaster.

Had the BBC producers looked a little closer, they would have noticed that the Web site bears the Dow logo, but actually spoofs the company's *lack* of ethics. It was a creation of the Yes Men, an activist group that specializes in performing high-profile "identity corrections" for ethically challenged companies.

With the major media so loath to spotlight the crimes of their advertisers and corporate sponsors, it has fallen to activists to break the sound barrier to bring attention to these hidden stories. The Yes Men use parody as a weapon to pierce the wall of silence imposed by the corporate media. As the Yes Men note, "In the U.S. at least, you can't cover the World Trade Organization (WTO) or the Bhopal anniversary just because they're tremendously important. We can provide the fodder, sometimes, that lets these subjects get covered." In 2004, the Yes Men "campaigned" in the United States for George W. Bush. They circulated petitions asking people to support global warming, and asked Bush supporters to sign a pledge agreeing to keep nuclear waste in their backyard and send their children off to war. In May 2006, the Yes Men, impersonating Halliburton officials, spoke at an insurance industry conference on "catastrophic loss." They demonstrated the Halliburton "survive-a-ball"—an orblike inflatable suit designed for corporate executives to survive a global warming–induced flood.

So when the BBC contacted dowethics.com, the Yes Men were ready. Servin threw on a cheap suit and went to the BBC's Paris studio, where he transformed into Dow spokesman Jude Finisterra. Here is what he announced in a live broadcast on the BBC on December 3, 2004:

JUDE FINISTERRA: Today is a great day for all of us at Dow, and I think for millions of people around the world, as well. It is twenty years since the disaster, and today I'm very, very happy to announce that for the first time Dow is accepting full responsibility for the Bhopal catastrophe. We have a $12 billion plan to finally, at long last, fully compensate the victims, including the 120,000 who may need medical care for their entire lives, and to fully and swiftly remediate the Bhopal plant site. . . . We have resolved to liquidate Union Carbide, this nightmare for the world and this headache for Dow, and use the $12 billion to provide *more* than $500 per victim, which is all that they have [received to date]—a maximum of just about $500 per victim. It is not "plenty good for an Indian," as one of our spokespersons unfortunately said a couple of years ago. In fact, it pays for one year of medical care. . . . When Union Carbide abandoned the site sixteen years ago, they left tons of toxic waste. The site continues to be used as a playground by children. Water continues to be drunk from the groundwater underneath. It is a mess, Steve, and we need a Dow—

BBC WORLD: It's a mess, certainly, Jude. That's good news that you have finally accepted responsibility. Some people would say too late, three years, almost four years on. How soon is your money going to make a difference to the people in Bhopal?

FINISTERRA: Well, as soon as we can get it to them, Steve. We have begun the process of liquidating Union Carbide. I would say that it is better late than never, and I would also like to say that this is no small matter, Steve. This is the first time in history that a publicly owned company of anything near the size of Dow has performed an action which is significantly against its bottom line simply because it's the right thing to do. And our shareholders may take a bit of a hit, Steve, but I think that if they are anything like me they will be ecstatic to be part of such a historic occasion of doing right by those that we have wronged.

BBC WORLD: And does this mean you will also cooperate in any future legal actions in India or the USA?

FINISTERRA: Absolutely, Steve. One of our nonfinancial commitments is to press the United States government to finally extradite Warren Anderson, who fled India after being arrested in 1984. He posted $2,000 bail on multiple homicide charges and fled India promptly. . . . We are going to release finally the full composition of the chemicals and the studies that were performed by Union Carbide shortly after the catastrophe. . . . And finally, we're going to . . . fund, with no strings attached, research into the safety of any Dow product. . . . We do not want to be a company that sells products that may have long-term negative effects on the world.

BBC WORLD: Jude, we will leave it there. Thank you for joining us. Just to reiterate what Jude Finisterra, the spokesman for Dow Chemical has just said, he says Dow Chemical now fully accepts responsibility for the events in Bhopal twenty years ago. And they will cooperate in future legal action.[5]

Could this be true: Dow Chemical taking responsibility and making restitution for the corporate crime of the century? As this historic event unfolded, the BBC flashed a "BREAKING NEWS" banner across the bottom of the screen. In Frankfurt, Dow's share price fell 4.2 percent in 23 minutes, wiping $2 billion off its market value before recovering all the day's losses three hours later.

Alas, it was but a fleeting mirage. An hour after the news segment aired, Dow spokesperson Marina Ashanin issued the following disclaimer:

This morning a false statement was carried by *BBC World* regarding responsibility for the Bhopal tragedy. The individual who made the statement identified himself as a Dow spokesperson named Jude Finisterra. Dow confirms that there was no basis whatsoever for this report, and we also confirm that Jude Finisterra is neither an employee nor a spokesperson for Dow.

Jacques Servin's nom de plume was carefully chosen: Jude is the patron saint of impossible causes, he explained to *Democracy Now!*, and Finisterra means "end of the earth," which the Yes Men declared "kind of represents the situation" in Bhopal.[6]

With their cover blown, the Yes Men decided to come clean . . . sort of. They issued a press release about the incident, purportedly from Dow, to clarify the company's stand on Bhopal. Many media outlets ran this as an actual statement from Dow Chemical:

> On December 3, 2004, a fake Dow spokesperson announced on *BBC World* television fake plans to take full responsibility for the very real Bhopal tragedy of December 3, 1984. Dow Chemical emphatically denies this announcement. Although seemingly humanistic in nature, the fake plans were invented by irresponsible hucksters with no regard for the truth.
>
> As Dow has repeatedly noted, Dow cannot and will not take responsibility for the accident. ("What we cannot and will not do . . . is accept responsibility for the Bhopal accident."—CEO Michael Parker, 2002.) The Dow position has not changed, despite public pressure. . . .
>
> To be perfectly clear:
>
> - The Union Carbide Corporation (UCC) will NOT be liquidated. (The fake "Dow plan" called for the dissolution and sale of Dow's fully owned subsidiary, estimated at US$12 billion, to fund compensation and remediation in Bhopal.)
> - Dow will NOT commit ANY funds to compensate and treat 120,000 Bhopal residents who require lifelong care. The Bhopal victims have ALREADY been compensated; many received about US$500 several years ago, which in India can cover a full year of medical care.
> - Dow will NOT remediate (clean up) the Bhopal plant site. We do understand that UCC abandoned thousands of tons of toxic chemicals on the site, and that these still contaminate the groundwater which area residents drink. Dow estimates that the Indian government's recent proposal to commission a study to consider the possibility of proper remediation at some point in the future is fully sufficient.

- Dow does NOT urge the US to extradite former Union Carbide CEO Warren Anderson to India, where he has been wanted for twenty years on multiple homicide charges. . . .

Most important of all:

- Dow shareholders will see NO losses, because Dow's policy towards Bhopal HAS NOT CHANGED. Much as we at Dow may care, as human beings, about the victims of the Bhopal catastrophe, we must reiterate that Dow's sole and unique responsibility is to its shareholders, and Dow CANNOT do anything that goes against its bottom line unless forced to by law.[7]

With a deft mix of humor, information, and theatrics, the Yes Men shifted the perspective of the reporting about the corporate crime of the century. For a brief moment, the world considered the Bhopal story from the perspective of the victims, and how long justice had been denied.

The Yes Men were criticized by some for raising false hopes among Bhopal survivors, and for tricking the BBC. "We may have given people two hours of false hope," Servin said of the Yes Men's action. "Dow has given them twenty years of suffering."[8]

A Stranger in Their Midst

It was billed by CNN as an International Town Meeting, a place in the heartland where Clinton administration officials could safely sell their plan to bomb Iraq. It was February 18, 1998, and Secretary of State Madeleine Albright was expecting the usual: handpicked questioners and carefully screened audiences to which she could present unchallenged the Clinton administration's case for attacking Iraq. The administration's push for war was sparked by confrontations with Saddam Hussein over keeping UN weapons inspectors in Iraq. As former UN weapons inspector Scott Ritter has argued on *Democracy Now!,* these confrontations were not "about disarming Iraq. It was about maintaining economic sanctions as a vehicle of containing Saddam until you could overthrow him."[9]

The controversy over UN inspections of Iraq occurred against the backdrop of Bill Clinton's mounting scandals. Indeed, impeachment hearings in the House of Representatives in December 1998 were delayed by a day when joint U.S.-British attacks were launched on Iraq just as the hearings were scheduled to get under way.

Albright, like other politicians who agree to participate in such purportedly unscripted encounters with the public, was assured that these events are carefully stage-managed. Albright had come to Ohio State University with National Security Advisor Sandy Berger and Defense Secretary William Cohen. This troika, the ABC of Clinton's war cabinet, was expecting a feel-good pep rally. As an account in the *Columbus Free Press* explained, "Unlike a real town meeting, admittance to this event was highly selective. First there were the red tickets given out for the 1,000 seats out on the arena floor. Red ticket holders would be the only ones with a chance to ask a question. (Yet everyone with a red floor ticket who wished to pose a question to the panel would first have to submit it in writing on a three-by-five card. If the White House or CNN didn't like your question, you didn't get to ask it.) Ohio State University would recommend certain local and university groups for red ticket eligibility and CNN would either approve or disapprove them. Groups receiving these red tickets included the ROTC, various veterans groups, active duty military, the League of Women Voters, university professors and staff. As well, forty student groups were approved. Yet many student groups, including two environmental groups, were disapproved and effectively barred. Then there were white tickets for the 6,000 seats in the bleacher stands. White ticket holders would absolutely not be allowed to ask questions . . ."[10]

So much for a freewheeling discussion. But community members were not so willing to play the part of cheerleaders. Concerned and skeptical citizens and activists lined up to get tickets to the event days in advance. The result: The Clinton officials came to sell war, but this audience wasn't buying. When Albright started to speak, some protesters began chanting, "One, two, three, four, we don't want your racist war." Others unfurled a banner: "No War."[11] CNN reported, "The heckling became so intense at one point that Albright interrupted CNN's Judy Woodruff and said, 'Could you tell those people I'll be happy to talk to them when this is over? I'd like to make my point.' "[12]

CNN handlers came out to negotiate with audience members who were angry that they could not ask questions. The network finally agreed to allow one person who was not in the preapproved front rows to ask a question. It fell to Jon Strange, a 22-year-old substitute teacher in the Columbus public schools, to take on the leading hawks of the Clinton administration. He walked to the front to ask his question:

JON STRANGE: Why bomb Iraq when other countries have committed similar violations? Turkey, for example, has bombed Kurdish citizens. Saudi Arabia has tortured political and religious dissidents. Why does the U.S. apply different standards of justice to these countries?

SECRETARY OF STATE MADELEINE ALBRIGHT: Let me say that when there are problems such as you have described, we point them out and make very clear our opposition to them. But there is no one that has done to his people and his neighbors what Saddam Hussein has done or what he is thinking about doing. . . .

STRANGE: What about Indonesia?

ALBRIGHT: . . . Saddam Hussein has produced weapons of mass destruction which he is clearly not collecting for his own personal pleasure, but in order to use. And therefore he is qualitatively and quantitatively different from every brutal dictator that has appeared recently. And we are very concerned about him specifically and what his plans might be.

STRANGE: What do you have to say about dictators in countries like Indonesia, who we sell weapons to, yet they are slaughtering people in East Timor? What do you have to say about Israel, who is slaughtering Palestinians and who imposed martial law? What do you have to say about that? Those are our allies. Why do we sell weapons to these countries? Why do we support them? Why do we bomb Iraq when it commits similar problems? [Audience cheers, applause, drowns him out.]

ALBRIGHT: There are various examples of things that are not right in this world and the United States is trying—[Shouting.] I really am surprised that people feel that it is necessary to defend the rights of Saddam Hussein when what we ought to be thinking about is how to make sure that he does not use weapons of mass destruction.

JUDY WOODRUFF, CNN: People are shouting . . . just a moment. . . .

STRANGE: I am not defending him in the least. What I am saying is that there needs to be a consistent application of U.S. foreign policy. We cannot support people who are committing the same violations because they are political allies. That is not acceptable. We cannot violate UN resolutions when it is convenient to us. You're not answering my question, Madame Albright. [Applause, cheers.]

ALBRIGHT: I suggest, sir, that you study carefully what American foreign policy is, what we have said exactly about the cases you have mentioned. Every one of them has been pointed out. Every one of them we have clearly stated our policy on. And if you would like, as a former professor, I would be delighted to spend fifty minutes with you describing exactly what we are doing on those subjects.[13]

The audience was shouting at Albright, and CNN host Judy Woodruff admonished them: "The more time you take shouting, the more time you take away from people who have questions." But then Woodruff picked up where Jon Strange left off:

WOODRUFF: Secretary, I do have a brief follow-up and that is on this point. There are many countries that have these biological and chemical weapons—six countries in the Middle East alone. You've stated why Saddam Hussein should be singled out. But it is puzzling to people who wonder why it's okay for other countries to have these biological and chemical weapons, but not for Iraq.

ALBRIGHT: I think that it is clear that other countries have weapons of mass destruction. It is a question of whether there is a proclivity to use them, and Saddam Hussein is a repeat offender. I think it is very important for us to make clear that the U.S. and the civilized world cannot deal with somebody who is willing to use those weapons of mass destruction on his own people, not to speak of his neighbors.

Jon Strange asked the impolite questions that all reporters should ask—making it safe for Woodruff to press the point. This was on live TV, so the Clinton administration officials could not hide from the anger sparked by their policies. Strange's challenge was heard by some 200 million people around the world. His exchange was followed by angry questions from other audience members shouted to the administration officials. CNN described a "heckler" criticizing the entire affair, saying it was not a town meeting but "a media event staged by CNN." The network also recounted how another "heckler" asked how Albright, Cohen, and Berger could sleep at night, knowing that innocent Iraqis would be killed and injured by any military strike.

The unidentified man in the audience addressed the trio: "We will not send messages to Saddam Hussein with the blood of the

Iraqi people. If you want to deal with Saddam, deal with Saddam, not the Iraqi people."

Albright shot back, "What we are doing is so that you all can sleep at night." She continued, shouting over the audience, "I am very proud of what we are doing. We are the greatest nation in the world. . . ."[14]

Albright hurried away immediately after the event. Jon Strange's promised fifty-minute lecture never happened.

The following day on *Democracy Now!*, Kathy Kelly, founder of Voices in the Wilderness, spoke from Iraq, where she was bringing food and medical supplies to hospitals that were suffering under sanctions. The CNN Town Hall was watched widely in Iraq. Kelly said, "I think many people here derived encouragement from it. People said to me 'There's no support for military strikes in the Middle East, and not even in the U.S.' . . . I spent most of the day in the hospital today, where mothers said to me, 'We need medicine. We need milk. We don't need bombs.' "[15]

This is how it is in our democracy today: Government leaders and the corporate media collude to protect those in power from being challenged. In a theatrical routine that has been perfected in recent years by the Bush administration, CNN and the Clinton administration used the trappings of participatory democracy as a prop behind which they could avoid having to answer tough questions. This is how the echo chamber of government and media works. People who disagree with the government are frozen out of the one-sided "debate" and are then reduced to having to shout their concerns or questions. They are labeled "hecklers," and caricatured and dismissed. Were they allowed to freely question their leaders—as the pro-war pundits get to do—they could be described differently: as concerned citizens.

Jon Strange was aware that his impertinent questions angered the administration and CNN. As he told *Democracy Now!* the next day, "I don't think this is what they had in mind."

Death-Defying Activism

In 1981, the Centers for Disease Control's newsletter reported five unrelated cases of pneumonia in homosexual men in the Los Angeles area. Two of them had already died. The report generated little interest. This was the quiet, deadly start of the AIDS epidemic.

As the death toll mounted, people with AIDS and their allies found themselves up against incredible odds: a government that refused to acknowledge the disease (President Reagan never mentioned AIDS publicly during his first term in office); government bureaucrats who dragged their feet on drug approval; right-wing leaders who called the disease "God's revenge on gays"; brutal police who wore rubber gloves while beating up activists; and a homophobic general population that stood by silently watching.

AIDS activists needed a way to break through this deadly complacency. Taking inspiration from the civil rights movement, their creative confrontations brought unprecedented attention to this hidden plague:

- *October 11, 1988:* The newly formed AIDS Coalition to Unleash Power—ACT UP—shuts down the Food and Drug Administration building in Washington. They demand increased funding for and easier access to promising AIDS drugs.
- *September 14, 1989:* ACT UP members stage a demonstration on the floor of the New York Stock Exchange, stopping trading for the first time in history. The activists demand that traders sell stock in Burroughs Wellcome (now GlaxoSmithKline), which was the only maker of the AIDS drug AZT, for which it charged exorbitant prices.
- *December 1989:* ACT UP members lie down in the center aisle of St. Patrick's Cathedral in New York City to protest the role of the Catholic church in interfering with AIDS education in the public schools.

As AIDS continued its deadly course, activists grew increasingly frustrated at how little the media covered the disease, and at the misplaced priorities of the government. The two issues converged in January 1991, when President George H. W. Bush launched the Persian Gulf War. John Weir, a member of ACT UP in New York City, was planning for a protest dubbed "Day of Desperation" in New York City, which aimed to protest both the war and the inadequate response to AIDS.

Weir and two other activists decided to make a surprise appearance on *CBS Evening News* with Dan Rather the night before the Day of Desperation. Another ACT UP member, Ann Northrup, was a former CBS producer. She provided them with directions to Rather's studio and an old CBS ID tag to gain entrance to the building.

On January 22, 1991, Dan Rather began his broadcast in the usual fashion: "This is *The CBS Evening News*, Dan Rather reporting. Good Evening—"

Suddenly, John Weir's head popped into the frame in front of Rather. "Fight AIDS not Arabs! Fight AIDS not Arabs!" he shouted with two others.

Rather stared straight ahead, but appeared startled. He announced urgently, "We're going to go to take a quick break for a commercial now." Studio technicians grabbed the men, hauled them off the set, and they were later taken to jail.

A grim-faced Rather appeared after the break. "I want to apologize to you for the way the broadcast came on the air tonight. There were some rude people here. They tried to stage a demonstration. They've been ejected from the studio, but our apologies for the way we began our coverage of the Gulf War. We will continue after these messages."

Meanwhile, another ACT UP group was staging an action a few blocks away at PBS, on the set of *The MacNeil/Lehrer Newshour*. Activists sat down during the live broadcast and chained themselves to chairs and a desk. The action prompted a discussion between the hosts. Robert MacNeil explained what happened to the viewing audience:

"There's been a demonstration in our studio. It was a group of nonviolent demonstrators from ACT UP who complained that we and the media are spending too much time and attention on the war in the Middle East, which they say will never kill as many people as are dying of AIDS. And I told them that this program has spent a lot of time on the AIDS matter and will be covering it more in the future."

On ACT UP's Web site, they recounted how a reporter questioned the disrupters afterward: "Don't you think this is an immature and silly way to get your point across to the country?"

The activists responded, "No, we think spending hundreds of billions of dollars bombing people in another continent is a silly and immature way to get a point across."[16]

As Ann Northrup recounted later on *Democracy Now!*, "I thought it was fantastic because this interruption of the CBS news was seen all over the world. CNN ran it as a story, and I remember the columnist Jimmy Breslin told me that he was in Israel at the time trying to cover the Gulf War and he saw it on CNN. This did make an impact everywhere.

"The whole point of all these actions was to get AIDS into the news, to get it talked about, to get it recognized and looked at as an issue," she explained. "Because what happens is these issues we care about get ignored by the mainstream media. What we've learned as activists is that we have to do things that will grab attention to get the issue covered. Our aim has always been not to be liked personally, but simply do whatever we need to do to get these things covered."

She said of ACT UP: "We do not defer to authority. And I think that's what has made us so effective. We are willing to speak the truth under any circumstances."

Some Unexpected *Crossfire*

Comedian Jon Stewart, host of *The Daily Show* on Comedy Central, has been making waves with his nightly parody of the day's news. His straight-faced takeoffs of journalists and politicians often serve as biting indictments of official hypocrisy and media complicity. That's what earned the fake news anchor an invitation to be a guest on CNN's *Crossfire*, a political show that featured hosts Tucker Carlson, the house conservative, and former Clinton aide Paul Begala.

But when Carlson and Begala began their live interview on October 15, 2004, they did not bargain for the political comedian aiming some sharp criticism at them. Here is an excerpt of their exchange:

JON STEWART: I made a special effort to come on the show today, because I have privately, amongst my friends and also in occasional newspapers and television shows, mentioned this show as being bad.

PAUL BEGALA: We have noticed.

STEWART: . . . It's not so much that it's bad, as it's hurting America. But I wanted to come here today and say: Stop, stop, stop, stop hurting America. . . .

Right now, you're helping the politicians and the corporations. And we're left out there to mow our lawns.

BEGALA: By beating up on them? You just said we're too rough on them when they make mistakes.

STEWART: No, no, no. You're not too rough on them. You're part of their strategies. You are partisan—what do you call it?—hacks. . . . It's not honest. What you do is not honest. What you do is partisan hackery. And I will tell you why I know it.

TUCKER CARLSON: You had John Kerry on your show and you sniff his throne and you're accusing us of partisan hackery?

STEWART: Absolutely.

CARLSON: You've got to be kidding me. He comes on and you . . .

STEWART: You're on CNN. The show that leads into me is puppets making crank phone calls! What is wrong with you?

CARLSON: Well, I'm just saying, there's no reason for you—when you have this marvelous opportunity not to be the guy's butt boy—to go ahead and be his butt boy. Come on. It's embarrassing.

STEWART: . . . You have a responsibility to the public discourse, and you fail miserably.

CARLSON: You need to get a job at a journalism school, I think.

STEWART: You need to go to one. The thing that I want to say is, when you have people on for just knee-jerk, reactionary talk . . .

CARLSON: Wait. I thought you were going to be funny. Come on. Be funny.

STEWART: No. No. I'm not going to be your monkey.

BEGALA: Go ahead. Go ahead.

STEWART: I watch your show every day. And it kills me.

CARLSON: I can tell you love it.

STEWART: It's so painful to watch. [Laughter.] You know, because we need what you do. This is such a great opportunity you have here to actually get politicians off of their marketing and strategy.

CARLSON: Is this really Jon Stewart? What is this, anyway?

STEWART: Yes, it's someone who watches your show and cannot take it anymore. I just can't . . .

CARLSON: I do think you're more fun on your show. Just my opinion. . . .

STEWART: You know what's interesting, though? You're as big a dick on your show as you are on any show. [Laughter.]

CARLSON: Now you're getting into it. I like that. Okay. We'll be right back.[17]

After the laughter died down, Stewart's criticism hit its mark. On January 4, 2005, CNN president Jonathan Klein canceled *Cross-*

fire and terminated Carlson's relationship with the network. The key reason cited by Klein: "I agree wholeheartedly with Jon Stewart's overall premise" that viewers are interested in information, not opinion.[18]

If only CNN applied the same standard to the rest of its coverage.

A Little "Truthiness"

Every year, the leaders of the corporate media gather for a ritual of schmoozing, backslapping, and joking around with the power elite they cover—and cover for. The occasion is the White House Correspondents' Association annual dinner, at which celebrities, journalists, and the president join for a lighthearted evening.

But by mid-2006, it was getting harder to joke about the lying, incompetence, and lawbreaking of the Bush administration. As the elites were dusting off their tuxedos, revelations were spilling forth daily about the relentless and unprecedented efforts by President Bush to claim dictatorial powers. In April 2006, the *Boston Globe* revealed that President Bush had "quietly claimed the authority to disobey more than 750 laws enacted since he took office"—one in ten of the laws introduced during his presidency—rendering the U.S. Constitution irrelevant.[19] Numerous retired generals were calling for the delusional defense secretary to be fired. As thousands of American and Iraqi bodies piled up in Iraq, Bush sought to change the subject—by preparing to attack Iran. At home, millions of immigrants protested new anti-immigration laws that threatened arrest and deportation for undocumented workers.

It was telling that at the White House Correspondents' dinner on April 29, 2006, with 2,600 of the media glitterati and their guests crowded into the Washington Hilton, the only one in the house willing to call out the president of the United States on his policies was . . . once again, a comedian. It fell to Stephen Colbert, the nebbishy, razor-witted host of *The Colbert Report*, the nightly fake news show on Comedy Central (it follows *The Daily Show*), to rain on the party.

President Bush opened the evening with a stand-up comedy routine with a Bush impersonator. He was greeted with howls of laughter from the assembled journalists. As Elizabeth Bumiller reported in the *New York Times,* the event was an opportunity for the president "to make fun of himself in an effort to establish his regular-guy credentials and ingratiate himself with the press." By that measure, it was another mission accomplished for the president.

Then it was Colbert's turn. Standing a few feet from George and Laura Bush, Colbert postured as Bush's number one fan. He launched in: "I know there are some polls out there saying this man has a 32 percent approval rating. But guys like us, we don't pay attention to the polls. We know that polls are just a collection of statistics that reflect what people are thinking in 'reality.' And reality has a well-known liberal bias.

"So don't pay attention to the approval ratings that say 68 percent of Americans disapprove of the job this man is doing. I ask you this: Does that not also logically mean that 68 percent approve of the job he's not doing? Think about it. I haven't."

Colbert continued, "I stand by this man because he stands for things. Not only for things, he stands *on* things. Things like aircraft carriers and rubble and recently flooded city squares. And that sends a strong message, that no matter what happens to America, she will always rebound—with the most powerfully staged photo ops in the world.

"The greatest thing about this man is he's steady. You know where he stands. He believes the same thing Wednesday that he believed on Monday, no matter what happened Tuesday. Events can change; this man's beliefs never will."

Noting the presence in the audience of several generals, including Gen. Peter Pace, chairman of the Joint Chiefs of Staff, Colbert declared, "They still support Rumsfeld! You guys aren't retired yet, right?"

Colbert then offered a suggestion "about how to handle these re-tired generals causing all this trouble: Don't let them retire! Come on, we've got a stop-loss program; let's use it on these guys." He said that instead of allowing generals to retire, they could still "stand on a bank of computers and order men into battle."

The faux right-wing populist then took aim at the media. "As ex-cited as I am to be here with the president, I am *appalled* to be sur-rounded by the liberal media that is destroying America, with the exception of Fox News. Fox News gives you both sides of every story: the president's side, and the vice president's side.

"But the rest of you, what are you thinking, reporting on NSA wiretapping or secret prisons in Eastern Europe? Those things are secret for a very important reason: They're *super-depressing*. And if that's your goal, well, misery accomplished. Over the last five years you people were so good—over tax cuts, WMD intelligence, the effect of global warming. We Americans didn't want to know, and you had the courtesy not to try to find out. Those were good times, as far as we knew."

Colbert then summarized the media's rules of engagement with Bush. "Let's review the rules. Here's how it works: The pres-ident makes decisions. He's the decider. The press secretary an-nounces those decisions, and you people of the press type those decisions down. Make, announce, type. Just put 'em through a spell check and go home.

"Because really," he added, motioning to administration offi-cials, "what incentive do these people have to answer your ques-tions, after all? I mean, nothing satisfies you. Everybody asks for personnel changes. So the White House has personnel changes. Then you write, 'Oh, they're just rearranging the deck chairs on the *Titanic*.' First of all, that is a terrible metaphor. This ad-ministration is not sinking. This administration is *soaring*. If anything, they are rearranging the deck chairs—on the *Hinden-burg!*" (A reference to the 1937 disaster in which the German zeppelin *Hindenburg* crashed and burned in New Jersey, killing 36 people.)

Speaking of Iraq, Colbert declared, "I believe that the government that governs best is a government that governs least, and by these standards we have set up a *fabulous* government in Iraq."

Colbert's blistering routine was greeted in the audience by muted laughter. This was in stark contrast to Bush's warm reception by media luminaries at another dinner in 2004, when they roared at a video skit that showed Bush searching in vain under papers and in drawers in the Oval Office for missing WMDs—just as U.S. soldiers were being cut down while pursuing a similar futile hunt in Iraq.

The corporate media acted as if Colbert's twenty-five-minute scorching of the president never happened: Bumiller's *New York Times* story on the dinner detailed the "love at first sight" that Bush felt for his impersonator, Steve Bridges, and quoted extensively from their skit together; Colbert was not mentioned. The *Washington Post* "Reliable Sources" column reported three days later that Colbert "fell flat." For proof, it quoted Bush's joke writer, and his impersonator. It wasn't until bloggers gave wide circulation to video footage of the Colbert routine on the Internet that the media was forced to report on it—and then to dismiss it as tasteless or say, as the *New York Times* declared, it "just was not funny."[20]

As for Bush, he was smiling at the beginning of Colbert's routine, but wasn't by the end. Aides reported that night, "He is pissed. . . . He is ready to blow."[21]

Colbert had some advice for media celebrities who couldn't take the heat. "Write that novel you got kicking around in your head. You know, the one about the intrepid Washington reporter with the courage to stand up to the administration. You know—*fiction!*"[22]

Voices of Hope and Resistance

At the risk of seeming ridiculous, let me say that the true revolutionary is guided by a great feeling of love. —**Ernesto "Che" Guevara (1928–1967), physician, revolutionary**

"During times of universal deceit," wrote George Orwell, "telling the truth becomes a revolutionary act."

Orwell's *1984* is a parable for our time. In the face of a 24/7 propaganda assault, war, a lawless American government, corruption, and state-sanctioned terror and torture—now, more than ever, we must speak truth to power. Around the globe, independent thinkers, artists, activists, journalists, and alternative media are doing just that.

From devastated New Orleans neighborhoods that are rising again, to people rebuilding homes in Gaza, to human rights activists fighting torture in the jails of Uzbekistan and the cages of Guantánamo, to brave unembedded journalists in Iraq, we draw inspiration from their vision and courage.

Hope lies in fighting back. Every day, *Democracy Now!* breaks the sound barrier by broadcasting a rich, dissenting, diverse range of voices. This includes the powerful and the grassroots, the banned, the celebrated, the despised, marginalized and ignored. These are the voices of people fighting to make the world a better, more humane, just, peaceful, and more compassionate place. Those who are scorned today are tomorrow's visionaries.

We have chosen a small sampling of some of the fighters, activists, journalists, and thinkers who have inspired and informed us. These are people who express their dissent in actions and words *when it matters.* They are all leaders: They take stands, risk ridicule, and in so doing change the way we see things. They open the political space for others to follow.

Here, in their own words from interviews with Amy that have aired on *Democracy Now!,* are just a few of the countless creative resisters who are lighting candles in the darkness. They help us to better understand our world, and in so doing, empower us to change it.

"There Is No Reason Not to Rebel"

Alice Walker is a renowned author, poet, and activist. She is perhaps best known for her book *The Color Purple,* for which she won the Pulitzer Prize in 1983, becoming the first African-American woman to win the prize for fiction. The novel was adapted into an Oscar-nominated film and was made into a Broadway musical. Her novel *Now Is the Time to Open Your Heart* was published in 2004. I interviewed Alice Walker in Oakland in February 2006 to mark the thirtieth anniversary of the media activist group Media Alliance. Over one thousand people crowded into the First Congregational Church.

One of the last times I had seen Alice was right before the invasion of Iraq. It was International Women's Day, March 8, 2003. She was standing in front of the White House with authors Maxine Hong Kingston, Terry Tempest Williams, and a number of other women. It wasn't a large group, about fifteen or so women, and they stood there, arms locked. I began interviewing them using my cell phone. I would call the control rooms of radio stations. As we went live, I'd put the phone to the mouths of the different women and ask them why they were risking arrest. As the police moved in, I tried to move out of the way. They arrested me and a cameraperson first. When Alice climbed into the police wagon, she said it was the happiest day of her life. In Oakland, I asked her to reflect back on that day.

"Actually I did feel incredibly happy," she said. "Because what happens when you want to express your outrage, your sorrow, your grief—grief is basically where we are now, just bone-chilling grief—when you're able to gather your own forces and deal with your own fears the night before, and you show up and you put yourself there, and you know that you're just a little person, and there's this huge machine that's going relentlessly pretty much all over the world. And then you gather with all of the other people who are just as small as you are, but you're together. And you actually do what you have set out to do, which is to express total disgust, disagreement, disappointment about the war in Iraq. All of these children, many of them under the age of fifteen, about to be just terrorized, brutalized, and killed—so many of them. So, to be able to make any kind of gesture that means that the people who are about to be harmed will know that we are saying we don't agree—just the ability to do that made me so joyful. I was completely happy. And I think that we could learn to live in that place of full self-expression against disaster and self-possession and happiness.

"I know I'm very soft-spoken. But I have endeavored to live my life by my terms. And that means that I am a renegade. An outlaw. A pagan."

Alice continued, "There is no reason not to rebel. I learned that really early. . . . Rebellion, any way you can manage it, is very healthy. Because unless you want to be a clone of somebody that you don't even like, you have to really wake up. I mean, we all do. We have to wake up. We have to refuse to be a clone."

When Alice Walker was arrested outside the White House, she made an unusual connection with the arresting police officer. "This African-American man truly did not want to arrest me," she said, recalling that he was "sort of apologizing." Later the officer confessed to her, "You know, when I told my wife that I had arrested you, she was not thrilled." The author continued, "He told me about his children, and I told him I write children's books. And so he said, 'Oh, you do? Because, you know, there's nothing to read. The children are all watching television.' . . . So it ended up with me sending books to them and feeling that this is a very good way to be with the police."

I asked Alice what good is the antiwar movement if it has failed to stop war?

"Sometimes you can't see tangible results," she explained. "You cannot see the changes that you're dreaming about, because they're internal. And a lot of it has to do with the ability to express yourself, your own individual dream and your own individual road in life. And so, we may never stop war. It isn't likely that we will, actually. But what we're doing as we try to stop war externally, what we're trying to do is stop it in ourselves. That's where war has to end. And until we can control our own violence, our own anger, our own hostility, our own meanness, our own greed, it's going to be so, so, so hard to do anything out there.

"So I think of any movement for peace and justice as something that is about stabilizing our inner spirit so that we can go on and bring into the world a vision that is much more humane than the one that we have dominant today."

Alice Walker closed by reading her poem "Be Nobody's Darling":

> Be nobody's darling;
> Be an outcast.
> Take the contradictions
> Of your life
> And wrap around
> You like a shawl,
> To parry stones
> To keep you warm.
>
> Watch the people succumb
> To madness

With ample cheer;
Let them look askance at you
And you askance reply.

Be an outcast;
Be pleased to walk alone
(Uncool)
Or line the crowded
River beds
With other impetuous
Fools.

Make a merry gathering
On the bank
Where thousands perished
For brave hurt words
They said.

But be nobody's darling;
Be an outcast.
Qualified to live
Among your dead.[1]

The State of Media

Allister Sparks gained fame as editor of South Africa's anti-apartheid newspaper, the *Rand Daily Mail*, in the late 1970s. His newspaper's investigative reporting helped bring down South African prime minister John Vorster in a government propaganda scandal. He also helped expose the death of anti-apartheid activist Steve Biko at the hands of South Africa's security forces. In 1995, South African president Nelson Mandela appointed Sparks to the Board of the South African Broadcasting Corporation.

Sparks also founded the Institute for the Advancement of Journalism, which has trained over thirteen thousand journalists from the African continent. He has written three books on South Africa.

As a veteran dissident journalist, Allister Sparks has a unique perspective on the current state of the media. I asked him his thoughts on the media today.

"You know, I think the media has always had a lot of problems, but after a long career as a journalist, there's one that I think has not received as much attention as it should. It's a two-edged factor. On the one hand, you have what Noam Chomsky has called the phenomenon of the elite consensus. That is simply the notion that journalists, especially senior journalists and beat journalists who are covering particular issues or subjects—White House correspondents, for example—become part of the elite. They live with them. They become friends. They start thinking the same way. And the reporters become dependent on their sources, the sources in turn dependent on them. It's a symbiotic relationship. It's rather like journalists embedded in the military. They become part of the group. They socialize together. Often, their children go to the same schools even. And they start thinking that way."

Sparks continued, "Above all, journalists of that sort need their sources. They need to maintain access to their sources. So the last thing they want to do is give offense to the source by suggesting that the source is not telling the truth. Now, you couple that with the fact that you get increasing sophistication with the spin-doctoring that every government and every government department now uses with increasing skill to put a particular spin on an event, particularly an embarrassing event. And more and more, it seems to me, the journalists who are so embedded with these sources—socially, culturally, professionally, in every way—they don't question that. They don't doubt that. They play along with it. They don't want to give offense. They want to maintain the access.

"That combination of the increasing skill of the spin doctoring and the dependence of the journalists on maintaining the source and becoming a friend of the source and part of that elite consensus—I think that is very much part of what has happened, particularly in the United States, where the spin doctoring skills are developed to a particularly high level. And journalists become reluctant to really go hard at it and crack that open and try and get to the truth.

"Of course, it's all magnified in times of war, when you have the additional pressures of patriotism, and the newspaper itself or the television network becomes fearful of being accused of being unpatriotic, of siding with the terrorists. These are knee-jerk responses."

Bucking the system, says Sparks, begins with an awareness that there *is* a system of going along to get along, of trading truth for access. "The individual journalist must become aware of the extent to which they're infected by it. And then the only way to do that is to determinedly revert to your professional instincts and to be questioning and to be bold enough to put up with the consequences. I think you've got to maintain that challenging spirit. Otherwise, you're finished."[2]

Crossing the Line

Amira Hass is one of Israel's leading journalists. She is a longtime correspondent for the Israeli newspaper *Haaretz*. The daughter of a Holocaust survivor, she is the only Jewish Israeli journalist who has spent the last decade living in Palestinian communities in the Gaza Strip and the West Bank. She visited *Democracy Now!* in 2005 while on a tour of the United States for her book *Reporting from Ramallah: An Israeli Journalist in an Occupied Land.*

We talked about her decision to live in the Occupied Territories. "I wanted to experience life under occupation day by day and night by night, not just on visits here and there. I never was satisfied with what I learned from Palestinians in my short visits. And that's how almost ten years ago, when I started going to Gaza, before I became a correspondent, I stayed more and more overnight at friends' places, first in Gaza City, then in refugee camps. Then I wanted to know more. And the more you know more, the more you realize that you need to know more."

Hass's work, and her decision to live among the people she is covering, has inspired strong reactions in Israel. "Some would say I'm a traitor. Some would be very proud of me. I have heard quite often from military officials that they know that I'm very accurate in the details that I bring. I think it has been proven that these details, this information that I gather, because I'm there on the ground and because I talk to people and collect testimonies, it has been proven how accurate it was. Things that were written—not only by me, but by others who go and speak directly to Palestinians, not through the channels of Israeli intelligence—so things that we wrote and said at the beginning of the Intifada [the Palestinian uprising] are common knowledge today, about the Intifada being a spontaneous outburst of Palestinians, about Arafat not planning it. In a way, [Yasir Arafat] was very scared by the Intifada, by the uprising. [Regarding] testimonies about the behavior of the Israeli army—now there are so many testimonies being exposed by Israeli soldiers in a group called Breaking the Silence, *Shovrim Shtika*.

"As for Palestinians, I have often also criticized the Palestinian Authority, Palestinian leadership. I am able to write things that maybe other Palestinian journalists think, but do not dare to write or do not have the place to write this criticism of the leadership. And I do hear people saying that this is good that at least I can write and express their criticisms. I don't think that the Palestinian Authority always likes what I write, and I wouldn't expect them to. I mean, I would have been worried if they liked everything which I wrote.

"As a whole, and it's true about me, and it's true about other journalists, and it's true also about Israeli activists who fight against occupation, that we turned out without planning to be the good messengers of Israel. Because it's through us that Palestinians know that Israelis are not only settlers and soldiers of occupation."

The *Jerusalem Post* criticized Hass for not being "objective." She responded, "I doubt if anybody can be objective. All of us who are

Israelis, we are part of this conflict. We cannot be objective. This is a myth, and it's a myth always taken by those who support the official policy. All of us have opinions. All of us have certain angles from which we view the situation. The thing is, if you report correctly, if you bring facts, if you allow different voices to be heard in your reporting, or to determine the reporting, and I think I have been trying to do this as much as I can and as much as my work requires."[3]

"You Must Challenge Power All the Time"

During the thirty years that he has been reporting on the Middle East, Robert Fisk of the London *Independent* has covered every major event in the region, from the Algerian Civil War to the Iranian Revolution, from the American hostage crisis in Beirut to the Iran-Iraq War, from the Russian invasion of Afghanistan to Israel's invasions of Lebanon, from the Gulf War to the invasion and ongoing war in Iraq. I asked Fisk to talk about the whole embedding process and the control of the media.

"It's not about embedding. It's about television's refusal to show the truth of war. Many of the worst pictures taken in the invasion of Iraq in 2003 . . . never saw the light of day. They couldn't be shown. They could—but they were not: 'Because of sensitivities.' 'Mustn't show this at breakfast time.' 'It's irresponsible to show the dead like this.' 'It's disrespectful.'

"If you saw what I saw when I go to wars when I'm on the front line—with or without soldiers or with civilians or the wounded in hospitals—you would never, ever dream of supporting a war again. Ever in your life. It's a remarkable thing that in the commercial cinema, feature films can now show the bloodiest, goriest themes which are quite similar to what we see in real life—*Saving Private Ryan*—the guts spilling out. And yet real war cannot be shown without censoring pictures which in many cases are exactly the same as what you see when you go to the cinema.

"If you go to war, you realize it is not primarily about victory or defeat. It is about death and the infliction of death and suffering on as large a scale as you can make it. It is about the total failure of the human spirit. We don't show that because we don't want to. And in this sense, journalists, television reporting, television cameras are lethal. They collude with governments to allow you to have more wars. Because if they showed you the truth, you wouldn't allow any more wars," he said.

"It seems somehow that modern-day politicians with, in many cases, the help, I'm afraid, of journalists, are able to continue to bamboozle people. 'We'll explain it tomorrow,' 'that's too secret to tell you,' 'secret intelligence officials insist.' Look at the *New York Times*'s first paragraphs over and over again: 'According to American intelligence officials.' 'American officials say.' I think sometimes the *New York Times* should be called 'American Officials Say.'

"Journalists like to be close to power. They know that if they want to be close to power, they mustn't challenge power. And that goes back to the Amira Haas definition of journalism, which I am a total devotee of: You must challenge power all the time, all the time, all the time. Even if the politicians and the prime minister, even if your readers hate you. You must challenge power."[4]

"The Whole World Is with Me"

In June 2002, a group of men gang-raped Mukhtar Mai near her home in Pakistan. The rape was ordered by her local tribal council as punishment for a crime allegedly committed by her 12-year-old brother. After her rape, Mukhtar Mai was forced to walk home nearly naked before a jeering crowd of three hundred onlookers.

On average, a woman is raped every two hours in Pakistan, and two women a day die in so-called honor killings. Most of the cases go unnoticed. But Mukhtar Mai, an illiterate peasant, defied tradition by fighting back against her attackers—in the courts. In August 2002, a lower court sentenced six men to death for raping her, but on appeal, a high court acquitted five of the men in 2005. Her case was still on appeal in mid-2006. Mukhtar Mai used compensation money that she received to open schools for girls in her village.

The Pakistani government has repeatedly tried to muzzle Mukhtar Mai. In January 2006, the Pakistani Embassy canceled a speech that she was to give at the UN, for fear it might embarrass them. In 2005, Pakistani president Pervez Musharraf personally banned her from traveling to speak in the United States because he felt she would "blacken" his reputation.

Mukhtar Mai talked about her experience, and about the problems of women in Pakistan, on *Democracy Now!*: "Women are facing a lot of problems here, not only at the workplace, but they're also facing domestic violence and abuses. I can only understand one reason for this: they think women are weaker than men. Men have all the controls in society. The second reason is illiteracy. Women are uneducated. They don't know their rights.

"The whole world is with me if you think about it. Not just Pakistan, but the whole world. And if I'm not getting justice, then there is little hope for other women going through the same kind of abuse. I don't think women are to blame for this. They don't get justice, and that's why they let these abuses go on quietly."

Speaking about her rape, she said, "The perpetrators of this crime were ignorant and illiterate people. But the judges at the high court were all educated people. I cannot imagine how they could have come to a conclusion like that. Afterwards I started hating education, as well.

"We say there is illiteracy and ignorance in this part of the world, and I believe that, too. But if the educated are doing it, what's there to stop the ignorant? . . . Don't they have their own daughters, mothers, and sisters? They should try to see it from their perspective. Today there is one Mukhtar, but tomorrow any girl can go through the same ordeal."

Mukhtar is determined to continue her work for women's justice, in spite of the challenges she confronts. "Of course, it hurts. You understand that, too, being a woman, the kind of hurt that a woman must feel after going through such violation. But I have to live. When it hurts really bad, I just go to my school, look at the girls, and spend time with them to help forget the pain. But I will go on until I have even the slightest hope of justice."[5]

"The World Can Change"

Eduardo Galeano is a Uruguayan writer, journalist, and historian. His work—from the trilogy *Memory of Fire* to the classic *Open Veins of Latin America*—ranges across the post-conquest Americas to uncover a heritage of oppression and resistance beneath the facade of official stories.

Born in 1940 in Montevideo, Galeano began writing newspaper articles as a teenager. By the age of 20 he became editor in chief of the influential weekly journal *La Marcha*, and a few years later, he took the top post at Montevideo's daily newspaper, *Epocha*. Following a 1973 military coup in Uruguay, he was imprisoned and then fled to Argentina, where he founded the magazine *Crisis*. After a bloody military coup in Argentina in 1976, Galeano's name was found on an official death list. He fled to Spain, where he wrote *Memory of Fire*. He returned to live in Montevideo in 1985.

I asked Galeano about how he dealt with censorship at his magazine, *Crisis*, in Argentina.[6] He explained, "*Crisis* was a very successful monthly magazine. We sold thirty-five thousand copies per month, which was incredible. But later when the military dictatorship came in Argentina, one of the first decrees was about the media, about communications, and it didn't allow any magazines or newspapers to publish.

"It was an incredible decree against the democratic right of expression. And *Crisis* was a very peculiar magazine, because we were writing about reality, but we were also trying to hear reality's voices. And therefore, almost half of the magazine was occupied not by professional writers, but just by people, people expressing themselves and saying things from their works, their homes, in the streets, in the cities—all of the thousands of ways in which people can express the horror and the wonders, the marvels of life. This was prohibited by the military. So, we tried to go on. It was each day more difficult because some members of our team were kidnapped or were killed or they were imprisoned or in exile.

"Finally, we decided to shut up. Because there is a certain point in which you should not go on fighting against censorship. You are obliged to choose silence. . . . Silence is also a language. . . . We were obliged to choose between lying or shutting up. And we decided to shut up."

When I asked Galeano about his biggest influences, he replied by talking about the small things. "I write because I feel the need to reveal the greatness hidden inside the small things—just the daily life—and to denounce at once the shallowness of some big things, the big powers, the big events."

Galeano continued, "I read everything: papers and newspapers, all kinds of things. Cheap magazines. I read a magazine when I came to New York some ten days ago. I discovered a story that may be read as a perfect metaphor for official history. It was a story in Maryland last May, there was a serial robber who robbed, assaulted, eleven stores. These guys dressed as Abraham Lincoln, with a beard, pipe hat, and cape.

"This was the perfect metaphor for official history. Kidnapping memory and manipulating heroes for their own purposes. The official history is something which is a big lie written by power to justify some privileges."

In Galeano's book *Embraces*, he described a piece of graffiti that he saw in Montevideo: "Assist the police. Torture yourself."

He explained, "There is a lot of marvelous graffiti. It is a way of expression of the so-called voiceless people. There are no voiceless people. Everybody has a voice. So, I try to multiply these voices which are really the voices which deserve to be heard. The voices of power lie. They are boring. The real purpose of everything that

I write is just to multiply the voices that deserve to be heard coming from the never-heard people."

"Voiceless people," Galeano said, "have their mouth shut by a system which concentrates the rights of expression to a few. Fewer people have the right to express themselves and to influence others, and to decide which opinions and information we will have. But it doesn't mean that people have no voice.

"The world can change. We are not doomed to accept it, even if there is a system that seems eternal. . . . Because tomorrow is not just another name for today."

"Seize the Time"

Arundhati Roy is an acclaimed author and activist from India. Her first novel, *The God of Small Things*, was awarded the 1997 Booker Prize. In India, she has been involved in the movement opposing hydroelectric dams that have displaced thousands of people. In 2002, she was convicted of contempt of court in New Delhi for accusing the court of attempting to silence protests against the Narmada Dam. She received a symbolic one-day prison sentence. She has also been a vocal opponent of the Indian government's nuclear weapons program, and of all nuclear programs worldwide.

In May 2003, six weeks after the United States invaded Iraq, Arundhati Roy spoke at Riverside Church in New York. *Democracy Now!* broadcast her powerful speech. Here is an excerpt of what she said:

> Some of you will think it bad manners for a person like me, officially entered in the Big Book of Modern Nations as an "Indian citizen," to come here and criticize the U.S. government. . . . But when a country ceases to be merely a country and becomes an empire, then the scale of operations changes dramatically. So may I clarify that tonight I speak as a subject of the American Empire? I speak as a slave who presumes to criticize her king.

So here we are, the people of the world, confronted with an Empire armed with a mandate from heaven (and, as added insurance, the most formidable arsenal of weapons of mass destruction in history). Here we are, confronted with an Empire that has conferred upon itself the right to go to war at will, and the right to deliver people from corrupting ideologies, from religious fundamentalists, dictators, sexism, and poverty by the age-old, tried-and-tested practice of extermination. Empire is on the move, and Democracy is its sly new war cry. Democracy, home-delivered to your doorstep by daisy cutters. Death is a small price for people to pay for the privilege of sampling this new product: Instant-Mix Imperial Democracy (bring to a boil, add oil, then bomb).

Apart from paying the actual economic costs of war, American people are paying for these wars of "liberation" with their own freedoms. For the ordinary American, the price of "New Democracy" in other countries is the death of real democracy at home.

It would be naïve to imagine that we can directly confront Empire. Our strategy must be to isolate Empire's working parts and disable them one by one. No target is too small. No victory too insignificant.

. . . An urgent challenge is to expose the corporate media for the boardroom bulletin that it really is. We need to create a universe of alternative information. We need to support independent media. . . .

The battle to reclaim democracy is going to be a difficult one. Our freedoms were not granted to us by any governments. They were wrested from them by us. And once we surrender them, the battle to retrieve them is called a revolution. It is a battle that must range across continents and countries . . . but, if it is to succeed, it has to begin here. In America. The only institution more powerful than the U.S. government is American civil society.

Hundreds of thousands of you have survived the relentless propaganda you have been subjected to, and are actively fighting your own government. In the ultra-patriotic climate that prevails in the United States, that's as brave as any Iraqi or Afghan or Palestinian fighting for his or her homeland.

If you join the battle, not in your hundreds of thousands, but in your millions, you will be greeted joyously by the rest of the world. And you will see how beautiful it is to be gentle instead of brutal. Safe instead of scared. Befriended instead of isolated. Loved instead of hated.

History is giving you the chance.

Seize the time.

Notes

Introduction

1. "U.S. Won't Ban Media from New Orleans Searches," CNN, September 11, 2005.
2. Meghan Martin, "FEMA: Photo Request Not a Directive," Poynter Online, September 8, 2005.
3. Eric Lipton, "Republicans' Report on Katrina Assails Administration Response," *New York Times,* February 13, 2006.
4. *Democracy Now!,* August 31, 2005.
5. Office of the Press Secretary, The White House, May 24, 2005.
6. "New Realities in the Media Age: A Conversation with Donald Rumsfeld," Transcript, Council on Foreign Relations, February 17, 2006.
7. Andrew Buncombe, "The U.S. Propaganda Machine: Oh What a Lovely War," *The Independent* (UK), March 30, 2006.
8. Ibid.
9. "New Realities in the Media Age: A Conversation with Donald Rumsfeld," February 17, 2006.
10. Thomas Ricks, "Military Plays Up Role of Zarqawi," *Washington Post,* April 10, 2006.
11. Ibid.
12. James Risen and Eric Lichtblau, "Bush Lets U.S. Spy on Callers Without Courts," *New York Times,* December 16, 2005.
13. "The Secret Downing Street Memo," London *Times,* May 1, 2005.
14. "If It's Sunday, It's Conservative," *Media Matters for America,* February 14, 2006. http://mediamatters.org/static/pdf/MMFA_Sunday_Show_Report.pdf

1: Outlaw Nation

1. Mark Danner, "Abu Ghraib: The Hidden Story," *New York Review of Books,* October 7, 2004.
2. "President Bush Discusses Freedom in Iraq and Middle East," Office of the Press Secretary, White House, November 6, 2003.

3. Arnon Regular, "'Road map is a life saver for us,' PM Abbas tells Hamas," *Ha'aretz*, June 26, 2003.

4. Stephen Grey, "United States: Trade in Torture," *Le Monde Diplomatique*, April 2005.

5. *Democracy Now!*, November 7, 2003.

6. Andrew Higgins and Christopher Cooper, "Cloak and Dagger: A CIA-Backed Team Used Brutal Means to Crack Terror Cell," *Wall Street Journal*, November 20, 2001.

7. Jane Mayer, "Outsourcing Torture," *The New Yorker*, February 14, 2005.

8. Higgins and Cooper, November 20, 2001.

9. "Arar Lawyers Criticize U.S. Envoy for Comments," Associated Press, December 27, 2005.

10. U.S. Department of State, "Country Reports on Human Rights Practices: Syria," *2001 Human Rights Report*, Washington, D.C., March 4, 2002. http://www.state.gov/g/drl/rls/hrrpt/2001/nea/8298.htm

11. *Democracy Now!*, February 27, 2006.

12. Tim Harper, "U.S. Ruling Dismisses Arar Lawsuit," *Toronto Star*, February 17, 2006.

13. Craig Whitlock, "Italians Detail Lavish CIA Operation; 13 Charged in '03 Abduction Allegedly Stayed in Finest Hotels," *Washington Post*, June 26, 2005.

14. Ibid.

15. Ibid.

16. Craig Whitlock, "CIA Ruse Is Said to Have Damaged Probe in Milan; Italy Allegedly Misled on Cleric's Abduction," *Washington Post*, December 6, 2005.

17. Ibid.

18. U.S. Department of State, "Country Reports on Human Rights Practices: Egypt," *2002 Human Rights Report*, Washington, D.C., March 31, 2003. http://www.state.gov/g/drl/rls/hrrpt/2002/18274.htm

19. *Democracy Now!*, December 7, 2005.

20. Whitlock, December 6, 2005.

21. Stephen Grey, "America's Gulag," *New Statesman*, May 17, 2004.

22. Whitlock, December 6, 2005.

23. Tracy Wilkinson, "Italy Seeks Former U.S. Diplomat in Kidnapping," *Los Angeles Times*, September 30, 2005.

24. Mayer, February 14, 2005.

25. Douglas Jehl, "Qaeda-Iraq Link U.S. Cited Is Tied to Coercion Claim," *New York Times*, December 9, 2005.

26. Douglas Jehl, "Report Warned Bush Team About Intelligence Doubts," *New York Times*, November 6, 2005.

27. *Democracy Now!*, December 7, 2005.

28. Dana Priest, "Wrongful Imprisonment: The Anatomy of a CIA Mistake," *Washington Post*, December 4, 2005.

29. Ibid.

30. Ibid.

31. Ibid.

32. "Extraordinary Rendition: Statement of Khaled El-Masri," American Civil Liberties Union, December 6, 2005. http://www.aclu.org/safefree/extraordinary rendition/22201res20051206.html

33. Ibid.

34. Priest, December 4, 2005.

35. Ibid.

36. Press Release, "ACLU Files Landmark Lawsuit Challenging CIA's 'Extraordinary Rendition' of Innocent Man," ACLU, December 6, 2005. http://www.aclu.org/natsec/emergpowers/22207prs20051206.html. Neil Lewis, "Federal Judge Dismisses Lawsuit by Man Held in Terror Program," New York Times, May 19, 2006.

37. "Rendition Revisited," CBS, 60 Minutes, December 18, 2005.

38. Richard Bernstein, "Skepticism Seems to Erode Europeans' Faith in Rice," New York Times, December 7, 2005.

39. Don Van Natta, "Germany Weighs If It Played Role in Seizure by U.S.," New York Times, February 21, 2006.

40. Scott Shane, "German Held in Afghan Jail Files Lawsuit," New York Times, December 7, 2005.

41. "Extraordinary Rendition: Statement of Khaled El-Masri," American Civil Liberties Union, December 6, 2005.

42. Peter Hart and Jim Naureckas, "The Consequences of Covering Up," FAIR Extra! Update, December 2005.

43. Democracy Now!, November 8, 2005.

44. Demetri Sevastopulo, "Amnesty's 'Gulag' Jibe Irks Rumsfeld," Financial Times, June 2, 2005.

45. E. J. Dionne, Jr., "Hyperbole and Human Rights," Washington Post, June 3, 2005.

46. Irene Khan, "A U.S. Gulag by Any Name," Letter to the Editor, Washington Post, June 2, 2005.

47. Democracy Now!, December 8, 2005.

48. Jan Silva, "Investigator: U.S. Outsourced Torture," Associated Press, January 24, 2006.

49. James Aronson, The Press and the Cold War, New York: Bobbs-Merrill, 1970, p. 166.

50. Ibid.

51. Ibid.

2: Watching You

1. Nat Hentoff, "J. Edgar Hoover Lives!" Village Voice, February 7, 2002.

2. Allan M. Jalon, "A Break-In to End All Break-Ins," Los Angeles Times, March 8, 2006.

3. Quoted in Hentoff, February 7, 2002.

4. "COINTELPRO: The FBI'S Covert Action Programs Against American Citi-

zens," *Final Report of the Select Committee to Study Governmental Operations with Respect to Intelligence Activities*, Vol. III, U.S. Senate, April 23, 1976. http://www.icdc.com/~paulwolf/cointelpro/churchfinalreportIIIa.htm

5. Jalon, March 8, 2006.
6. Ibid.
7. Eric Lichtblau, "FBI Goes Knocking for Political Troublemakers," *New York Times*, August 16, 2004.
8. Press Release, ACLU of Colorado, March 28, 2006.
9. *Democracy Now!*, August 19, 2004
10. John S. Friedman, "Spying on the Protesters," *The Nation*, September 19, 2005.
11. *Democracy Now!*, October 9, 2003.
12. "The Denver Police Spy Files," ACLU of Colorado. http://www.coloradoaclu.org/spyfiles/fbifiles.htm
13. Friedman, September 19, 2005.
14. Ibid.
15. Nicholas Riccardi, "FBI Keeps Watch on Activists," *Los Angeles Times*, March 27, 2006.
16. Ibid.
17. Ibid.
18. Walter Pincus and Dan Eggen, "325,000 Names on Terrorism List," *Washington Post*, February 15, 2006.
19. Lisa Myers, Douglas Pasternak, Rich Gardella, "Is the Pentagon Spying on Americans?" *NBC News*, December 14, 2005.
20. Transcript, Senate Appropriations Committee Hearing, March 9, 2006. http://leahy.senate.gov/press/200603/030906.html
21. Lowell Bergman, et al., "Spy Agency Data After Sept. 11 Led FBI to Dead Ends," *New York Times*, January 17, 2006.
22. Spencer Hsu and William Branigan, "GAO: Customs Failed Dirty Bomb Test," *Washington Post*, March 29, 2006.
23. Nina Totenberg, "O'Connor Decries Attacks on Courts," *NPR Morning Edition*, March 10, 2006.

3: News Fakers

1. "Media Contracts: Activities and Financial Obligations for Seven Federal Departments," Government Accountability Office, January 2006.
2. James Glanz, "Iraq Utilities Are Falling Short of Prewar Performance," *New York Times*, February 9, 2006.
3. Mark Mazzetti and Borzou Daragahi, "U.S. Military Covertly Pays to Run Stories in Iraqi Press," *Los Angeles Times*, November 30, 2005.
4. Jeff Gerth, "Military's Information War Is Vast and Often Secretive," *New York Times*, December 11, 2005.
5. Andrew Buncombe, "So, Just Who Is Christian Bailey?" *The Independent* (UK), December 17, 2005.

6. Mark Mazzetti and Kevin Sack, "Planted PR Stories Not News to Military," *Los Angeles Times*, December 18, 2005.

7. Buncombe, December 17, 2005.

8. Gerth, December 11, 2005.

9. Mazzetti and Sack, December 18, 2005.

10. Mazzetti and Daragahi, November 30, 2005.

11. Ibid.

12. Ibid.

13. *Democracy Now!*, January 14, 2004.

14. Peter Slevin, "Iraqis Unhappy with U.S. Signals," *Washington Post*, May 26, 2003.

15. Bruce B. Auster, "Iraq: Broadcast Blues," *U.S. News & World Report*, January 26, 2004.

16. Katrin Dauenhauer and Jim Lobe, "Massive Military Contractor's Media Mess," *Asia Times*, August 16, 2003.

17. Dean Calbreath, "SAIC Rejoins Pentagon's Media Blitz," *San Diego Union-Tribune*, June 18, 2005.

18. Daniel Williams, "Staffers Quit at U.S.-Backed Paper," *Washington Post*, May 5, 2004.

19. Noelle C. Haner, "How Harris Became a Major Media Player," *Orlando Business Journal*, December 12, 2004.

20. Ibid.

21. Mark Mazzetti, "Planted Articles May Be Violation," *Los Angeles Times*, January 27, 2006.

22. Mark Mazzetti, "PR Meets Psy-Ops in War on Terror," *Los Angeles Times*, December 1, 2004.

23. Howard Kurtz, "Journalists Worry About Limits on Information, Access," *Washington Post*, September 24, 2001.

24. Jack Fairweather, "Heroes in Error," *Mother Jones*, March/April 2006.

25. Ibid.

26. Jeff Gerth and Scott Shane, "U.S. Is Said to Pay to Plant Articles in Iraq Papers," *New York Times*, December 1, 2005.

27. David S. Cloud and Jeff Gerth, "Muslim Scholars Were Paid to Aid U.S. Propaganda," *New York Times*, January 2, 2006.

28. "What the Iraqi Public Wants," Program on International Policy Attitudes, University of Maryland, January 31, 2006. http://www.worldpublicopinion.org/pipa/pdf/jan06/Iraq_Jan06_rpt.pdf

4: Unreality TV

1. David Barstow and Robin Stein, "Under Bush, a New Age of Prepackaged TV News," *New York Times*, March 13, 2005.

2. "U.S. Screeners Miss One in Four Bombs," *Daily Telegraph* (London), October 16, 2004.

3. Barstow and Stein, March 13, 2005.

4. Ibid.

5. Ibid.

6. "Video News Releases: Unattributed or Prepackaged News Stories Violate Publicity or Propaganda Prohibition," U.S. Government Accountability Office, May 12, 2005. http://www.gao.gov/new.items/d05643t.pdf

7. Memorandum from Joshua Bolton, White House Office of Management and Budget, March 11, 2005. http://www.whitehouse.gov/omb/memoranda/fy2005/m05-10.pdf.

8. Barstow and Stein, March 13, 2005.

9. Ibid.

10. Ibid.

11. Ibid.

12. Ibid.

13. GAO, May 12, 2005, p. 1.

14. Alvin A. Snyder, "U.S. Foreign Affairs in the New Information Age: Charting a Course for the 21st Century," The Annenberg Washington Program in Communications Policy Studies of Northwestern University, 1994.

15. "Fake TV News: Widespread and Undisclosed," Center for Media and Democracy, April 6, 2006. www.prwatch.org/fakenews

16. *Democracy Now!*, April 6, 2006.

17. Office of Inspector General, Department of Education, "Review of Formation Issues Regarding the Department of Education's Fiscal Year 2003 Contract with Ketchum, Inc. for Media Relations Services," April 2005, ED-OIG/A19-F0007, p. 11.

18. Ibid., p. 16.

19. Armstrong Williams, "Secretary Paige and Mayor Williams Fight for Change," syndicated column, January 7, 2004. http://www.townhall.com/columnists/Armstrongwilliams/aw20040107.shtml

20. "Department of Education—Contract to Obtain Services of Armstrong Williams," GAO, September 20, 2005, p. 6.

21. Ibid., p. 5.

22. Howard Kurtz, "Writer Backing Bush Plan Had Gotten Federal Contract," *Washington Post*, January 26, 2005.

23. Ibid.

24. Maggie Gallagher, "A Question of Disclosure," United Press Syndicate, January 25, 2005. http://www.uexpress.com/maggiegallagher/index.html?uc_full_date=20050125

25. Kurtz, January 26, 2005.

26. Eric Boehlert, "Third Columnist Caught with Hand in the Bush Till," salon.com, January 27, 2005. www.salon.com/news/feature/2005/01/27/mcmanus/index.html

27. Office of Inspector General, "Review of Department Identified Contracts and Grants for Public Relations Services," U.S. Department of Education, September 2005, p. 14. www.ed.gov/about/offices/list/oig/aireports/i13f0012.doc

28. Press Release, Rep. George Miller, "Department of Education Pays for Op-Eds, Ads That Promote Bush Policies, Do Not Reveal Federal Government as Funding Source," September 6, 2005. www.house.gov/apps/list/press/ed31_democrats/rel9605.html

29. "And now, the counterfeit news," Editorial, *New York Times,* March 16, 2005.

30. Mike Allen, "Bush's Isolation from Reporters Could Be a Hindrance," *Washington Post,* October 8, 2004.

31. David Margolick and Richard Gooding, "Jeff Gannon's Public Blogging," *Vanity Fair,* June 2005.

32. Maureen Dowd, "Bush's Barberini Faun," *New York Times,* February 17, 2005.

33. *Real Time with Bill Maher,* October 28, 2005.

34. Ann Coulter, "Republicans, Bloggers and Gays, Oh My!," February 23, 2005. http://www.anncoulter.com/cgi-local/article.cgi?article=43

35. *Democracy Now!,* April 8, 2004.

36. Russell Mokhiber, "Scottie and Me: White House Press Briefing with Scott McClellan," commondreams.org, September 2, 2003. www.commondreams.org/scottie/0902-10.htm

37. Ibid., February 1, 2005. www.commondreams.org/scottie/020105.htm

38. Associated Press, October 13, 2005.

39. *Democracy Now!,* October 14, 2005.

40. Jim VandeHei, "Troops Put in a Good Word to Bush About Iraq," *Washington Post,* October 14, 2005.

41. The Harris Poll # 95, December 29, 2005. http://www.harrisinteractive.com/harris_poll/index.asp?PID=623

42. John Zogby, "A Letter from the Troops," tompaine.com, March 1, 2006. http://www.tompaine.com/articles/2006/03/01/a_letter_from_the_troops.php

5: The Mighty Wurlitzer

1. John M. Crewdson and Joseph B. Treaster, "Worldwide Propaganda Network Built by the CIA," *New York Times,* December 26, 1977.

2. Carl Bernstein, "The CIA and the Media," *Rolling Stone,* October 20, 1977.

3. Crewdson and Treaster, December 26, 1977.

4. Bernstein, October 20, 1977.

5. Ibid.

6. Ibid.

7. Ibid.

8. Ibid.

9. Ibid.

10. Ibid.

11. Crewdson and Treaster, "Worldwide Propaganda Network Built by the CIA," *New York Times,* December 26, 1977; and Crewdson and Treaster, "The CIA's 3-Decade Effort to Mold the World's Views," *New York Times,* December 25, 1977.

12. Crewdson and Treaster, December 25, 1977.

13. Ibid.
14. *Democracy Now!,* February 17, 2006.
15. Bernstein, October 20, 1977.
16. Judith Miller, "A Personal Account: My Four Hours Testifying in the Federal Grand Jury Room," *New York Times*, October 16, 2005.
17. James Rainey, "*New York Times* Story on Leak Raises Questions," *Los Angeles Times*, October 18, 2005.
18. Howard Kurtz, "The Judy Chronicles," *Washington Post,* October 17, 2005.
19. John M. Crewdson and Joseph B. Treaster, "CIA Established Many Links to Journalists in U.S. and Abroad," *New York Times,* December 27, 1977.

6: Hijacking Public Media

1. *Democracy Now!,* July 22, 2005.
2. "Review of Alleged Actions Violating the Public Broadcasting Act of 1967," Office of Inspector General, Corporation for Public Broadcasting, November 15, 2005, p. 3.
3. Timothy Karr, "The Karl and Ken Show," *Media Citizen,* November 6, 2005. http://mediacitizen.blogspot.com/2005/11/karl-and-ken-show.html
4. Brian Lowry, "Tuning In," *Variety,* January 30, 2006.
5. Frank Rich, "The Armstrong Williams NewsHour," *New York Times,* June 26, 2005.
6. News Release, Senator Byron Dorgan, June 30, 2005. http://dorgan.senate.gov/newsroom/record.cfm?id=239955
7. Eric Boehlert, "Fair and Balanced—The McCarthy Way," Salon.com, May 25, 2005.
8. Wes Vernon, "Voice of America Struggles with Its Own 'Anti-American' Arrogance," NewsMax.com, October 16, 2002. http://www.newsmax.com/archives/articles/2002/10/15/213933.shtml
9. *Democracy Now!,* July 12, 2005.
10. Paul Farhi, "A Different Reception for Public Broadcasting," *Washington Post,* May 20, 2005.
11. Sarah McBride, "As Sponsorship Sales Blossom, Public Radio Walks a Fine Line," *Wall Street Journal,* March 27, 2006.
12. Chris Mooney, "Some Like It Hot," *Mother Jones,* May/June 2005.
13. Ross Gelbspan, "Snowed," *Mother Jones,* May/June 2005.
14. Maxwell T. Boykoff and Jules M. Boykoff, "Balance as Bias: Global Warming and the U.S. Prestige Press," *Global Environmental Change,* July 2004, pp. 125–136.
15. Mooney.

7: Whitewashing Haiti

1. Paul Farmer, "What Happened in Haiti?" in *Getting Haiti Right This Time,* ed. Noam Chomsky, Paul Farmer, and Amy Goodman, Common Courage Press, 2004, pp. 13–14.

2. Ibid., p. 15.

3. *Democracy Now!*, February 16, 2004.

4. *Democracy Now!*, February 18, 2004.

5. AP, AFP, "Aristide Flees Country," *Herald Sun* (Australia), March 1, 2004.

6. Christopher Marquis, "The Aristide Resignation: The Finale," *New York Times,* March 1, 2004.

7. Michael Wines, "If You're Thinking of Living in Exile," *New York Times*, March 7, 2004.

8. *Herald Sun* (Australia), March 1, 2004.

9. Farah Stockman and Susan Milligan, "Before Fall of Aristide, Haiti Hit by Aid Cutoff," *Boston Globe,* March 7, 2004.

10. Farmer, p. 19.

11. Max Blumenthal, "The Other Regime Change," Salon.com, July 16, 2004.

12. Walt Bogdanich and Jenny Nordberg, "Mixed U.S. Signals Helped Tilt Haiti Toward Chaos," *New York Times,* January 29, 2006.

13. *Democracy Now!*, July 20, 2004.

14. Bogdanich and Nordberg, January 29, 2006.

15. Ibid.

16. Dennis Bernstein and Anthony Fenton, "Denial in Haiti: AP Reporter Régine Is Wearing Two Hats," *Flashpoints,* Pacifica Radio, December 29, 2005. http://haitiaction.net/News/FP/12_29_5/12_29_5.html

17. *Democracy Now!*, February 8, 2006.

8: Witch Hunt

1. James Risen and Jeff Gerth, "U.S. Says Suspect Put Code on Bombs in Unsecure Environment," *New York Times*, April 28, 1999.

2. James Risen and Jeff Gerth, "Breach at Los Alamos: A Special Report; China Stole Nuclear Secrets for Bombs, U.S. Aides Say," *New York Times,* March 6, 1999.

3. Matthew Purdy, "The Making of a Suspect: The Case of Wen Ho Lee," *New York Times,* February 4, 2001

4. Risen and Gerth, March 6, 1999.

5. Ibid.

6. Ibid.

7. Purdy, February 4, 2001.

8. Ibid.

9. Robert Scheer, "The Real Scandal: A Scientist Slandered," *Los Angeles Times*, October 7, 1999.

10. James Risen, "U.S. Fires Scientist Suspected of Giving Bomb Data," *New York Times,* March 9, 1999.

11. Risen and Gerth, April 28, 1999.

12. Mary Dejevsky, "How the New York Times Said Sorry (and Lost Its Reputation)," *The Independent* (London), October 3, 2000.

13. David A. Vise, "President 'Troubled' by Lee Case," *Washington Post,* September 15, 2000.

14. James Sterngold, "Nuclear Scientist Set Free in Secrets Case; Judge Attacks U.S. Conduct," *New York Times,* September 14, 2000.

15. "Statement by Judge in Los Alamos Case, with Apology for Abuse of Power," *New York Times,* September 14, 2000.

16. Cited in Robert Scheer, "No Defense," *The Nation,* October 23, 2000.

17. Bob Drogin, "Zeal to Catch 'Spy' Created Shaky Case That Finally Crumbled," *Los Angeles Times,* September 18, 2000.

18. James Sterngold, "U.S. to Reduce Case Against Scientist to a Single Charge," *New York Times,* September 11, 2000.

19. Vise, September 15, 2000.

20. "An Overview: The Wen Ho Lee Case," *New York Times,* September 28, 2000.

21. "From the Editors: The Times and Wen Ho Lee," *New York Times,* September 26, 2000.

22. "An Overview: The Wen Ho Lee Case," September 28, 2000.

23. Robert Scheer, "All the Secrets Unfit to Print," *Pittsburgh Post-Gazette,* February 8, 2001.

24. "FAIR Calls for Revealing Sources in Plame, Lee Cases," Media Advisory, FAIR, August 19, 2004. http://www.fair.org/index.php?page=1830

25. *Democracy Now!,* September 22, 2005

26. Vernon Loeb, "Pentagon: Deutch Did No Harm," *Washington Post,* February 1, 2001.

27. Rowan Scarborough, "Islamic Chaplain Is Charged as Spy," *Washington Times,* September 20, 2003.

28. Oliver Burkeman, "He Is Not Guilty and He Is Not Innocent," *The Guardian,* March 30, 2004.

29. John Mintz, "Clashes Led to Probe of Cleric," *Washington Post,* October 24, 2003.

30. Ibid.

31. Burkeman, March 30, 2004.

32. John Mintz, "Plea Deal Erases Charges of Spying," *Washington Post,* September 23, 2004.

33. Eric Schmitt and Tim Golden, "U.S. Concedes to Force-Feeding Detainees," *New York Times,* February 22, 2006.

9: The Torturers' Apprentice

1. Ken Auletta, "Fortress Bush," *The New Yorker,* January 19, 2004.

2. "Vice President for Torture," Editorial, *Washington Post,* October 26, 2005.

3. *Democracy Now!,* November 9, 2005.

4. Ibid.

5. Ibid.

6. Alfred W. McCoy, "Why the McCain Torture Ban Won't Work," TomDispatch .com, February 8, 2006. http://www.tomdispatch.com/index.mhtml?emx= x&pid=57336

7. *Democracy Now!*, February 17, 2006.

8. Michael Scherer and Mark Benjamin, "What Rumsfeld Knew," Salon.com, April 14, 2006.

9. Ibid.

10: Exporting Abuse

1. *Democracy Now!*, December 20, 2005.

2. "A Macabre Assembly Line of Death: Death Penalty Developments in 1997," Amnesty International USA, 1997. http://www.amnestyusa.org/children/ document.do?id=8DA10EEF6D68397A802569000068A28F

3. Robert Dvorchak, "Brutality Probe Targets Up to 40 Guards at SCI Greene," *Pittsburgh Post-Gazette*, April 10, 1998.

4. Mike Bucsko and Bob Dvorchak, "Firings, Charges Shake Up SCI Greene," *Pittsburgh Post-Gazette*, August 9, 1998.

5. Dvorchak, April 10, 1998.

6. Pennsylvania Department of Corrections, December 2005. http://www.cor .state.pa.us/portal/lib/portal/Execution_List.pdf

7. Ibid.

8. Richard C. Dieter, "The Death Penalty in Black and White," Death Penalty In- formation Center, June 1998. http://www.deathpenaltyinfo.org/ article.php? scid=45&did=539

9. U.S. Department of Justice, *Capital Punishment 2004*, Bureau of Justice Statistics Bulletin, November 2005. http://www.ojp.gov/bjs/pub/pdf/cp04.pdf

10. "Death by Discrimination: The Continuing Role of Race in Capital Cases," Amnesty International USA, April 24, 2003. http://web.amnesty.org/library/ index/engamr510462003.

11. U.S. Department of Justice, *Capital Punishment 2004*.

12. Robert Dvorchak, "State-of-Art SCI Greene Criticized as Repressive," *Pittsburgh Post-Gazette*, August 10, 1998.

13. Ibid.

14. Bureau of Justice Statistics, Press Release, Department of Justice, May 21, 2006.

15. Thomas Bonczar, "Prevalence of Prison in the U.S. Population, 1973–2001," Bu- reau of Justice Statistics, Department of Justice, August 2003. http://www.ojp .usdoj.gov/bjs/pub/pdf/piusp01.pdf

16. Daniel P. Mears, *Evaluating the Effectiveness of Supermax Prisons*, Justice Policy Center, Urban Institute, June 2005, p. 6. http://www.ncjrs.gov/pdffiles1/nij/ grants/211971.pdf

17. Siobahn McDonough, "U.S. Prison Population Soars in 2003, 2004," Associated Press, April 28, 2005.

18. "Lawsuits Challenge Prison Conditions," Associated Press, March 9, 2005.

19. Dvorchak, August 10, 1998.

20. *Democracy Now!*, December 20, 2005.

21. "Order at SCI Greene; Changing the Culture at an Unruly State Prison," Editorial, *Pittsburgh Post-Gazette*, August 13, 1998.

22. Paul von Zielbauer and James Dao, "Guard Left Troubled Life for Duty in Iraq," *New York Times*, May 14, 2004.

23. *Paula Zahn Now*, CNN, May 27, 2004.

24. Von Zielbauer and Dao, May 14, 2004.

25. *Democracy Now!*, June 2, 2004.

26. MTC Web site, http://www.mtctrains.com/company/

27. Dan Frosch, "Exporting America's Prison Problems," *The Nation*, May 12, 2004.

28. *Democracy Now!*, June 2, 2004.

29. Office of Inspector General, "A Review of ICITAP's Screening Procedures for Contractors Sent to Iraq as Correctional Advisors," U.S. Department of Justice, February 2005, p. 21. http://www.usdoj.gov/oig/special/0502/final.pdf

30. *Democracy Now!*, June 2, 2004.

31. Office of Inspector General, p. 27.

32. "New Realities in the Media Age: A Conversation with Donald Rumsfeld," Transcript, Council on Foreign Relations, February 17, 2006.

33. Seymour M. Hersh, "The Gray Zone," *The New Yorker*, May 24, 2004.

34. Press Release, "U.S. Operatives Killed Detainees During Interrogations in Afghanistan and Iraq," ACLU, October 24, 2005. http://www.aclu.org/intl humanrights/gen/21236prs20051024.html

35. *Democracy Now!*, October 26, 2005.

36. "Docket: Center for Constitutional Rights Seeks Criminal Investigation in Germany into Culpability of U.S. Officials in Abu Ghraib Torture," Center for Constitutional Rights, 2005.

37. Press Release, American Civil Liberties Union, March 1, 2005. http://www.aclu .org//safefree/general/17594prs20050301.html

38. Press Release, Death Penalty Information Center, November 16, 2005. http:// www.deathpenaltyinfo.org/122Exoneration.pdf

11: Unembedded in Fallujah

1. Kerry Kennedy, *Speak Truth to Power*, Crown: New York, 2004, p. 195.

2. Joshua Chaffin, Salamander Davoudi, and Nicolas Pelham, "U.S. Army Promises Punishment and Pacification after Fallujah Killings," *Financial Times*, April 2, 2004.

3. Rory McCarthy and Julian Borger, "Defiant U.S. Says Fallujah Dead Were Rebels," *Guardian* (UK), April 12, 2004.

4. Jeffrey Gettleman, "Into the Heart of Falluja," *New York Times Magazine*, May 2, 2004.

5. Kevin Maguire, "Law Chief Gags the *Mirror* on Bush Leak," *Daily Mirror* (UK), November 22, 2005.

6. Arthur Neslen, "Reality Television," *Guardian* (UK), April 21, 2004.

7. "Iraq: Journalists in Danger," Committee to Protect Journalists, 2006. http://cpj.org/Briefings/Iraq/Iraq_danger.html

8. "The War in Iraq: The Most Deadly One for the Media Since Vietnam," Reporters Without Borders, May 3, 2005. http://www.rsf.org/IMG/pdf/ Etude_Irak_Eng_PDF.pdf

9. Ann Cooper, "Jailing Iraqi Journalists," *Dangerous Assignments*, Committee to Protect Journalists, Fall/Winter 2005. http://cpj.org/Briefings/2005/DA_fall05/ DA_fall-05_FINAL.pdf

10. Jamie Doward, et al., "The Leak That Revealed Bush's Deep Obsession with Al Jazeera," *The Observer* (UK), November 27, 2005.

11. Jeremy Scahill, "The War on Al Jazeera," *The Nation*, December 19, 2005.

12. Peter Johnson, "U.S. Says Al-Jazeera Putting Troops at Risk," *USA Today*, April 19, 2004.

12: Oil Profiteers

1. Patricia Wilson, "Bush Focuses On Energy Bill's Economic Impact," Reuters, August 8, 2005.

2. Elisabeth Bumiller, "Bush Admits to 'Mixed Signals' Regarding Laboratory on Renewable Energy," *New York Times*, February 22, 2006.

3. "Email from Release of Energy Department Documents," Judicial Watch. http://www.judicialwatch.org/1770.shtml

4. Letter from *Public Citizen* to the Senate Committee on Energy and Natural Resources, February 11, 2003.

5. Center for Responsive Politics. http://www.opensecrets.org/politicians/ allindus.asp?CID=N00007997

6. Dana Milbank and Justin Blum, "Document Says Oil Chiefs Met with Cheney Task Force," *Washington Post*, November 16, 2005.

7. "Maps and Charts of Iraq's Oil Fields," Judicial Watch. http://www.judicial watch.org/iraqi-oil-maps.shtml.

8. "The Best Energy Bill Corporations Could Buy: Summary of Industry Giveaways in the 2005 Energy Bill," *Public Citizen*, August 29, 2005.

9. "Campaign Contributions to Members of the House-Senate Energy Bill Conference Committee," *Public Citizen*, July 18, 2005. http://www.citizen.org/cmep/ energy_enviro_nuclear/electricity/energybill/2005/articles.cfm?ID=13728

10. Susan Milligan, "Energy Bill Highlights Influence of Texas," *Boston Globe*, August 4, 2005.

11. "Press Gaggle by Trent Duffy," White House Press Release, August 8, 2005. http://www.whitehouse.gov/news/releases/2005/08/20050808-8.html

12. Center for Responsive Politics, 2005.

13. Paul Brown, "Republicans Accused of Witch-Hunt Against Climate Change Scientists," *The Guardian* (UK), August 30, 2005.

14. Edmund Andrews, "Vague Law and Hard Lobbying Add Up to Billions for Big Oil," *New York Times*, March 27, 2006.

15. Ibid.

16. Chris Mondics, "Energy Bill Stokes Nuclear Power," *Philadelphia Inquirer*, July 29, 2005.

17. "The Best Energy Bill Corporations Could Buy," *Public Citizen*, August 29, 2005.

18. "Summary of Harmful Provisions in the Energy Bill," Alaska Wilderness League, et al., July 26, 2005. http://www.citizen.org/documents/harmful provisions.pdf

19. Jad Mouawad, "For Leading Exxon to Its Riches, $144,573 Per Day," *New York Times*, April 15, 2006.

20. "Exxon Chairman's $400 Million Parachute," *ABC News*, April 14, 2006.

21. Simon Romero and Edmund Andrews, "At ExxonMobil, a Record Profit but No Fanfare," *New York Times*, January 31, 2006.

22. Ralph Nader, "Open Letter to the New ExxonMobil Chairman, Rex Tillerson," commondreams.org, April 1, 2006. http://www.commondreams.org/views06/0401-26.htm

23. Brad Foss, "Boone Pickens Sees Oil Prices Going Higher," Associated Press, June 22, 2005.

13: Cindy's Crawford

1. Cindy Sheehan, "The Dangerous Gold Star Families," commondreams.org, January 24, 2005. http://www.commondreams.org/views05/0124-20.htm

2. Stan Goff, "The Spectacle," *Counterpunch*, January 22, 2005. http://www.counterpunch.org/goff01222005.html

3. Leon Alligood, "Nashville Soldier Asks Rumsfeld, Why Can't We Get Armor We Need?" *The Tennessean*, December 9, 2004.

4. *Democracy Now!*, August 31, 2005.

5. Ibid.

6. *Democracy Now!*, August 25, 2005.

7. *Democracy Now!*, August 19, 2005.

8. Ken Herman, "An Exercising Bush," *Atlanta Journal-Constitution*, August 15, 2005.

9. "Secretary Rumsfeld Remarks to National Council of State Legislatures," News Transcript, U.S. Department of Defense, December 12, 2003.

10. "The Final Word Is Hooray!," *FAIR*, March 15, 2006. http://www.fair.org/index.php?page=2842

11. Ibid.

12. Cindy Sheehan, "Casey Austin Sheehan: May 29, 1979–April 04, 2004," commondreams.org, March 31, 2006. http://www.commondreams.org/views06/0331-28.htm

14: Anti-Warriors

1. Bertolt Brecht, *Gedichte*, Vol. 4. Suhrkamp Verlag, 1961. Reprinted by permission of Suhrkamp Verlag.

2. John Zogby, "A Letter from the Troops," Tompaine.com, March 1, 2006. http://www.tompaine.com/articles/2006/03/01/a_letter_from_the_troops .php

3. Gordon Trowbridge, "Troops Sound Off," *Military Times*, January 3, 2006. http://www.militarycity.com/polls/2005_main.php

4. T. Trent Gegax, "Wartime Stress," *Newsweek*, April 2, 2004.

5. Iraq and Afghanistan Veterans of America is a successor to Operation Truth, also founded by Rieckhoff.

6. Jeffry House, personal communication, April 1, 2006.

7. Bill Nichols, "8,000 Desert During Iraq War," *USA Today*, March 7, 2006.

8. Monica Davey, "Former GIs, Ordered to Fight, Fight Not to Go," *New York Times*, November 16, 2004.

9. Nichols, March 7, 2006.

10. James McKinley, Jr., "Mexican Pride and Death in U.S. Service," *New York Times*, March 22, 2005.

11. Camilo Mejia, "Peace Doesn't Come Easily." www.freecamilo.org

12. Quoted in War Resisters Support Campaign, "Declaration." http://www.resisters .ca/declaration.html

13. Chet Barfield, "Navy Petty Officer Refuses Duty," *San Diego Union Tribune*, December 6, 2004.

14. *Democracy Now!*, March 28, 2005.

15. *Democracy Now!*, May 13, 2005.

16. Joe Garofoli, "Anti-War Sailor Lifts Foes of Iraq Policy," *San Francisco Chronicle*, May 28, 2005.

17. Seth Hettina, "Sailor Who Refused to Deploy Sentenced to Hard Labor," Associated Press, May 12, 2005.

18. Damien Cave, "For a General, a Tough Mission: Building the Army," *New York Times*, February 5, 2006.

19. Shankar Vedantam, "A Political Debate on Stress Disorder," *Washington Post*, December 27, 2005.

20. News Release, "DoD Announces Recruiting and Retention Numbers for September," Department of Defense, October 11, 2005. http://www.dod.mil/ releases/2005/nr20051011-4881.html

21. Charles A. Krohn, "Finding Our Next Army," *Washington Post*, June 26, 2005.

22. Robert Burns, "Army Offers New Plan to Boost Recruiting Numbers," Associated Press, October 11, 2005.

23. Ann Scott Tyson, "Youths in Rural U.S. Are Drawn to Military," *Washington Post*, November 4, 2005.

24. Robert Sappenfield, "Short of Recruits, Army Redoes the Math," *Christian Science Monitor*, December 15, 2005.

25. Michael Bronner, "The Recruiters' War," *Vanity Fair*, September 2005.

26. "Army Recruiters Face Investigation," CBS News, May 2, 2005.

27. Lizette Alvarez, "Army Effort to Enlist Hispanics Draws Recruits, Criticism," *New York Times*, February 9, 2006.

28. Leslie Wayne, "America's For-Profit Secret Army," *New York Times*, October 13, 2002.

29. Michael Gilbert, "Army Tries Civilian Recruiters in Ten Areas, Including Tacoma, Wash.," *News Tribune*, August 5, 2002.

30. Press Release, Serco, November 23, 2005. http://www.serco-na.com/r-news-2005-11-23.asp

31. Juan O. Tamayo, "Private Firms Take On Jobs, Risks for U.S. Military in Andes Drug War," *Miami Herald*, May 22, 2001.

32. Jonathan Krim, "More than 100 Groups Launch Campaign to Dismantle Database," *Washington Post*, October 19, 2005.

33. JAMRS Web site, "Affiliations." 2006. http://www.jamrs.org/about/affiliations.php

34. JAMRS Web site, "Market Research and Studies: Mothers' Attitude Study— Video Preview." http://www.jamrs.org/programs/mktrs/mother_study.php

35. *Democracy Now!*, June 24, 2005.

36. "DOD Database Campaign Coalition Letter," Privacy Coalition, October 28, 2005. http://www.privacycoalition.org/nododdatabase/letter.html

37. James Gillaspy and Dan McFeely, "Military Recruiter Accused of Sex Assaults," *Indianapolis Star*, March 1, 2005.

38. Press Release, "Teens' Support for the War in Iraq Weakens," Teenage Research Unlimited, May 10, 2004, Web site accessed 1/20/2006. http://www.teen research.com/PRview.cfm?edit_id=204

15: Human Wrongs

1. "Uzbekistan," *World Report 2006*, Human Rights Watch, January 2006.

2. Craig Murray, "Speech to Freedom House," October 17, 2002, on the Web site of Craig Murray. http://www.craigmurray.co.uk/archives/2002/10/speech_by_ambas.html

3. Robin Gedye, "FO Backs Down over Envoy's Sacking," *Daily Telegraph* (UK), November 7, 2003.

4. "The Murray Torture Telegrams," http://chris-floyd.com/telegrams/feed/#docs.

5. "Confidential Letters from Ambassador Craig Murray," March 18, 2003. www.craigmurray.co.uk

6. Robin Gedye, "The Envoy Silenced after Telling Undiplomatic Truths," *Daily Telegraph* (UK), October 23, 2004.

7. Gedye, November 7, 2003.

16: Bravo Bush!

1. "60 Stops in 60 Days Accomplishments," Social Security Information Center, April 27, 2005. http://www.strengtheningsocialsecurity.gov/60stops/accomplishments_042705.pdf

2. Jonathan Weisman, "Cost of Social Security Drive Cited," *Washington Post*, April 7, 2005.

3. "President Discusses Strengthening Social Security in Colorado," Office of the Press Secretary, White House, March 21, 2005. http://www.whitehouse.gov/news/releases/2005/03/print/20050321-13.html.

4. *Democracy Now!*, April 8, 2005.

5. Dana Milbank, "The Tenacious Trio," *Washington Post*, June 22, 2005.

6. E. J. Dionne, "Stepford Town Meetings," *Washington Post*, April 1, 2005.

7. Richard Morin and Jim VandeHei, "Social Security Plan's Support Dwindling," *Washington Post*, June 9, 2005.

8. Howard Pankratz, "Bush Staffers Ejected 3 at Speech," *Denver Post*, March 20, 2006.

9. News Release, ACLU Foundation, November 21, 2005.

10. Cassie Tomlin, "UA Young Democrat Banned from Forum," *Arizona Daily Wildcat*, March 22, 2005.

11. Josh Marshall, "Public Forums Are No Place for Bush's Thought Police," *The Hill*, April 7, 2005.

12. "33 on List Connected to Fargo-Moorhead Democracy Group," *Fargo Forum*, February 3, 2005.

13. Dave Roepke, "Local Volunteer at Root of Do-Not-Admit Buzz," *Fargo Forum*, February 4, 2005.

14. Ken Herman, "How to Get Straight to the People: Control the Message, Stage the Event," *Cox News Service*, February 14, 2005.

15. Jeff Jones, "GOP Says Pledge Allegiance," *Albuquerque Journal*, July 30, 2004.

16. Steve Larese, "Bush-Backers-Only Policy Riles Voters at RNC Rallies," *Boston Globe*, August 9, 2004.

17. Leslie Linthicum, "I Really Like This Crowd," *Albuquerque Journal*, August 1, 2004.

18. "Teachers' T-shirts Bring Bush Speech Ouster," KGW-Newschannel 8 and Associated Press, October 15, 2004.

19. Kera Abraham, "An Unwelcome NO," *Eugene Weekly*, February 9, 2006.

20. Larese, August 9, 2004.

21. "Grieving Mom Heckles Laura Bush," CBS News, September 17, 2004. http://www.cbsnews.com/stories/2004/09/17/politics/main644005.shtml

22. Ibid.

23. Center for Public Integrity, 2006.

24. *Democracy Now!*, February 8, 2006.

25. *Special Report with Brit Hume*, Fox News, February 8, 2006.

26. *Media Matters*, February 9, 2006. http://mediamatters.org/items/200602090006

27. *Hannity & Colmes*, Fox News, February 8, 2006.

17: We Interrupt This Program . . .

1. "What Happened in Bhopal," The Bhopal Medical Appeal & Sambhavna Trust. http://www.bhopal.org/whathappened.html#_ftnref2

2. Saheed Shah, "New documents will threaten US giant's defence on Bhopal disaster," *The Independent* (U.K.), December 6, 2004.

3. Pierre Prakash, "In Bhopal, the Poison Still Flows," *La Liberation*, December 3, 2003. http://www.truthout.org/docs_03/120503G.shtml

4. Shah, December 6, 2004.

5. *Democracy Now!*, December 6, 2004.

6. Ibid.

7. "Dow 'Help' Announcement Is Elaborate Hoax," The Yes Men (Web site). http://www.dowethics.com/r/about/corp/bbc.htm

8. Shah, December 6, 2004.

9. *Democracy Now!*, October 21, 2005.

10. David Evans, "Heckled in Columbus," *Columbus Free Press*, February 25, 1998. http://www.freepress.org/Backup/UnixBackup/pubhtml/iraq/heckled.html

11. *Cleveland Plain Dealer*, February 19, 1998.

12. "U.S.'s Iraq Policy Catches Flak in Ohio," CNN, February 18, 1998. http://www.cnn.com/WORLD/9802/18/town.meeting/

13. *Democracy Now!*, February 19, 1998.

14. CNN, February 18, 1998.

15. *Democracy Now!*, February 19, 1998.

16. "Day of Desperation," ACT UP Web site. http://www.actupny.org/diva/synDesperation.html

17. "Jon Stewart's America," *Crossfire*, CNN, October 15, 2004. http://transcripts.cnn.com/TRANSCRIPTS/0410/15/cf.01.html

18. Bill Carter, "CNN Will Cancel 'Crossfire' and Cut Ties to Commentator," *New York Times*, January 6, 2005.

19. Charlie Savage, "Bush Challenges Hundreds of Laws," *Boston Globe*, April 30, 2006.

20. Jacques Steinberg, "After Press Dinner, the Blogosphere Is Alive with the Sound of Colbert Chatter," *New York Times*, May 3, 2006.

21. Paul Bedard, "Skewering Angers Bush and Aides," USNews.com (*U.S. News & World Report*), May 1, 2006. http://www.usnews.com/usnews/news/articles/060501/1whwatch.htm. E&P Staff, "Colbert Lampoons Bush at White House Correspondents Dinner—President Not Amused?" *Editor & Publisher*, April 29, 2006.

22. Transcript of Colbert speech on DailyKos, May 2, 2006. http://dailykos.com/storyonly/2006/4/30/1441/59811

Conclusion: Voices of Hope and Resistance

1. *Democracy Now!*, February 13, 2006. "Be Nobody's Darling," by Alice Walker. Reprinted with permission of the author.
2. *Democracy Now!*, February 23, 2006.
3. *Democracy Now!*, April 12, 2005.
4. *Democracy Now!*, October 20, 2005.
5. *Democracy Now!*, June 21, 2005.
6. *Democracy Now!*, August 28, 2001.

Index

©ROBERT KIM

Amy Goodman has been confronting the Washington establishment and its corporate sponsors while giving voice to the ordinary citizens and activists who are fighting for a better, more peaceful world. Her daily international radio and TV show, *Democracy Now!*, began in 1996 and is now carried on about 500 stations and on www.democracynow.org. It is the largest media collaboration in North American public broadcasting. *Democracy Now!* is more than a show—it's a movement.

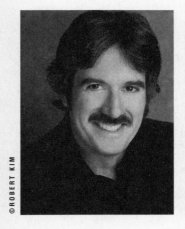

©ROBERT KIM

David Goodman is an award-winning investigative journalist, author of six books, and a contributing writer for *Mother Jones*. His articles have appeared in the *Washington Post, Outside, The Nation,* and numerous other publications. His reporting is included in the American Empire Project book *In the Name of Democracy*. He lives with his wife and two children in Vermont.

Visit www.democracynow.org